Practical Golf Course Maintenance

Practical Golf Course Maintenance

The Art of Greenkeeping

Fourth Edition

Michael Bavier

and

Luke Cella

WILEY

Published by John Wiley & Sons, Inc., Hoboken, New Jersey
Published simultaneously in Canada

For general information about our other products and services, please contact our Customer Care Department within the United States at (800) 762-2974, outside the United States at (317) 572-3993 or fax (317) 572-4002.

Wiley publishes in a variety of print and electronic formats and by print-on-demand. Some material included with standard print versions of this book may not be included in e-books or in print-on-demand. If this book refers to media such as a CD or DVD that is not included in the version you purchased, you may download this material at http://booksupport.wiley.com. For more information about Wiley products, visit www.wiley.com.

Library of Congress Cataloging-in-Publication Data applied for

ISBN 9781119823346 (Hardcover)
ISBN 9781119823360 (ePDF)
ISBN 9781119823353 (ePub)

Cover Design: Wiley
Cover Image: Courtesy of Luke Cella

 M WEP270001 120324

Dedicated to

all those who give rise to the art of greenkeeping. . .

Contents

Preface

As an end user of the first three editions of *Practical Golf Course Maintenance,* I was honored when asked by Mike Bavier to help with the update for the 4th edition. Both he and Gordon Witteveen (deceased) are giants in the world of turfgrass maintenance. The original text was the first of its kind written as a guide to the fascinating and often complicated world of golf course maintenance. It's not a technical book that is difficult to understand but is based on science and real-world applications in the golf maintenance trade. It provides simple, common-sense turf management ideas and protocols that are drawn from many technical sources and years and years of practical knowledge and experience. It has been a pleasure to be a part of the 4th edition, updating the work with new images, ideas, and practices, while preserving the history and documenting the evolution as golf course maintenance continues to advance today.

Golf is a sport that connects people to the outdoors. We were reminded of this as the COVID pandemic swept through the world and many searched for safe respites and havens outside. Golf course superintendents never stopped knowing and understanding the connection their chosen profession has with the environment, working in harmony with the earth, providing a haven for not only people, but so many other members of the plant and animal kingdom. *Practical Golf Course Maintenance* expounds on this connection and explains how superintendents work with nature to provide golfers and their communities a valuable resource and retreat from the ever-developing world.

Practical Golf Course Maintenance is an easy read and thorough introduction for all superintendents, general managers, golf professionals, and for all their assistants, as well as club officials, and golfers who are searching for information and want to know and learn about all aspects of greenkeeping. As the title indicates, the approach is practical, based on the experience of its superintendent/authors. In each edition, everyday English was used and the use of any technical terminology was avoided, and this approach has been maintained in the fourth edition.

The original text was based on a series of talks that Mike and Gordon developed from their experience as superintendents, their visits to golf courses around the globe, and their interactions with countless others in the industry. Their talk was titled the "Magic of Greenkeeping" a subtitle that was used in the first three editions of this book. One of the two cents that I added to the 4th edition was to change the word *Magic* to

Art. While "magic" was a suitable word used in the past, I felt "art" was a much more descriptive term that compiles all of the know-how and experience, materials and processes, plants, and the environment, and finesses them into a landscape for the purpose of people to play and enjoy. Superintendents use all of their available resources to sculpt and shape the course and the golfing experience, and that can only be called an art.

Many will say the superintendent profession is unlike any other because of the willingness of any superintendent to share their knowledge, ideas, and experience with others in the golf maintenance industry. There are virtually no trade secrets among the society of golf course superintendents. There is nary a need for nondisclosure agreements in our profession, and this book is a testament to all those in our industry who strive to provide the best playing conditions for their golfing communities and never think twice about helping their fellow superintendent in need. *Practical Golf Course Maintenance* is a collection of experiences and knowledge for those who want to know how to manage a golf course using practices that improve with time. The 4th edition captures the new ideas and processes that are used to create the finest playing surfaces in the world.

Luke Cella

Practical Golf Course Maintenance

1

Greens

Of all the playing areas on the golf course, the most significant is the green. Nearly 40 percent of all golf shots are played on and around the green. Golfers may tolerate mediocre fairways, inferior bunkers, and sparse tees, but they expect, and deserve, puttable, near-perfect greens. When a golf ball rolls onto the green toward the hole, nothing must impede it from its true path. The factor that most affects the roll of the ball is the smoothness of the putting surface. The final step of preparing a green for play is mowing and needs to be done with a sharp mower by a well-trained operator that will ensure that the surface allows the golf ball to roll accurately and effortlessly.

All other work that is done to a green – such as topdressing, aerating, fertilizing, spraying, rolling, and watering – are wasted unless the green is cut to perfection. No matter how healthy the green, its dark green color, its long root system, or the absence of disease, if the green is not cut perfectly, golfers will condemn it, and much work will have been in vain. Topdressing, aerating, fertilizing, spraying, rolling, and watering are all important, and then there is the icing on the cake – the cutting of the green to perfection, which is the glorious culmination of all the hard work that has been completed. That is why proper cutting is so vitally important in maintaining golf course greens in tiptop condition. Golf course superintendents are judged by the putting surfaces they produce, and the quality of ball roll should be the number one concern of a superintendent.

KEEPING THE MOWERS SHARP

Just as it is impossible to obtain a clean shave with a dull razor, it's not possible to mow a green successfully with a dull mower, so the putting green mowers must be kept sharp at all times. To check whether a mower will cut grass, simply insert a strip of paper between the bed knife and the mowing cylinder, and watch the blades shear it off. If the paper is creased and not cleanly cut, more than likely the same will happen to the grass when the mower traverses a green.

If in doubt, get down on your hands and knees and examine the grass with a magnifying lens. Getting down on your hands and knees is a tried-and-true way of examining the turf for most situations. A grass blade that is poorly cut will look bruised, with the veins in the leaf blade sticking out like damaged protrusions or tiny hairs. The collective effect of the bruised hairs is the appearance of a light sheen over the entire surface of the grass. This phenomenon is not limited to greens alone, but may also occur on tees, fairways, and roughs. It is a common problem that can easily be corrected by adjusting the cutting edge of the mower and/or by sharpening the mower. It is well to remember that dull mowers usually are a major factor in reducing the speed of greens. This is particularly important on greens in southern locales that are overseeded for winter play.

There are two fundamentally different methods of sharpening mower reels: spin grinding and relief grinding. The first method, spin grinding, sharpens all the blades equally in a perfect cylinder with the entire width of the blade touching the cylinder and, subsequently, the bed knife. The second method, relief grinding, results when single blades of the mower are ground on an angle and only the front edge of a blade touches the bed knife. Both methods have their adherents, and both camps tend to believe in the superiority of their particular way.

Equally important to the cutting cylinder is the bed knife, which depending on one's school of thought, can be sharpened with or without a relief angle. One thing everyone agrees on is that the front edge or the face of the bed knife must also be kept sharp. When the front tip of the bed knife becomes rounded, it will once again result in bruised grass blades. The grinding of bed knives and cutting cylinders is usually done during the off-season, and is repeated often during the regular season. Once the grass is cut on a regular basis, the cutting cylinders need periodic attention and are occasionally back-lapped with a grinding compound to maintain their edge. The grinding compound is applied lightly with a brush as the reel turns backward. This process tones the cutting edges of both the reel blades and the bed knife and results in a superior quality of cut. The front edge or face of the bed knife may be touched up at this time with a specially designed facing tool for use between major sharpenings. Those who prefer spin grinding over relief grinding often do away with back-lapping, claiming that it is messy, bad for the mower bearings, and unnecessary.

CUTTING THE GREENS

Cutting the green is accomplished by well-trained, conscientious operators who understand the importance of the task at hand. Recognizing and removing hazards such as stones from adjacent bunker shots or twigs and other debris is paramount to a consistent and uniform cut and ultimately a smooth ball roll. One small rock can nick a mower blade or knock the unit out of adjustment, causing and uneven surface wasting all other inputs and efforts to produce the best putting surfaces possible.

The Height of Cut

A cutting unit that traverses across a grass covered area is supported by a front and a rear roller. These two rollers touch the ground, and the cutting cylinder turns between the rollers at some distance above the ground. This distance, known as the height of cut, is expressed in parts of inches or millimeters, depending on the country in which the course is located. For repair or adjustment of a cutting unit, it is tilted backward or upside down on a workbench. A straightedge is placed across the front and rear rollers; the distance between the straightedge and the top or front edge of the bed knife represents the height of cut. Measuring the height of cut is made infinitely easier by using a solid steel bar and a micrometer attachment. Because the height of cut is measured on a workbench, the resulting measurement is known as the *bench setting,* which often differs from the actual, on the green, cutting height. Why is this so? Superintendents discovered long ago that a cutting height of $\frac{3}{16}$ inch produced different results on different makes of mowers. Obviously, mowers made by different manufacturers are constructed differently and perform in their own peculiar ways, which are rarely similar. There is a device that makes it possible to measure the actual height of cut on the green. It consists of a triangular prism that is placed on the putting surface with the edge touching the soil. The height of the grass mat is projected against incremental graduations, thus revealing the actual in-the-field height of cut. During the same process, one can observe the quality of cut, which can be just as important.

Heights of Cut on Greens

Imperial	Decimal	Metric
$\frac{3"}{16}$	0.188"	4.76 mm
$\frac{1"}{8}$	0.125"	3.18 mm
$\frac{1"}{10}$	0.100"	2.54 mm
$\frac{1"}{16}$	0.063"	1.59 mm

At most golf courses, greens are cut at ³⁄₁₆ inch or less. Above that height, the speed of the green slows dramatically and the enjoyment of golf, and particularly of putting, is reduced. A cutting height somewhere between ⅛ inch and ³⁄₁₆ inch is acceptable to the vast majority of golfers. However, the recent introduction of dwarf species of bent and Bermuda grasses for putting greens has mandated the need to cut the grass at or below ⅛ inch.

Mowers and Cutting Patterns

Though robotic green mowers have been developed in recent years, their entry into to the golf course market has been met with many obstacles. There will come a time when science and technology will push forward and introduce an autonomous green mower that will free up employees to do other tasks. Until then, there are two basic types of green mowers used on putting greens worldwide: riders and walkers. The first reel-type mower was patented in England in 1830, and although many changes and improvements have been made since then, the basic principle of having a cutting cylinder with blades shearing off the grass above the bed knife remains the same.

At first, walk-behind greens mowers needed to be pushed. Later, engines were added, as well as many other refinements that made it possible to cut at lower heights. In spite of this progress, cutting greens with walkers remained a slow and laborious process. Not surprisingly, when the first riding triplex greens mower came on the scene in 1963, its introduction was an immediate success. Large numbers of golf courses discarded their walkers and switched over to the riders (Figure 1.1). Quickly it became evident that the riding mowers had certain drawbacks. The heavy machines caused compaction, which often created wear patterns. Serious hydraulic leaks occurred from time to time and left streaks of ugly dead grass in their wake. Today, the problems with hydraulic leaks have been minimized on new machines and eliminated when battery-operated triplex greens mowers are utilized.

The walk-behind greens mowers have made a comeback and are now widely used on traditional golf courses with small greens, even more so with the reintroduction of an efficient battery-operated version similar to ones used in the early 1960s. Golf courses with larger greens, 5,000 square feet and more, find the riders more economical. The quality of cut from both types of units is comparable. In fact, many superintendents use riders and walkers alongside each other. Occasionally, the main body of a green is cut with a rider, and a walker is used for the cleanup pass. When sufficient workers are not available during shoulder seasons or on weekends, riders are used and walkers the rest of the time.

Figure 1.1 *Triplex greens mower in operation.*

The distinctive checkerboard cutting pattern on putting greens is a desirable feature, very much appreciated by golfers. Although both riders and walkers are capable of producing these patterns, the use of walkers, because of their narrow tracks, produces a far more eye-catching design.

Cutting the Green: 10 Steps to a Perfect Putting Surface

1. *Check the mower's performance.* It is customary for the equipment manager or technician to check the mower for its ability to perform as expected. The first function of the greens mower operator is to double-check to make sure that everything is in order. While a gas-fueled mower is still in the maintenance area, the engine oil should be checked and the gas tank topped off. If using a battery-powered mower, it is important to check that the battery is fully charged.

2. *Before commencing cutting, inspect the green.* Walk and scan the putting surface, looking for stones and debris that need to be removed. In the process, fix ball marks and check the height of hole plugs that have been replaced by the cup changer, and make sure that the new plugs are level with the putting surface. Remove the flagstick and put it aside. Some fast operators believe that they can remove the stick as they pass by, but this is seldom a good idea and quite often leads to accidents.

3. *The direction of cut varies and is generally determined by the superintendent.* It is important that it be different from that of the previous day. The direction of cut is changed every day to help reduce the buildup of grain. The grain on a green is the direction in which the grass leans, much like the nap of a living-room rug. Change the cut every day, and, ideally, grain will be eliminated or at least reduced.

4. *Straight cutting lines are essential.* For the first pass, pick a tree on the horizon or some other feature in the landscape, and keep looking at it as you mow a strip across the green. A straight line will result. For subsequent passes, it is no longer necessary to look at the horizon. Instead, focus on the straight line that has been completed at the far end of the green.

5. *Novice cutters should overlap several inches.* Experienced cutters may reduce the overlap to a narrow strip. The markings on the baskets can be helpful in determining the degree of overlap. Missing a small strip of grass because of insufficient overlap is a cardinal sin against good greenkeeping. This results in golf balls jumping on the green and losing their direction, which becomes a golfer's nightmare.

6. *It is important to make long, wide turns.* Think of the shape of a light bulb or a teardrop while making the turn. Short, quick turns tear the turf on the apron. If a sand bunker or other obstruction is in the way of completing the turn, maneuver away from the hazard and turn in the adjacent rough. Operators should be cautious when making turns on wet aprons. Mowers may slip and slide on the damp turf. Some operators will use turning mats (Figure 1.2) where there is little room between the putting surface and an obstacle to make their turn and not damage the turf.

7. *Check the basket for clippings while the green is being cut.* Clippings tell a story: Uneven distribution within the basket means the cutting unit is set improperly. Unbalanced quantities between the baskets on a rider may indicate differing heights of cut. Likewise, when using a walking mower, the quantity and distribution of the clippings in the basket is a sign of how the mower is cutting. If you think the green has been cut perfectly and the mowers are truly sharp, come back in the evening to make an assessment. With the setting sun over your shoulder, every imperfection on the green is clearly visible, and suddenly what was the perfectly cut green does not look as perfect anymore.

8. *Always empty the baskets before they become too full.* Baskets laden with wet grass affect the quality of cut. If policy dictates that clippings be spread, learn the sweeping but coordinated motion of the upper body, arms, and hips that results in the perfect dispersal

Figure 1.2 *Walking greens mower utilizing turning mats to minimize the wear on the collar of the putting green.*

of the grass clippings. The clippings should be spread in the rough behind the green, *never* on the fairway in front of the green or in wildlife areas. At some golf courses, the clippings are collected and composted instead of being spread in the rough.

9. *At the completion of the back-and-forth cutting pattern, the outer edge of the green must now be cut.* This process is known as the *cleanup pass,* and it requires great diligence on the part of the operator. A cut into the adjacent apron will result in an ugly brown streak. Alternatively, to leave a few inches uncut can result in experiencing the superintendent's wrath. Instead, slow the mower down to a crawl and concentrate on the edge. Superintendents from time to time – and especially during the first mowings of the season – will mark the perimeter of the green with small dots of paint. This process will help to keep the shape of the green intact. The cleanup pass may be omitted from time to time to prevent the buildup of wear patterns along the edge of the green.

10. *Listen to the mower.* Although many operators now use earplugs to protect their ears from excessive noise, it is still important to listen to the sound of the mower, especially the purr of the reels touching the bed knives, which will give a hint if the reels are maladjusted or if an unseen object is struck.

When the green has been completely cut, replace the flagstick. Last but not least, take a whipping pole and brush away the clippings that may have fallen off the mower during cutting near the edge of the green and on the apron. Then, stand back for a few seconds and admire your work in the hope that your supervisor will, from time to time, praise you for your outstanding greens-cutting ability.

The Sequence of Cutting Greens

When golfers arrive at the club in the morning, they typically can tell whether the superintendent has the interests of the golfers in mind. It has been said, "If the putting green has been cut, it shows that the superintendent cares about the golfers." We agree, and we strongly recommend that the putting green be among the first greens that are cut in the morning, certainly before the golfers start arriving at the golf shop.

When using riding greens mowers, it is relatively easy to stay ahead of the players. Riding mowers cut faster than most golfers can play. Superintendents should be aware that some golfers may start play on the back nine, and the needs of those golfers should be taken into account when the superintendent schedules cutting. Checking the schedule with the pro shop is beneficial. When using walker-type greens mowers, three to four operators may be needed to cut all 18 greens, as well as the putting and pitching greens. This will keep green mowing ahead of the golfers. The cutting sequence is then determined based on the superintendent's familiarity, and the sequence will vary from course to course.

When greens are mowed (or any other hole-by-hole maintenance) after play has begun, it is best to change the sequence in which they are cut. Start with the 18th green and work backward so as to avoid bothering the same foursome more than once during the course of their game.

During the height of the golfing and growing season, the greens are frequently cut on a daily basis, but prudent greenkeepers know the beneficial effects of skipping a cut on occasion. Every mowing injures the turf. This practice can be compared to a man not shaving his face for a day after routinely doing so every morning. The skin on the jowls immediately improves after a day of rest. It feels softer and healthier. So it is with a green that has been given a rest from daily mowing. In lieu of mowing on a skip day, some greenkeepers will roll the putting surfaces before play, removing the morning dew and giving the turf an extra day to recover. Skipping a day during the busy golf season is not always conceivable, but a rainy day when cutting is not possible will provide the same result.

The First Cut of the Spring

Superintendents in northern regions look forward to the first cut of the spring. The harbinger of a new season brings with it anticipation and great expectations for the months ahead. Many superintendents enjoy making the first cut themselves. The thrill of trying new mowers, combined with the fragrance of the freshly cut grass, brings memories of past seasons and lost youth. At the same time, there is a wonderful opportunity to outline the greens.

During the previous season, the greens may have lost some of their shape because cautious operators made them smaller with each successive cutting. In the process, curves and shapes were unintentionally altered. Spring is a good time to cut into the apron and reoutline a green, returning it to its original configuration. Small adjustments can be made while using the mower, but if the green will be substantially enlarged, it is best to outline the change with a paint gun. It may be necessary to mark the new outline several times before it becomes established.

Cutting the apron or collar to greens height is a drastic measure that should be performed only during the spring when the grass plants have an inner drive to recreate themselves and are able to recover from the severe scalping. At any other time of year, such treatment could result in instant death of the grass plants, but in the spring the grass will manage to survive.

Many superintendents like to cut greens themselves from time to time during the season, even at large operations where there are plenty of staff, not only for exercise, but also to get a feel for the course. It is part of the mystique of being a golf course superintendent and having a love affair with one's golf course. Such a relationship needs constant nurturing on the part of the superintendent, and cutting greens from time to time is an important part of that process.

TAKING CARE OF WEAK GREENS

Not all greens are created equal. Certain greens may have been constructed from the same material and in the same manner, but there are other factors that cause greens to perform differently, not only during the growing season but also when the grass is dormant. Foremost among these factors is location. Greens exposed to the north tend to be colder and green up more slowly in the spring. The soil on greens that face the south tends to be much warmer, and the growth on such a green is more substantial. Another factor is shade. As a general rule, grasses don't grow well in the shade, and Bermuda grass needs more sun than any other turf. Therefore, greens that are surrounded by trees often struggle for survival. Trees should not be planted near greens. If they have been so established by well-meaning but ill-informed committees, then the trees should be trimmed regularly to reduce shading and the roots pruned to keep the nutrients and moisture levels acceptable on the greens. The early morning sun is particularly important for the health of the green.

Greens that become weaker during the progression of the golfing season should be treated gingerly. There are several steps that can be taken to prevent the further decline of a weak green:

1. Use only walkers on weak greens; they are lighter and cause less mechanical damage and compaction (Figure 1.2).
2. Periodically, roll instead of cutting.
3. Remove the dew on weak greens as early in the morning as possible. Dry greens are less subject to fungal diseases.
4. Cutting weak greens when the grass is virtually dry is beneficial.
5. During extreme conditions of high temperature and humidity, consider cutting the green in late afternoon, early evening, or not at all.
6. Syringe lightly during the hottest part of day. This will help to cool the turf. Syringe refers to a light watering either by hose or a quick irrigation cycle.
7. Spread the wear by changing the hole daily, even twice daily if needed.
8. Choose hole locations that are easier for the golfer to make putts and minimize traffic on the green.
9. Raise the height of cut ever so slightly.
10. Cut with solid rollers instead of grooved rollers. Do not use groomers.
11. Go easy on fertilizer (organic sources of fertilizer are less phytotoxic) and pesticide applications. Stay away from cocktail mixes. A mixture of pesticides, wetting agents, and liquid fertilizer is known colloquially as a "cocktail mix."
12. Improve the internal and subsurface drainage of a weak green by removing water on an as-needed basis with a roller or squeegee. Other methods of draining the greens are included in a later chapter.

On which days should superintendents choose not to cut their greens? Usually a day or time is selected that is the least busy on the course. It may also be a rainy morning, or a cloudy day with no dew on the grass. Other factors enter into the decision as well. Clever superintendents who wish to survive the pitfalls of club politics should be aware of the playing schedules of the owners and club officials and other VIPs. Communication with the pro shop on special events and play can also help dictate what days a superintendent may skip a mow.

SPIKE MARKS AND BALL MARKS (OR PITCH MARKS)

The introduction and the acceptance of nonmetal or soft spikes have improved the day-to-day condition of golf greens immeasurably. Gone are the days of spike-marked greens and putts deflected on the way to the hole as golfers are now permitted to tap down any imperfections on their putt line. Ball marks continue to scar and mar otherwise perfect greens. These marks are caused by high-flying golf balls leaving ugly indentations on a soft green. Ball marks are rarely a problem on firm greens; however, when greens are moist from rain or excessive irrigation, ball marks can become problematic.

Ball marks left unrepaired become the responsibility of the superintendent and the greens crew. On a daily basis, the task of repairing them falls to the greens cutter and/or the hole changer. Some superintendents assign special staff to fix ball marks with a mix of seed and green sand, or other various types of divot mix according to the composition of the green. In severe cases, periodic topdressing alleviates the problem. The ball marks on some of the newer cultivars of bentgrass don't heal as quickly and it is up to the superintendent to develop a course of action to address this putting green infliction. Of course, we can also appeal to the golfers to repair the damage resulting from their actions. All golf courses, without exception, encourage players to repair ball marks. In fact, the practice is a principal part of the codes of conduct and ethics everywhere.

DEW REMOVAL

On mornings when greens are not to be cut and there is dew on the turf, it should be removed for the benefit of the golfers as well as for the health of the grass. Wet turf provides an ideal breeding ground for disease development, and drying the grass early in the morning either by means of dew whipping or simply by cutting the green is an essential part of disease prevention.

Methods of Dew Removal

We know from experience that courses that religiously practice dew removal spend less on chemicals for disease prevention than those

Figure 1.3 *A fiberglass-tipped pole is used to wipe the dew off greens and to scatter grass clippings on the collars and can be used to mask a skipped cleanup pass.*

courses that never remove dew. Using one of these "green" methods of dew removal will more than likely result in long-term cost saving on the chemical budget:

1. Whipping with a fiberglass-tipped pole (Figure 1.3)
2. Using roller squeegees, like those used on tennis courts
3. Dragging a rubber hose, weighted rope, or similar device across the green
4. Running the syringe cycle on the irrigation system

THE TRIPLEX RING SYNDROME

When a riding greens mower cuts the same swath day after day along the outer edge of the green, the tires of the mower are on the same track each time. If, in addition, the green is small or has been designed with many exotic curves, the weight of the mower and the wrenching action of the tires making tight turns will quickly injure the grass. Ugly dead or brown concentric rings, the dreaded "triplex ring syndrome" (TRS), will result. This is not some mysterious disease related to fairy rings, but pure and simple mechanical damage caused by the overuse of a mower.

TRS Prevention

Most superintendents, at the first sign of TRS damage, will switch back to walk-behind greens mowers. This is not always possible, nor is it wholly necessary. Many superintendents have successfully eliminated the triplex ring by the simple expedient of skipping the cleanup pass every other day. Even for one day on a weekend, the cleanup pass can be conveniently forgotten. It is amazing how quickly the stressed-out grass responds to, and recovers after, a rest from the regimen of the daily routine. Removing groomers and replacing grooved rollers with smooth rollers on the greens mowers will help eliminate triplex ring damage.

Golfers generally don't notice that the grass has not been cut for the first 3 to 4 feet near the edge of the green, and if they do, they probably won't mind. Golf balls that are putted from this area are rarely deflected in the initial stages, when they are traveling at their greatest velocity on their way to the cup. Possibly the grass along the outer edge of the green may look shabby as a result of omitting the cut. This is especially true during times of heavy dew on the grass. Carrying a whipping pole and brushing the greens along the outside perimeter will address this shortcoming.

Another method simply involves disengaging the mower reels prior to turning, but not lifting the cutting units. This helps stop the clippings from falling off the rollers and leaving a mess along the outside of the green.

From time to time, a good practice is to move the cleanup pass in from the edge of the green between the extents of 1 to 2 feet. This method results in the tracks of the wheels being straddled and, thus, helps prevent the buildup of the triplex ring. Perhaps the best method of eliminating the triplex ring is to use walkers for the cleanup pass.

Architects wanting to break the monotony of round and oval greens continue to design fancy-shaped greens with many tight turns, much to the frustration of the superintendent. Superintendents, however, have many golf architect friends who are sympathetic to this hardship and refuse to make curves on greens that have a radius of less than 25 feet. That makes the development of a triplex ring virtually unlikely.

Strategies to Prevent Triplex Ring Damage

Any one or more of the following can be used to help prevent triplex ring damage:

1. Skip the cleanup pass on alternate days.
2. Use walkers for the cleanup pass.

3. Move the cleanup pass away from the outer edge periodically.
4. Disengage the outer reel when using a rider.
5. If necessary, engage a golf architect to redesign the perimeter of the green, thus reducing the severity of the curve.

Repairing Triplex Ring Syndrome Damage

In the initial stages, when a triplex ring is just starting to show, it is relatively easy to stop the damage from becoming serious. Simply using a walker on such greens will do the trick. Once the grass has become seriously injured, however, more drastic measures are needed. Aerating with minitines and overseeding (a process that is described in detail in Chapter 9) are probably sufficient to promote the recovery of the turf. In really serious cases, the affected part may actually have to be resodded. Whether seeding or sodding, the portion of the green that is being treated should be roped off and put out of play until recovery is complete.

HYDRAULIC SPILLS

A most unpleasant occurrence in using a riding triplex greens mower is the occasional bursting of the hydraulic hose. This usually happens when least expected and often goes unnoticed until it is too late. The results can be disastrous. A careless operator might not notice a hydraulic leak until the machine actually stops functioning. A perfect pattern of brown lines may result on several successive greens. Most often, the burn of the grass is limited to a single narrow strip across a green or on the apron.

There have been many miracle cures advocated by fast-talking salespersons to save the grass from hydraulic burns: activated charcoal, liquid soap, kitty litter, and strips of felt tissue, to name but a few. These do not work adequately. These quick fixes can make the superintendent or the greenkeepers feel better for a little while, because at least they are doing something, but there are no magic cures that can bring dead grass back to life. The hydraulic oil from the mower that is squirted onto the green because of a loose-fitting or broken hose is very hot. It is so hot, in fact, that the grass immediately singes and dies upon contact with the oil. It may still look green, and a bit shiny at that, but it will certainly be brown in just a few days. The damage can be mitigated, however, if the area is washed off with a powerful spray of water during the initial stages. Adding a wetting agent at this point may also help, but it also needs to be washed off. Others use a peat product immediately after a spill, which absorbs much of the oil and lessens the damage.

Some superintendents now use vegetable oils in their hydraulic systems. These oils are biodegradable and less caustic to the grass. Battery-operated mowers in use at a number of courses have helped to alleviate the wrath of the hydraulic spills.

Prevention

It all starts at the "grounds maintenance facility" (see Chapter 20), the maintenance headquarters, with a good, well-qualified mechanic, the unsung hero in the golf course maintenance industry. A conscientious mechanic will regularly check and repair the hydraulic hoses on all machinery, but especially on the mowers. When a particular hose becomes worn or breaks, the mechanic should order one or even preferably two replacement hoses. Hence, it's important to have a supply of spare hoses is in the parts room.

In some instances, the mechanic and an assistant will work together to put out all machinery from the storage area in the morning. It is helpful to start the engines to warm up the machines before they are taken out onto the course. Each operator should be responsible for checking that his machine is in proper running condition, which includes looking for small drops of oil as well as gasoline leaks that are telltale danger signs before taking mowers out. A small drip can be an indicator of a loose fitting. Fixing it, then and there, can prevent a disaster on the greens later.

Mixing a dye into the hydraulic oil makes it somewhat easier to see a leak, and this can help to prevent running the hydraulic tank completely dry. Some superintendents and mechanics have installed elaborate alarm systems that will immediately detect a drop in hydraulic pressure and signal the operator. Such systems are very expensive, but the cost can be justified in terms of avoiding damage to a precious green, tee, or fairway.

As long as there are cars on our highways, there will be accidents. As long as we use mowers equipped with numerous hydraulic lines, there will be mishaps and damaged turf. It is inevitable. Operator training should cover all aspects of hydraulic leaks, starting from what to look for after each mowing pass to where to move the mower once a leak is detected, such as a cart path, rough, or even sand bunker in some cases. A printed, detailed plan of action should be conveniently available so that when a hydraulic spill does occur, immediate remedies can be executed.

Repairing Burnt Grass Caused by Hydraulic Spills

Quick action and clear thinking are necessary to cope with unexpected hydraulic spills. Several key members on the greens staff should be familiar with one or all of the following steps:

1. *Remove the excess oil by spreading Turface or kitty litter over the affected area or applying Peat-sorb.* Any one of these materials will soak up much of the oil and prevent the burn area from becoming a much wider strip than it needs to be. Applying a solution containing a wetting agent will further dilute the remaining oil. If a wetting agent is not available, use hand or dish soap and dilute with water.
2. *Use an aerator with pencil tines or minitines closely spaced, about 1 inch apart and no deeper than 1 inch.* A tine hole deeper than 1 inch will prevent the seedling from reaching the surface of the green once it has germinated. Make a double pass to ensure that there is plenty of seed bed. Hand-forking is an alternative method. Apply seed, making sure that some of it ends up in the tiny aerator holes. The seed that falls on the surface is mostly wasted, but the seed in the aerator holes has found a growth chamber. Below the surface, in a moist and warm environment, it will quickly germinate and sprout up. The small tufts of grass, firmly rooted below the surface, will withstand golfer and mower traffic and rapidly join together to make an acceptable turf. In four to six weeks, the ugly scar will disappear. Frequent topdressings will speed the process. Unfortunately, this practice is not an option on Bermuda grass greens.
3. *If you absolutely must, take a sod cutter and remove the affected area and replace it with new sod.* This is a drastic measure that will affect the putting surface much longer than seeding. Try to obtain a sod cutter with a narrow cutting blade. Make sure that the sod is cut thicker than normal, so that the sod won't shift under the golfers' feet or the greens mower. If there is no sod nursery from which to take the sod, consider taking it from the putting green or along the edge from the back of a regular green. Taking sod from the back of the damaged green will guarantee that you will have the same turf that is already on the green that is being repaired. This not only will be visually more appealing but will offer a more consistent playing surface. The sod should be carefully laid and tamped down just a fraction of an inch below the adjacent surface. After sodding has been completed, the strip must be topdressed and rubbed with the back of an aluminum rake or, better yet, with a Levelawn. This makes for a perfectly smooth surface that will quickly grow in and become part of the regular green. Although a mechanized

sod cutter can be used, hand-pushed, narrow-bladed sod cutters are available and are ideally suited for this type of repair.

The problem with the sodding process is that the sod needs regular watering until it becomes firmly rooted. This means that someone has to be available to water it, even on weekends and perhaps during late afternoons and evenings. If the sod were to die, it would be one mistake compounding another and a crisis difficult to survive, especially for novice superintendents.

4. *Repairing turf on damaged tees and fairways is slightly less cumbersome because these surfaces are not as critical as the green.* In many cases, when the scar is narrow, the adjacent turf will grow in quickly. It may still be necessary to either seed or sod or even use a divot mix to help promote growth. In any case, it is always better to repair the damage than to let the visual effects of the dead turf linger. Golfers will lose their patience with superintendents who are indecisive or procrastinate.

CLIPPINGS

Clippings can be spread in the rough behind the green or in the rough between two fairways as long as it is done properly. Leaving clumps of clippings in the playing areas interferes with the game and is not acceptable. As stated previously, many superintendents collect the clippings and compost them on-site or have them hauled away to a waste area.

We have already discussed the significance of constantly checking the grass clippings in the basket(s) of the mower when cutting greens. Important information can be gleaned from uneven distribution inside the basket. This may indicate that the mower is dull or out of adjustment, but there is more to be learned from the clippings.

Grass clippings have an odor all their own. When the grass is healthy, it releases a very pleasant fresh smell, but when the green is sick, the odor of the clippings is very pungent. Early warnings of a pending fungus disease outbreak can often be detected by simply sticking your nose into a handful of clippings. A foul odor is a sure giveaway that disease is trying to gain a foothold. Old-time greenkeepers knew this secret long ago and could often be seen on all fours, sniffing a green and trying to learn about pending problems. In the baskets, among the clippings, look for adults of the hyperodes weevil or the ataenius beetle insect species. Keeping track of the number of bugs found in the clippings may help to determine the need for spraying an insecticide.

Clippings can also reveal the succulence of the turf. Overfertilized greens produce an abundance of fat, juicy snippets of grass. Lean greens make for wiry, stringy leaf blades. If there are fertilizer granules mixed in with the clippings, it probably means that the green should have been cut with the baskets off after applying fertilizer. Even the small-particle, homogenous fertilizers get caught in the reels and end up in the baskets. It makes no sense to pick up the expensive nutrients from the greens and spread them in the roughs. Better to remove the baskets for a couple of days and water in the fertilizer.

Emptying the baskets (Figure 1.4) is a common practice after cutting the green. If the baskets need emptying before the green is finished, it probably means that the green is overfertilized. If, however, the baskets still do not need to be emptied after four or five greens are cut, it indicates that the turf is lean and thin and possibly did not need cutting at all. A light rolling with a high-speed greens roller might have been a better method of creating a perfect putting surface.

Greens rollers were first used on lawn bowling greens in Australia. The original models were 6 feet across, much too wide to cope with undulations of putting greens but ideal for flat bowling greens. Their purpose was to speed up the green without cutting it. Lawn bowling greens are frequently maintained at the very edge of survival in order to be hard and fast. Cutting greens maintained under such stressed-out conditions would almost certainly mean instant death to the grass. A light rolling achieves the desired result without removing any of the grass growth.

Figure 1.4 *Grass clippings are mostly water and will decompose quickly when spread out properly in the rough or other out-of-play areas.*

Australian golf course superintendents, who often manage bowling greens as well, adopted the speed roller for putting greens by the simple expedient of making it narrower. Such rollers quickly became a hit in North America and are now widely accepted all over the world.

FAST GREENS

Television golf and the Stimpmeter have combined to put pressure on superintendents to provide faster greens – greens so fast that, according to some witty tour players, a dime left as a ball marker would slide off the green. That is an exaggeration, of course, but with an element of truth. Greens have been cut to the quick, rolled, and left to dry, all in a quest for speed. It is a miracle that the poor grass plants manage to survive, and all too often they do not.

The Stimpmeter is a device used to measure the speed of a green in feet and inches. A ball is rolled from a slotted steel bar at a predetermined height, and its progress is measured on the green. The direction is reversed, and the process repeated two to four times. Several measurements are averaged to arrive at a length to calculate the speed for a particular green. The Stimpmeter should be used on a flat portion of the green. That may present a problem, inasmuch as many greens have severe undulations and with only a few flat areas available to measure the speed.

It is becoming more common for greens to reach speeds of 12 to 13 feet. The stage is set every spring during the Masters at Augusta National, where quick greens are commonplace. Golfers from all parts of the world watch and then demand that their superintendents emulate the course conditions and also the lightning-fast greens. Those weak-willed souls who give in to the golfers and cut their greens to the root hairs usually lose their grass and their jobs at the same time.

Until the advent of the dwarf cultivars, no grass, whether it was Bermuda, bent, or *Poa annua,* could survive being cut at ⅛ inch for any length of time. Yet rookie superintendents kept on trying at their own peril. They accommodated the club champion and the captain, but completely forgot about the needs of the grass and perhaps the majority of the golfers. In the horribly hot and dry summer of 1995, when grass across the continent was dying by the acre on the golf courses, many greens could have been saved if they had just been cut a little higher. The introduction of high-density dwarf varieties of both bent and Bermuda grasses improved the situation. Cutting heights below ⅛ inch are commonplace for these grasses – indeed a necessity – and green speeds of 12 to 13 feet can be maintained for extended periods.

The major factors that affect the speed of a green are the height of cut and the rolling of the green. Superintendents should select mower settings that will ensure the survival of the grass and produce a green speed that is acceptable to the majority of the golfers. A dry wind on a sunny afternoon can speed up the greens as much as 6 inches on the Stimpmeter, at the same time stressing the grass.

For special events, such as club competitions and tournaments, the green speed can be increased a trifle by the simple expedient of double cutting. This is an old trick that smart superintendents have known about for years. The double cut results in a smoother and faster putting surface. The entire green can be double cut, but this is not always necessary. Three or four cuts on either side of the cup could be adequate. Remember, the ball is most likely to deviate from its true path as it slows near the cup. This is all the more reason that the turf should be perfect near the hole, so that more putts will drop and golfers will applaud the greens staff.

There is one machine that helps speed up the greens without cutting the grass and is used by most golf course superintendents. As discussed earlier, the greens roller was first used on bowling greens in Australia and later adapted for more undulating golf greens. These fast-moving machines (Figure 1.5) can roll a green quickly and can appreciably increase the Stimpmeter readings (Figure 1.6). The greens rollers have been refined and

Figure 1.5 *Greens rollers are a great tool to even out putting surfaces and increase green speed.*

Figure 1.6 *The Stimpmeter is a tool that is used to measure green speed and helps golf course superintendents make sure all the greens on the course putt the same.*

are very user friendly. One crew member can roll a green quickly that will create a fast, smooth putting surface. After a rolling, the grass blades are still there, to breathe and keep the plant alive. The greens roller is a useful tool and can be used occasionally instead of cutting, or on a regular basis in addition to cutting. We know of superintendents double cutting and double rolling the greens daily for extended periods, but such practices are hazardous, particularly when both the temperature and the humidity are on the rise.

MEDIUM-SLOW GREENS

Amazingly, there are some golf clubs that don't want any part of fast greens. Such courses take pride in having slow greens. Using the United States Golf Association's (USGA) guidelines, a green that measures between 6 and 7 feet on the Stimpmeter is considered medium-slow. In terms of height of cut, this translates to ³⁄₁₆ inch, or 4.76 mm.

The problem with slow greens is that they tend to develop thatch and grain. Superintendents who cut their greens at the ³⁄₁₆-inch height should be vigilant about the potential formation of a heavy layer of mat or thatch. On such greens, the groomer attachments on the mowers should be used on a regular basis. Verticutting and topdressing frequently is important to prevent the buildup of thatch and encourage the grass to grow upright.

OVERSEEDED GREENS

Bermuda greens in the transition zone, south of the Mason-Dixon Line in the United States, experience a period of dormancy during the winter months. Golfers do not like to putt on brown grass, and turf managers respect their wishes by overseeding the greens with northern grasses such as rye grass, *Poa trivialis*, and bentgrass, or any combination of these three. During the overseeding period, grass is left to grow at a higher height of cut and greens are watered several times daily to promote seed establishment. Once the seed is actively growing, the height of cut is reduced to acceptable putting levels, but rarely low enough to satisfy all golfers. Overseeded greens have a reputation of being slow and inconsistent, but recent advances in plant breeding have resulted in superior species of grass for the purpose of overseeding. In addition, superintendents have become more adept at establishing and maintaining overseeded greens.

At the conclusion of the winter months the reverse transition from winter to summer grasses is encouraged by methods that favor Bermuda grass and are harmful to northern turf grasses. This involves reducing the height of cut, verticutting, and controlling nutrient intake.

TEMPORARY GREENS

There are times when the regular green cannot or should not be used. On such occasions, the ingenuity of the superintendent is called on to create a temporary green. If the temporary green is to be in use for only a few hours or perhaps even a day, it is simply a matter of moving the pin of the regular green and cutting a hole in the fairway. A sign explaining the reason for the temporary green is advisable, and the best place to put the sign is on the tee of the hole that is under repair.

Golfers will accept a temporary green far more readily if they know the reason. Another little trick that will put a smile on a golfer's face is to use a larger-than-normal cup on a temporary green:

1. Use an 8-inch hole auger for the initial cut.
2. Use a standard hole cutter to cut inside.
3. Place the cup inside the regular hole.
4. Place the flag inside the cup.

Even a square hole that can be made with the help of an Australian Turf Doctor, a handy turf repair tool invented by an Aussie greenkeeper, can be used to give an unusual twist to a temporary green.

When a temporary green is planned to be in use for an extended period, more care should be taken in its preparation – golfers deserve a decent putting surface at all times. If possible prepare the temporary green several months in advance of its intended use. Select a level portion of the fairway and mark out the green with a paint gun. It is very important that even this temporary green be of sufficient size, as large as the space permits but at a minimum of 1,500 to 3,000 square feet. Double-cut the temporary green about ⅛ inch lower than the existing fairway. The new putting surface is then verticut in two different directions. In northern climates, the temporary green should also be seeded. In southern regions, a Bermuda turf will gradually adjust to the new cutting height. Fertilize moderately with a starter fertilizer and topdress heavily. For such a relatively small green, it is best to work the topdressing in with the backside of an aluminum rake or, better still, with a Levelawn. If there are old divot marks in the green, these should be repaired with a hole cutter or similar tool.

At this time, it is important that the green be soaked thoroughly. This can best be done with a hose attached to a roller-base sprinkler that is connected to a fairway outlet. Next, fence off the temporary green with stakes and ropes, and declare the area as "Ground Under Repair," or GUR for short. A sign placed on the green explaining to the golfers what you are trying to do is appreciated. The golfers will gladly take a free lift as long as they know its purpose.

Over the next six to eight weeks, institute a regular cutting regimen, lowering the height of cut gradually every week until the desired cutting height is reached. In the meantime, topdress and verticut at least two more times; also consider aerating at least once prior to opening up the green to golfers. Temporary greens have to be treated with loving care by the superintendent and greens staff. They should be inspected frequently to ensure their health and condition. If the reason for a temporary green is the rebuilding of an existing green, then a near-perfect putting surface on the temporary green is extremely important. There will be less pressure on the superintendent to open the new green prematurely if birdie putts are frequent on the temporary green.

Steps to Establish a Temporary Green

When a temporary green is necessary, the following steps should be taken to establish and maintain the green:

1. Select a suitable location that is reasonably flat and spacious.
2. Outline the green, rope it off, and declare it as GUR.
3. Double-cut the existing turf at a slightly lower height and remove clippings.
4. Double-aerate and then verticut the entire area.
5. Apply seed, starter fertilizer, and topdressing.

6. Keep the green moist by watering when necessary.
7. Gradually reduce the height of cut weekly.
8. Continue topdressing.
9. Fine-tune to putting green quality.
10. When the temporary green is in play, remind the players that it is in use so they are aware and can adjust their game or play.

DOUBLE GREENS

Ever since St. Andrews was established along the shores of the North Sea, double greens have been a part of golf. In North America, double greens are an occasional oddity that attracts attention but also presents potential injury liabilities. To prevent the danger of golfers hitting into each other, double greens tend to be of immense size. Double greens seem to take forever to cut. Although much of the grass is never used, double greens are visually spectacular and exciting to play. The perceived saving in maintenance is frequently not realized. Therefore, sometimes double greens are abandoned after just a few years and converted to separate greens.

SAND GREENS WITHOUT TURF

Years ago, sand greens without turf were quite prevalent. These greens were easy to maintain and cost effective. Now they are usually found in arid areas and extreme climate regions in the world where growing grass greens are just too difficult or too expensive. Until recently, sand greens were quite commonly found in the prairieland sections of the United States and the provinces of western Canada. There were even sand greens at some of the more exotic golf courses in the world, including the Royal Kathmandu Golf Course in Nepal, although many of these have since been converted to grass. The firm surface of a sand green is created by the addition of old engine oil or diesel fuel. When sand greens are used, local rule permits players to smooth the putting line to the hole by dragging a small mat over the intended line of play.

HIGH-SAND-CONTENT GREENS

The trend toward high-sand-content greens had its beginning in California, where it was believed that so-called dirty sand (containing small amounts of other soils, such as peat, clay, etc.) would make the ideal matrix for growing grass on putting greens. Dirty sand occurred naturally in many places and was an easy shortcut for the construction of golf greens. When dirty sand was not available, superintendents used washed sand and added peat or similar organics to duplicate the dirty sand.

Initially, sand had been one of the three components of the ideal greens growing mix; it quickly became the major component, and in some cases, the only component of the growing medium. Sand has several advantages:

- It drains well and rarely becomes saturated.
- Sand is difficult to compact and needs little aeration.
- Sand greens hold golf shots, even when dry.

GREENS FOR HOMEOWNERS

Superintendents are often asked to build a putting green in someone's backyard. The temptation to accept the assignment can be flattering and often irresistible. Ardent and enthusiastic golfers have a way of making otherwise rational superintendents surrender to the homeowner's desires. We have constructed several backyard greens during our extensive greenkeeping careers, and the most successful ones are those that are located in the backyards of the golf superintendent's home. Greens are the pride of their owners, but rarely do they last beyond a few years. Over a period of time, the unkempt greens are usually inundated by an overabundance of *Poa annua* and other noxious weeds. They are frequently converted to flower beds, swimming pools, or outdoor living space around the home.

The Expense of Building a Backyard Putting Green

Obtaining cups and flagsticks is probably the least expensive and least important aspect of building a backyard putting green. Making sure that the maintenance work is done on a regular basis requires lots of time and funds:

1. When homeowners dream of a putting green for their backyards, they think in terms of one similar in size to their living room or master bed room, and that is just too small. The minimum size for a backyard green is 1,500 square feet. Twice as large would be better. Invariably, the existing soil needs to be modified, which means importing several truckloads of sand and topsoil.
2. Putting greens require a lot of sun, and most home yards are too heavily shaded, most often by trees that cannot be removed.
3. Keeping the green irrigated is a must. An automatic irrigation system is most desirable. It may be possible to modify an existing

sprinkler system, but undoubtedly several new irrigation heads, new pipe, and a new controller may be needed.

4. Although seeding the new green is initially less expensive than sodding, both methods require expertise and much can go wrong before a desired result is achieved.

5. Maintenance involves buying a new or used green mower and then cutting the green four to five times a week. Perhaps it is best to use a push-type mower for a small backyard green. Using such a mower would provide an opportunity for regular exercise. Maintenance also includes fertilizing, spraying with pesticides, and topdressing the green on a regular basis. Spraying for diseases should be postponed as long as possible.

Homeowners should analyze their reasons for wanting a backyard putting green. Some want to improve their putting and chipping skills, and others just want to live on a golf course. Most golf course superintendents discourage golfers from building backyard putting greens. In the case where a golfer has completely lost his or her senses and insists on proceeding, as a last resort, we advise our colleagues to inform them of the high maintenance costs, which include labor and chemicals, involved with a backyard putting green. Hopefully, this will bring the overenthusiastic golfer back to reality. Another option is now readily available and should be discussed with the homeowner – the installation of a synthetic or artificial putting green.

Artificial turf products have improved in quality. There are now many ready-made contoured greens completely made from artificial materials. Such greens are used as target greens on driving ranges and are ideally suited for backyard use. Like artificial Christmas trees, they have all the same advantages: they look just like the real thing, are much less expensive, and require very little upkeep.

SUMMARY

We must assume that the great majority of golfers will want to continue putting on grass greens and that these greens must be smooth and reasonably fast and consistent throughout the course. A superintendent's greatest accomplishment will be to provide such greens. In the process, the superintendent walks a fine line between ultimate success and utter failure in balancing the needs of the grass with those of the golfers.

Superintendents must remember that nearly 40 percent of all golf shots are played on and around the green. Therefore, to keep the golfers happy, the greens should be kept in as perfect condition as possible.

2

Tees

Although all tees are important, the most significant is usually the first tee. Golfers receive their first impression of a course on the first tee, unless they are playing in a shotgun tournament or are starting on the back nine. We want our golfers to feel comfortable on the first tee. Everything possible should be done to alleviate fear and anxiety, so that the golfer will be relaxed and able to execute a near perfect drive from the first tee. Such a marvelous beginning sets the tone for the rest of the game.

Golf course superintendents contribute much to a golfer's happiness or, at times, to his or her despair. What do golfers expect, and what can the superintendent provide on the tees, particularly the first, that will put them in a positive frame of mind?

1. *The surface of the tee ought to be as flat and even as possible.* The tee may tilt slightly forward, backward, or sideways, depending on the architect's specifications. No bumps or hollows are permitted; no sudden grade changes are allowed. The reason is obvious: the golfer needs a level stance to make a perfect shot.

    When the architect designs a tee to incline one way or another, the slope should be unnoticed by the golfer. The design should be such that with a heavy rain the water flows toward an area that the golfers are unlikely to walk over when approaching or leaving the tee.

2. *On elevated tees, the surface may tilt slightly forward.* Golfers often have a better view of the fairway when the tee markers are placed at the rear of such a tee. On fairways that slope uphill, the tee should also have a built-in incline. The advice of an architect or a golf course builder should be sought before determining the incline of

the teeing surface, but regardless, the tee surface itself should always be flat and on a consistent plane.

3. *Most golfers are apprehensive about driving from the first tee.* Having to hit one's drive in front of a critical gallery can be nerve-racking. Offering a degree of privacy on the first tee for the golfers is helpful. Superintendents should work with architects to provide some privacy while avoiding the creation of shady conditions that are detrimental to the growth of healthy turf. Once away from the clubhouse, tees should be as open as possible, keeping trees and shrubs a reasonable distance away from the tees.

4. *Tees should not be cramped, but spacious and sufficiently large to accommodate 200 to 300 golfers a day.* The hope is that some of the players will use the forward tees, and some will even play from the championship tees. The main tee, from which the majority of players will hit their drives, should be at least the same size as the corresponding green. On par 3 holes, the teeing area should be twice the size of the green. On par 4 and par 5 holes, the teeing area should be around the same size of the green. Whatever rule is applied, tees are rarely too large.

   The main tees on the first and tenth holes should be larger than most others. Many golfers coming to the first tee, or tenth tee if they are playing the back nine first, want to warm up. Often, they carelessly swing and frequently damage the turf on these tees. Provide plenty of space, and these tees can be repaired on a regular basis and recover quickly.

5. *The slopes surrounding the tees should be gentle, so that golfers can easily walk to the teeing area without having to climb a steep grade and be out of breath before driving the ball.* Although steps and stairs are objectionable around tees for a variety of reasons (expensive to maintain and aesthetically unappealing), in some cases, the elevation of a particular tee makes it necessary to provide a way for a golfer to get up to the tee. In this situation, it is the superintendent's responsibility to construct something that is functional and not too obnoxious (Figure 2.1).

6. *A tee should be firm, for better footing, but not so hard as to make it impossible to get a tee into the ground.* The grass on tees is usually cut somewhat longer than on greens. Keeping the grass sufficiently short ensures that there is never any grass between the clubhead and the ball at the time of address.

7. *The tee should also be free of ugly divot scars, especially the first tee, for that all-important first impression.* The previous day's divots should be filled and tee markers moved on a scheduled rotation to provide adequate turf recovery.

Figure 2.1 *Tees that have steep slopes require the superintendent to come up with ways to ease the climb in a safe manner.*

When all is said and done, golfers of all calibers will agree that the tee surface ought to be perfectly flat in order to execute a flawless shot. Golfers will accept divot-scarred tees, worn tees, hard tees, or soft tees, but never tees with too many undulations. After all, the Rules of Golf allow the player to adjust their lie on the tee to their liking. Superintendents must do everything in their power and employ all their skills as greenkeepers to make sure that tees are kept flat and firm and have an adequate cover of grass throughout the golfing season.

Tees are rarely constructed with the same degree of diligence that is devoted to the creation of greens. Tees seldom have a network of tile or a bed of gravel in their base, and as a result, the drainage on most tees is usually mediocre in comparison to that of greens. However, if a new tee is constructed with all sand or a high sand ratio mix, it is highly recommended that tile lines are installed. Years ago the process for the construction of tees entailed pushing up adjacent earth for use on the finished grade. Today, soil mixes are used for tees and are composed of an improved combination of mixes that help to reinforce and encourage compaction of the tees. The new mixes have enabled tees to retain their shape and grade. This is quite a contrast to earlier construction in years past, when only the adjacent soils were used to make a tee.

CUTTING TEES

Tees are generally elevated and are inherently difficult to cut, more so than putting greens. Tees with steep slopes entail making tighter turns while cutting, making it more difficult for operators to retain control of their mowers. Cutting a tee perfectly is very important; a shoddy job of mowing will destroy its appearance.

Walk around the tee and look for broken tees, branches and twigs, and other debris before beginning the cut. Everything must be picked up and properly discarded prior to cutting the tee. Make a mental note of any other abnormalities or hazards to avoid when mowing, such as steep slopes or even sprinkler heads.

The mowing direction of the tees should be changed frequently to prevent grain, and encourage upright growth. Usually, on the day before the weekend, the tees are cut lengthwise or from back to front. The striping that points to the center of the fairway assists the golfer subconsciously to drive the ball in that beneficial direction.

Many superintendents use riding greens mowers on the tees, but on smaller tees, walk-behind mowers are preferred (Figure 2.2). Because tees are usually not cut on a daily basis and the mowing height is greater, the triplex ring is not a serious problem. When it does develop, omitting the cleanup pass will quickly remedy the situation.

Figure 2.2 *Cutting the tee with a walk-behind mower is preferred. It takes a skilled operator to keep square tees well groomed.*

Frequency of tee mowing coincides with the growing season. It is important that they are mowed often enough to not remove too much of the leaf surface at any one mowing. Mowing tees on long weekends in season should be scheduled to keep them looking pristine. This creates a favorable condition from a golfer's point of view.

We have already mentioned the slopes that make cutting tees a difficult operation. There are other obstacles on and around tees, such as benches, ball washers, trash receptacles, and divot boxes, which must be removed before cutting or avoided while cutting tees. In addition, there are tee blocks that need to be set aside before the tee is cut, and reset with a careful eye to line up with the center of the fairway. For all these reasons, cutting tees requires not only great dexterity but also much savvy and experience. Cutting tees is a job for the most capable golf course workers and using rookies for the job only as a last resort.

In 1992, the US Open was played at Pebble Beach, which first featured televised play on tees that were cut in a rectangular shape. Since then, many golf course architects and superintendents have mimicked these tee borders that can be lined up perfectly with the fairways. This is not possible with banana-shaped or free-form tees; however, the practice still continues and takes special care to mow each corner.

Golf courses with modest budgets may decide that cutting tees with greens mowers is too expensive for their liking and thus choose less-sophisticated mowers. Some will use utility reel-type mowers or trim mowers, sacrificing the quality of cut for speed and a higher mowing height. Golfers can adjust by using a longer tee.

Many otherwise near-perfect tees are spoiled because the surrounds have not been trimmed adequately. Long grass at the front of a tee may impede a low ball that has been driven from the tee. Low-hanging tree branches and long grass at the back of a tee may hinder the golfer's backswing. Superintendents should be vigilant about such adverse conditions and make sure that the surrounds of tees are trimmed regularly, especially on forward and championship tees in out-of-the-way places that may not be used regularly. Hitting corridors or chutes created by trees creep inward and need to be trimmed back to make the whole fairway accessible from the whole teeing area.

TIP: Review sight lines and ball flight line two times a year to make sure trees are not encroaching the normal ball flight path from a properly struck tee shot.

THE HEIGHT OF CUT ON TEES

The demands of the game dictate that a ball on a peg is sufficiently elevated above the grass, so that it can be cleanly struck with a driving club. The large heads of contemporary driving clubs have made it all the more important that the grass be closely cropped. The grass mat on today's tees is of the same quality as the greens of yesteryear. In fact, at some very exclusive golf clubs, tees are cut very close to the same height as the greens.

Today, some golf courses have the height of cut on tees as low as ¼ inch, but far more often it will be in the ½ inch range. When we get away from bent and Bermuda grasses and get into the fescues, bluegrasses, ryes, and even kikuyu turf, the height of cut could fluctuate nearly ½ inch. A cut that is much higher than that will make for many unhappy golfers.

FORWARD TEES

The golf experience should be fun and friendly for all calibers of players. Forward tees became part of the game to encourage play and make the game more enjoyable for beginners, ladies, and senior golfers. Some of these tees were added without proper consultation and planning and have actually made the hole more difficult for the unexperienced player because they don't line up properly with the hole and are too small. These tees should be evaluated and corrected to make certain the game is enjoyable for all. On set days when families come out and play together tee blocks are placed in the fairway for the very new players so they may experience the joys and thrills of the game.

PRACTICE RANGE TEES

Practice range tees take more abuse and are more difficult to maintain than other tees. The primary reason is that many practice tees are far too small for the daily traffic. Another reason is that there is not enough time for the grass to recover before it must be used again. For these reasons, superintendents often use a combination of artificial turf and natural grass. By switching between the two, the life of the grass tee can be extended. If you closely watch golfers practice, you will see that some remove the turf systematically. Divot by divot they destroy a measurable area in a matter of minutes. Fortunately, there are many other golfers who treat the turf gently and kindly. In any case, the practice range tee needs constant attention. It would be beneficial if the golf professional, superintendent, or range attendee could encourage golfers on the practice tee to move the location of their ball with every shot, thus preserving patches of grass between the divots, which will increase the likelihood that the grass will grow back at a faster rate. The divots must be swept or blown off daily and the scars refilled with seed, fertilizer, and topsoil.

While some superintendents battle with bentgrass on the driving range tee, others have switched over to rye grass that grows faster and fills in more quickly. In recent years, seed producers have developed bluegrasses that are being installed on range tees that recover well, tolerate close mowing and traffic, and can germinate in as little as 10 days. Whatever the case, growth of the turf must be encouraged with proper fertilizer and timely irrigation. Just as on all other tees, the grass should be cut on a regular basis.

WHAT SUPERINTENDENTS CAN DO TO IMPROVE EXISTING TEES

Superintendents can improve the teeing area by means of installing proper drainage, grading, enlarging, and leveling the playing surface, by properly locating sprinkler heads and properly training staff to place tee blocks that get the most out of every teeing area.

1. *Tees that hold water can usually be remedied by installing drain tile*. It is common for tees to hold water, so installing drainage is routine maintenance. Superintendents should make sure that the committee responsible for this maintenance is informed of its benefits. These are beneficial projects that can often be completed in the off-season in-house. In northern climates, improving the drainage will also reduce the damaging effects of soil that heaves as a result of deep ground freezing.
2. *Regrade the top surface of the tees so that they are perfectly level*. The first course of action is to remove all the sod before starting the grading operation. Grading equipment or outside contractors using GPS and laser technologies are well worth the investment to rent or employ for this process. The turf can be replaced if it was salvageable or a newer cultivar(s) may be desirable to grow on the newly leveled tee. Maintaining the edges of the tee is an important step during the grading process to ensure the flatness of the teeing deck all the way to the edge.
3. *Enlarging an existing tee by adding earth can be tricky*. It is almost impossible to match and marry the old and the new tee perfectly. The extended portion of the tee will probably settle somewhat, and the joint will become clearly visible over time. It is better to strip the turf, add the extension and regrade the entire surface before installing a new stand of high-quality turf. When it is not possible to regrade the entire tee, some sod should be removed a few feet away from the edge of the existing tee before adding the new strips of sod to the existing tee. Blending the existing tee surface and the additional new area will create a level tee area that is more acceptable.

4. *Once a perfectly flat top has been established, it is necessary to keep it that way.* Applying topdressing improperly will distort the flat surface. How is this possible? This is usually caused when topdressing mix is applied mechanically and worked in haphazardly. This occurs in small amounts over time until the sudden realization that the tee deck is no longer level. Greenkeeping tools such as drag mats, the backs of aluminum rakes, and Levelawns should be used at all times on the surface, and to avoid crowning used evenly near the edge (Figure 2.3). Brushes may adequately work soil mixes into the grass mat but can often leave small waves and undulations that grow with successive applications of topdressing. We have also seen tee surfaces that have been ruined by the improper application of divot mixes.

5. *The location of sprinkler heads can be a nuisance on tees.* All sprinklers need repair and maintenance from time to time, and this may involve digging a deep hole in the middle of a tee. Consider the consequences should this happen during an important event! Therefore, if at all possible, sprinklers should be located off to the side of the tees. On large, wide tees, this may not be possible, nor is it nearly as critical.

Figure 2.3 *A Levelawn is used after aerification of a tee to break up the cores while working the sand back into the holes.*

6. *Training employees to properly set up tees each day can reduce wear and tear not only on the tee but also the turf areas leading to the tee.* It is imperative that the tee blocks are pointed directly to the center of the fairway target line and golfers are given adequate space between and behind them (Rules of Golf, two club lengths.)

BUILDING NEW TEES

1. Site selection is best left to a golf course architect, who should be encouraged to make the forward or additional tees part of the overall master plan. Naturally, the superintendent may have some input in the decision inasmuch as he or she is familiar with the property, the drainage, and the irrigation lines.
2. It is vitally important that the new tee is properly aligned with the center of the landing area.
3. Construction can be done either in-house or by a reputable golf course contractor. Tees should be at least 20 × 30 feet, and preferably 30 × 30 feet. Small tees are difficult to cut and are tricky for sprayers, aerators, and mowing equipment to get around. The importance of good drainage and high-quality topsoil has already been stated.
4. Seed, sod, or sprig the new tee (see Chapter 13).
5. The tendency to plant hedges or shrubs on the sides of the tees should be resisted. Inevitably, such growth reduces the amount of usable space on the tees. Similarly, stairs leading to the teeing deck, by their very nature, restrict traffic and cause ugly wear patterns. No amount of expert greenkeeping can avoid the development of bare areas near the top or the bottom of the stairs. If possible, for that reason alone the slopes around tees should be gentle enough so that stairs are unnecessary.
6. Tees and trees are not compatible. It may be desirable for golfers to enjoy the shade of a tree while waiting to tee off, but the grass on the tee will not tolerate shade, and roots from the tree will absorb the nutrients and water that are essential for the health of the turf. Every effort should be made for tees to be in the open and free from the harmful effects of nearby trees.

SUMMARY

Once superintendents understand the importance of the need for perfectly flat tees and assume responsibility for creating and maintaining such tees, they will also make some of these recommended procedures part of the maintenance regimen. Superintendents are often at the mercy of the architect who has created the course. During the career span of an ambitious superintendent, however, there are many opportunities to work with the architect to address the golfers' concerns and design features.

Practicing the game on a driving range is becoming more and more popular. The overall management of the driving range tee and surrounds cannot be overlooked. Superintendents should employ the use of systematic hitting area rotations, enhanced divot mixes, and artificial turf areas after heavy rains or event play. Next to the clubhouse landscaping, the driving range tee provides one of the first impressions the golfer receives and should, therefore, be kept up and very meticulously maintained. In addition to the driving range tee, a golf course with many tees that provide panoramic views will always be a favorite with the golfers.

3

Fairways

The improvement in turf quality and playability of the course has been the most evident on the fairways. Next to the putting greens, the conditioning of the fairway turf and its ability to support the golf ball is most significant when it comes to playing the game. The golfer has to "play it as it lies," and when a fairway is in top condition, it presents the ball for the golfer to get the full clubface on it during the swing. This is the reward for hitting the ball into the fairway and avoiding hazards that may produce a poor lie. Keen superintendents are aware of this and place the conditioning of their fairways just below putting greens. Remember, a golfer can manipulate their lie on a tee, but not on a fairway.

Not long ago, fairways were cut with tractor-drawn gang mowers, much like the mowers that had been pulled with leather-shod horses prior to World War II. Little changed over the years, until the 1950s and 1960s, when large tractors equipped with multiple hydraulic cutting units made their appearance. These behemoths struggled with our fairways, twisting and turning, and many times tearing, the tender turf in the process. Although these cumbersome mowers cut a wide swath in quickly, their excessive weight caused serious compaction and subsequent turf damage.

Golf itself was undergoing a change of sorts. Wide-open spaces became passé, and target areas were being defined with well-placed bunkers, trees, and water hazards. Fairways became contoured, and the total area was reduced. Superintendents needed lightweight mowers, and some experimented with the riding greens mowers. At first, these handy units were tried on aprons or collars as well as on tees. The riders were ideally suited for this new application. They proved to be fast, relatively maintenance-free, and, above all, user-friendly. The next step was to extend the aprons on the par 3 holes. The results were spectacular; the closely cut grass with the clippings removed looked amazing and were a delight to play. Golfers loved it!

It was not surprising, then, that enterprising superintendents began cutting entire fairways with triplex greens mowers. These gentle machines cut the grass beautifully and produced a playing surface of outstanding quality. Initially the intent was to remedy a difficult mowing problem on a single fairway, but it quickly became apparent that all fairways would benefit from the new practice. Outstanding displays of striping were created in the process – at times so breathtaking that country club golfers applauded the work of their superintendents and raved about the new fairways to their friends and their fellow players (Figure 3.1A). At first, the professionals on tour were reluctant to accept the new cutting patterns, and for a while, tours demanded "plain" fairways, without striping. Eventually, tour officials relented, and with some prodding from television producers, superintendents were given a free hand to use their imagination. Interestingly, some traditional courses have maintained their fairways the old-fashioned way by cutting half the fairway in one direction and the other half the opposite way (Figure 3.1B). Many courses have had their maintenance budgets reduced, and this practice is more and more common because of its cost-effectiveness.

Figure 3.1A *Outstanding displays of striping the fairways attracts the attention of golfers*

Figure 3.1B *Cutting half the fairway in one direction and the other half the opposite way. AKA: there and back.*

There was an unexpected and beneficial side effect of cutting fair-ways with riding triplex greens mowers (Figure 3.2) and removing the clippings. Superintendents in northern regions who had been struggling with *Poa annua* infestation in their bentgrass turf noticed that the bentgrass thrived, once the switch was made to lightweight mowers. After only a single season of regular cutting with the riding greens mowers, bentgrass could be seen spreading and outgrowing the *Poa annua*. This was most remarkable, and a huge bonus for superintendents who wanted to promote bentgrass at the expense of *Poa annua* without resorting to costly and unpredictable herbicides.

Since the use of lightweight mowers, bentgrass has been able to outperform the *Poa annua*. We do not know of any good reason that this occurs. Little scientific research has been done at our colleges and universities to explain this phenomenon. We suspect, however, that it is related to compaction in the surface layer of the soil. Bentgrass grows best on loose soils, and *Poa annua* is one of only a few grasses that will survive on compacted soils. Lightweight mowers, by their very nature, cause less compaction than the heavy tractors of years past, and hence the bentgrass has a better chance to prosper. Now, because of the presence of lightweight mowers, new courses that are seeded with bentgrass have been able to maintain homogenous cultures with little invasion of *Poa annua*.

Figure 3.2 *Using triplex greens mowers to cut fairways creates striping effects that are extraordinary.*

Superintendents who were progressive thinkers during the early 1980s and switched to the new cutting methods deserve a great deal of credit for their foresight and determination. At first, those individuals were ridiculed and berated by their colleagues for catering to the whims of finicky golfers. They received little support from their colleagues and professors who at that time did not understand the new method and thought that this concept was just a passing fad. The industry was also slow to recognize the potential benefits. Eventually, the manufacturers of triplex greens mowers saw the benefits and advantages of the lightweight mowers and produced a fiveplex mower (Figure 3.3) that gained wide acceptance in the industry. These lightweight fairway mowers have become the norm in the industry for mowing fairways. Manufacturers continue to improve these mowers by increasing the quality of cut, the mowing speeds, and traction for wet or hilly terrain while using alternative fuel and electric to power the units.

Figure 3.3 *The use of fiveplex mowers enables fairways to be cut in a very short time.*

On southern courses, Bermuda fairways have long provided extraordinary playing conditions for skilled golfers. The turf is cut very closely, at less than ½ inch, and provides tight lies that enable golfers to aptly spin the ball. Another benefit is that the closely cut fairways allow plenty of roll for well-struck shots. There may be times during the season when the grass is growing so fast that the height of cut should be raised on Bermuda fairways in order to avoid scalping. Kikuyu and Zoysia, both warm-season grasses, provide high-quality turf but at a much greater height, which allows golfers to scoop their shots while retaining spin. In the northern climatic zone, bluegrass cultivars, which also provide for excellent playing conditions, are often used instead of the tenuous bentgrass, but, again, these cultivars require a higher cutting height. Recently, many low-cut bluegrass cultivars have been introduced that are quite acceptable and are well suited for a lower cut of height on fairways. These new cultivars are gaining favor in northern climates.

Ryegrass was once used as an alternative when neither bentgrass nor Bermuda grass filled the bill, but has since lost favor because of its susceptibility to gray leaf spot, a devastating disease that wiped out many fairways in the late 1990s. Ryegrass is still used in conjunction with other species or alone as in overseeded winter turf.

CUTTING FAIRWAYS

The objective is to provide the golfers with a consistent playing surface, and consistency can be provided only when the grass is mowed regularly and with expertise. The height of cut must be sufficiently low to ensure that there is no grass between the ball and the clubhead at the time of impact. The ball should sit up perfectly on closely groomed turf. Low-handicap golfers and golf professionals prefer tight lies with very little grass between the ball and the earth. From such lies they make the golf ball spin when it lands on the green. Higher-handicap golfers tend to be happier with more turf under the ball so that they can scoop or sweep the ball with a fairway wood or a low iron. Achieving these conditions for all types of golfers, of course, is nearly impossible, and we must also compromise, somewhat, by taking into account the needs of the grass.

The following factors should govern the decisions that prudent superintendents must make when cutting fairways:

1. *The height of cut on fairways should be $^5/_8$ inch or less.* Golfers the world over demand closely cropped turf on the fairways. They want tight lies and lots of roll. There are certain species of grass that do not tolerate such a shortcut and the cutting height needs to be raised. Such is the case on bluegrass fairways in the northern zone. Not every golf course wants or needs close-cut fairways. Various bluegrass mixes make an excellent turf that is quite playable for even the most discriminating golfers. The coolseason fescues and ryes are also often cut at below 1 inch. Fairways that are overseeded with rye and *Poa trivialis* in the southern states during the winter season are also cut at the ½-inch height. Superintendents who, for whatever reasons, wish to grow 1-inch grass on their fairways should expect to struggle with their bosses, committees, and the golfing community. At many golf courses fairways are cut at less than ½ inch. Both bent and Bermuda grasses can tolerate the lower height with minimal ill effects. Although visually appealing, maintaining a lower height of cut may not be a cost-effective approach for many golf-course budgets. Fairways that are cut extremely short will virtually have a turf quality that is similar to that of the greens.

2. *The frequency of cut is determined by the rate of growth of the turf.* The faster the grass is growing, the more often it needs to be cut. When the grass is fertilized regularly and growing actively, it may need to be cut every other day. Many superintendents cut fairways Mondays, Wednesdays, and Fridays. At times, the grass is growing so vigorously that three times per week is just not enough. Arrangements then have to be made to cut the fairways on weekend mornings or to add

an extra day to the weekly schedule. The use of growth regulators has significantly reduced the rate of growth on fairways and the need to cut as often. Clipping disposal has become much less of a problem on fairways treated with these products for the simple reason that substantially fewer clippings are removed.

3. *Pattern cutting on fairways is a matter of personal choice, and done with some degree of imagination, or television-fed golfers will soon find a superintendent who can provide picture-perfect cut grass.* Straight cutting lines on fairways are as important as they are on greens and tees. The age-old method of cutting toward a tree on the horizon will provide a straight line every time. Of course, there are courses without trees, and in such cases, another feature or focus point will do just fine. Sometimes, instead of cutting a straight line, superintendents have been known to follow the contour of a water hazard. This makes for an interesting deviation from the more commonly used checkerboard pattern.

4. *The fairway edge has become an important feature of the golf hole.* The contrast between the short, light green fairway and the much darker and longer rough is startling and provides subconscious boundaries in the golfer's mind. Sometimes there is an intermediate cut, or step cut, to make the shapes and the shading even more interesting and pronounced. Golfers like this transitional cut, as it reduces the severity of the penalty between a heavenly lie on the fairway and a difficult shot from an ankle-deep rough. Over time, the repeated cutting of fairways, as with greens, often results in the fairways losing their shape. The best way to correct this situation is to employ an experienced golf course architect to recreate fairways with sweeping curves. It takes a special talent, as well as expert knowledge, to make the curves suit the needs of the game of golf. Architects are authorities on where fairways should be cut narrow or wide, and where they should bell out or crimp in. The preferred solution to make these corrections in design is to hire an architect, but if this is not possible, then two other methods of restoring the contour should be considered. The first would be to use a long hose to form the proposed outline of the new curve, and the second method is to place stakes outlining the proposed new form. In either case, after deciding the proper location of the new curves, white paint should be applied to outline the proposed contour. Cutting a strip of sod along the intended curved line and replacing the extended fairway area with similar fairway turfgrass will ensure that the new curves will be clearly visible for many years to come.

5. *An extension of the fairway, the short turf that surrounds the green is usually cut at an even lower height than the fairway.* It is sometimes

described as *collars, aprons,* or *frogs' hair.* At some courses, the collar may just be one cut around the outside of a green, usually at a height slightly higher than the green and somewhat lower than the fairway. At other courses, the collar, which now becomes an apron, is extended somewhat, especially at the front where it is cut in such a fashion that it blends in with the fairways. Yet another method involves using a walk-behind greens mower for the collar and the transition zone between the fairway and the green. Turf maintained in this fashion encourages golfers to putt from these areas. Superintendents all have their own particular preferences and are usually assisted by their green committee or golf architect advisors in determining what's best for the golfers and course.

6. *Mower operators should be wary of sprinkler heads that they are apt to encounter when cutting fairway grass.* Sprinkler heads are ideally leveled so that the operator can drive over the top without worrying about cutting a sprinkler instead of the grass. If necessary, slow down on the throttle and ever-so-gently glide over the sprinkler, but if the sprinkler head is higher than the grass, then there is no choice but to cut around the obstacle. Operators should report all improperly adjusted heads to the superintendent, especially raised sprinkler heads that should be adjusted immediately before disaster strikes. When a mower swallows a sprinkler, all sorts of horrible things are apt to happen. At best, the mower will just take a bite from the collar of the sprinkler – no big deal, just an ugly scar. At worst, the sprinkler will be torn from its subterranean mountings, which is immediately followed by a geyser of water nearing Old Faithful proportions.

   Good greenkeeping calls for level sprinkler heads that are neatly trimmed on the fairways, on the tees, as well as the collars around the greens. If the sprinklers have been pushed out of kilter by vehicles or in some northern areas by thawing and freezing of the ground, they should be readjusted on a regular basis. There is no excuse for this condition to persist on any golf course.

7. *When clippings are picked up as part of the fairway cutting process, they must be removed in some manner that is economical and expeditious.* Some superintendents have arrangements that include a large dumpster to be emptied at a local waste disposal site. This method tends to be costly and can be malodorous during the warm summer months when the dumpster cannot be picked up as often as needed. A more environmentally friendly method involves composting the clippings and, in the process, mixing fresh soil with the grass snippets. A large area is required for this method, and the resulting "green" mixture of humus-rich topsoil can be put to good use in flower beds, planters, gardens, and even divot mix.

If the rough is spacious, the clippings from the fairways may be spread there without having any adverse effect on the play of the game. Keep in mind that the clippings disposed of in the roughs get chopped up by the mowers on a regular basis. Of all the ways to spread the fairway clippings, scattering them in the adjacent rough is probably the most economical, but care must be taken that they are disposed of properly. Operators who just dump the grass will cause grief to the golfer whose ball rolls into the areas that have clumps of clippings that are not evenly distributed, which makes for unplayable lies. When piles of clippings are left for any length of time, the grass underneath will smother and die and becomes unsightly. Merely dumping clippings in naturalized areas is sloppy maintenance and is an unacceptable greenkeeping practice.

DEW REMOVAL AND DRAGGING

The formation of dew on grass during the early morning hours makes for all kinds of unpleasantness:

- Dew on the grass makes for an ideal environment for the growth of different fungal diseases. It is easy to identify the mycelia of Dollar Spot and Pythium as they spread on the wet turf. Actually, the best time to scout for disease is during the early morning, while the dew is still on the grass.
- Heavy dews impede the quality of cut of the fairway mowers. It's always best to mow dry grass as opposed to wet turf. Many superintendents have begun the practice of mowing fairways in the early evenings when golfers are finished with their round and the grass is still dry.
- Golfers dislike dew-covered fairways, not only because the roll of the golf ball is slowed, but also because the moisture can cause wet shoes.

For those reasons alone, many superintendents have resorted to dew removal in the morning before the golfers arrive and before the cutters mow the fairways. One way to remove the dew is to use a heavy rubber hose that is strung between two maintenance carts and then is dragged across the turf. The dew is dispersed and slithers down among the blades of grass. In place of a rubber hose, a thick polypropylene rope embedded with a lead cable can be used (Figure 3.4). Yet a third method is to drag a heavy net behind a truckster. It is best to drag from the green to the tee, in the opposite way that the grass leans, which is caused from cart traffic moving from tee to green. This will also pull the grass up a bit while removing the dew. Don't be afraid to include the green and even

Figure 3.4 *Dragging the fairway in the early morning knocks the dew off the leaf blade and helps to disperse clippings, worm casting, and slows the spread of disease.*

the tee in the dragging process. It takes only a few extra minutes. Two experienced workers can drag all 18 fairways in just over an hour.

When worm casts are a problem, dragging will break up the casts and turn the messy little piles into beneficial topdressing. On some courses when clippings are not collected, dragging will help to scatter the wet clumps of clippings that were left behind. The greatest benefit of dragging is expediting the drying of the grass for golfers and the cutters, and in the process helping to diminish the spread of disease.

UNEVEN FAIRWAYS

On older courses it is often common to find irregular depressions, aka "bird baths," on the fairways. Such areas are difficult to cut smoothly, and their uneven growth spoils the appearance of otherwise perfect fairways. Low areas should be raised to blend in with the surrounding terrain. This work is best done during the shoulder season when nature provides ideal conditions for growth. Do not wait for an unsolicited complaint. Instead, take the initiative and improve the appearance and the playability of the golf course. If it is not possible to correct all fairways in one season, start raising or leveling the uneven surfaces of a few fairways each season. Continue the process seasonally, until all fairways are smooth and blend with the surrounding terrain. Starting the process on the 18th fairway will leave the golfer as he finishes the game with a favorable impression of the course.

SUMMARY

Fairways are prime play landing areas and, as such, ought to be in excellent condition at all times. The simple rule governing golf – you must "play it as it lies" – requires superintendents to manage fairway conditions often beyond that of tees, where a golfer may move the ball to any position he or she likes. Superintendents should remember that the number of times a fairway is cut relates to its smoothness. Smooth conditions aid the balls to roll a few extra yards and provide a platform to position the ball for the next important golf shot. The importance of dew removal as a method of disease prevention cannot be overemphasized. Anyone who has witnessed the ugly mycelium on damp grass in the morning will know precisely what we mean and will be motivated to make dew removal part of the fairway maintenance program. A well-cut fairway, exquisitely striped, is a magnificent piece of turf that even the most discriminating golfers will find irresistible. Keep in mind, however, that although very enticing, striping the fairways may be costly and timely, and alternatives should be considered if the budget is restrictive.

4

The Rough

When superintendents speak of the rough, they are referring to the grassed areas immediately in front of the tee, adjacent to the fairways, and on both sides of, as well as behind, the green. Today, the rough on North American courses is, as a rule, maintained in the 2-inch range, fertilized, watered regularly, and is comparable in quality to the lawns of many homes. Currently, many North American courses also include areas in the rough that are environmentally friendly that contain native grasses, wildflowers, pollinator plants, bird sanctuaries, and other animal habitats. The rough may render distinct impressions on various golf courses around the world. The rough area may include unkempt grass, gorse, heather, shrubs, and also naturalized areas.

The rough on our courses in North America is very much like the fairways of a half-century ago. During the growing season, the rough is trimmed regularly, often twice a week, and also fertilized so that it will be thick. The weeds in the rough are sprayed as needed, and occasionally the turf is treated for disease. The golfers in America are amongst the most pampered players in the world. They play on the slickest greens, the flattest tees, and the smoothest fairways, but nowhere are they more spoiled than by the grooming of the rough. Golfers on our courses rarely lose a ball unless it is hit into the water or out of bounds. Clearly, the rough receives a great deal of care.

DEFINING THE ROUGH AREA

In terms of the total area of the golf course, the rough occupies the largest acreage. A typical 18-hole course is built on approximately 150 acres. Following is a breakdown of the land area devoted to each playing area:

Greens:	2–3 acres	2%	Water/Wetland:	5–15 acres	9.3%
Tees:	3–4 acres	3%	Naturalized Areas:	10–25 acres	11%
Fairways:	25–35 acres	20%	Rough:	80–95 acres	54%
Sand:	1 acre	0.7%			

These are approximate figures that can vary somewhat from course to course. In any case, because of the large area it encompasses, maintaining the rough when it is actively growing is a mammoth job. When the rough cutters go out in the morning, they are like a swarm of locusts, devouring the long grass in front as they move and leaving behind a sward of neatly trimmed grass that pleases even the most particular golfer.

CUTTING THE ROUGH

Rough needs to be cut routinely and when properly maintained will help the speed of the game. Some superintendents will mow a secondary cut, also known as an intermediate cut, which is cut higher than the fairway and shorter than the height of the rough. This cut is approximately 5–6 feet wide, or the width of a typical mower, along the outside edge of the fairway that transitions into the rough. This additional process will help golfers with their shot as they hit off the secondary cut. The cut needs to be uniform so that playing conditions do not vary throughout the course.

In prior years, a set of tractor-drawn reel mowers were often used. Now this piece of equipment is seldom found in the maintenance inventory, mostly because of the increased cost of upkeep and newer, more efficient equipment that has been introduced. To cut the rough, superintendents use a combination of some of the following pieces of equipment:

- Several rotary-type mowers of varying widths, either self-propelled or tractor-drawn
- One or more riding triplex or fiveplex reel-type mowers, also known as trim mowers
- Several hand rotary mowers as well as a number of string trimmers

An 18-hole course, especially in the springtime when the grass is actively growing, may require a larger-than-normal share of the crew to cut the rough. With familiarity of the rough area and an understanding of the work at hand, a well-organized superintendent will be able to coordinate the responsibilities of all the workers.

It stands to reason that the largest area should be cut by the fastest and the largest machine. In most cases, this is a self-propelled rotary mower with multiple decks, a set of tractor-drawn rotary mowers (Figure 4.1), or a combination of the two mowers. The smaller rotaries are used to cut around and between trees. The riding triplex rotary mowers or reel-type mowers are ideal for steep banks around tees and bunkers. Also, hand trimmers and hand-pushed rotary mowers are useful to pick up the grasses that are left behind by the other mowers. Cutting the rough is a team effort, and the results are best when all well-trained participants know their assignments and work together. In that manner, the work gets completed quickly and the entire course is constantly kept trimmed.

In the spring when there are sudden surges of growth the rough will need to be cut often. The challenge is to maintain the rough by keeping the crew one step ahead of the growing grass. The worst scenario imaginable is a warm rain on a Thursday in spring, followed by a long weekend. In just hours, the grass will burst from its roots and provide a thick green carpet that grows faster than the mowers can cut. Changes in the weather can cause rapid growth and the golfers will experience inconsistencies in the playing conditions: In some areas, the rough will be freshly cut and of perfect playing height; in other parts of the rough the grass will be much too long and golfers will waste time looking for balls adding to the conundrum of slow play. Therefore, turf managers should be prepared for long weekends or any weekends in the spring that coincide with periods of rapid growth. The greens crew should be willing to work overtime, or the rough will get out of hand and the superintendent is likely to receive phone calls and emails from angry golfers.

Figure 4.1 *Tractor drawn rough mower decks are still in use and can mow a lot of rough very quickly.*

Riding mowers on steep slopes present a distinct problem. The turf must be dry when sloped areas in the rough are to be cut. Because of safety concerns and the high degree of difficulty, the slope should be cut only by the most experienced operators (Figure 4.2). The machines need to be in the best of mechanical condition, each with the required safety equipment for the trained operator. Manufacturers employ the use of rollover protection systems (ROPS) and operators should always use them as they are intended. Steep slopes can be very dangerous; all precautions should be used when mowing, and if at all possible the slope should be left to grow naturally. Steep, grassy banks in the rough are especially difficult to keep trimmed.

The wheel-less "Flymo" performs admirably in such areas, but it is an arduous task to handle such a mower on a continuous basis. These areas can also be trimmed with the use of string trimmers (Figure 4.3). Both pieces of equipment should be operated by expert handlers, otherwise the end result will be a series of scalps and misses that will continue to look ugly long after the work has been completed.

Those who watch televised golf on the weekends may notice the beautiful striping exhibited at tournament sites not only on the fairways but also in the rough. Turf managers talk about this decorative method as striping, which refers to the creation of alternate light and dark green stripes. Striping can be enhanced by installing solid rollers on rotary-cutting units.

Figure 4.2 *The rough includes the surrounds of green complexes and requires specialized rotary mowers capable of mowing uneven terrain.*

Figure 4.3 *Steep grassy areas can be maintained by using string trimmers or hover mowers, as shown here.*

Some superintendents will encourage their workers to imitate the different art designs by the use of striping at their place of work. Golfers will also be impressed by and appreciative of the creations.

THE DEW OR PRO WALK

Superintendents at many courses now cut a strip from 5 to 8 feet wide through the rough from the front edge of the tee to where the fairway starts. This path is for the golfers who walk, so they won't get their feet wet, and is, therefore, known as a dew walk. It is maintained like the fairway but cut at a slightly higher height, and it is watered and fertilized in a like manner. It may be necessary from time to time to move the path a few feet in either direction, so that the turf will not wear out and die. The practice of cutting a dew walk has spread rapidly as a result of televised golf (hence the name Pro walk) and has gained wide acceptance among golfers. If the superintendent is apprehensive about introducing a dew walk, one might consider adding one or two walks to see if they are acceptable to the golfers. Caddies who don't wear waterproof shoes will thank the superintendent, too.

MAINTAINING SMALL BUT DIFFICULT ROUGH AREAS

No matter how diligently the cutters operate large mowers in the rough, there is always some long grass left behind in areas that can only be cut with small rotary mowers or with string trimmers. At every golf course, there is a routine of trimming around trees and other hard-to-get-at places. The course takes on an unkempt appearance when such routines are not followed. The best time to complete this work is immediately following the operation of the larger rough-cutting units. In this manner, the entire area will look uniformly maintained.

Most important, the rotary crew should be led by an experienced person. The leader will look after fueling the machines, making small repairs and adjustments, and most important, making decisions about what area needs to be cut next. Aspiring assistants often get their first experience at personnel management as rotary crew leaders. We emphasize that such a leader should be a working leader and not someone who stands around idly while others labor.

Careless rotary mower operators can easily cause damage to the bark of small trees. The threat is even greater with the use of string trimmers. The small trees can be protected by surrounding the trunks with mulch or placing short pieces of flexible drainage tile around the base. Superintendents, in an effort to save time, will spray around the bases of trees with herbicide, which eliminates the use of trimmers and, thus, prevents damage to the bark. This widely used grass killer affects only the grass and not the bark of the trees or the roots. This application must be sprayed by an experienced technician, and precautions must be taken when moving with the sprayer from tree to tree so that the drippings of the liquid from the sprayer do not fall on desirable turf. One or two applications around the tree bases during the course of a season will eliminate the need for trimming.

TIP: In some instances, superintendents will employ the use of growth regulators around trees and other areas that require hand trimming to slow down the growth of the grass and alleviate some of the periodic attention required to keep all things cut.

THE FESCUE ROUGH

Recently, fescue rough has come in vogue on golf courses, and golf course architects now often specify seeding some of the secondary rough with homogenous stands of fescue grass. Such turf requires infrequent cutting and can look quite spectacular, especially when the wind blows and moves the stems and seedheads like waves on water. This action brings an element of tranquility to a golf course that may have once been absent (Figure 4.4).

Superintendents who think that fescue rough is maintenance-free are sadly mistaken. Very quickly, the sparse turf is invaded by a variety of weeds that make the fescue rough unsightly. Such weeds must be removed, and because weed spraying in fescue rough is not always advisable, burdocks, goldenrod, and thistles are often pulled out by hand – an arduous job, to say the least.

When the fescue rough encroaches on the playing areas, it results in golfers losing balls and slowing down the pace of play. Superintendents should be observant and look for excessive concentrated foot traffic in the long grass, which is an indication that many golfers are looking for lost balls. Sometimes these areas are unintentionally irrigated, which adds to the unruly thick swards of turf that are close to the line of play. These areas should be evaluated and possibly trimmed shorter to speed up play. Rough areas that are out of play add an element of beauty to golf, but if allowed to expand and start to interfere with the regular flow of the game, such beauty can quickly become a trodden-down, unattractive hazard.

From time to time, the fescue rough may also need to be cut to preserve the natural look. The fescue can be cut with a tractor-driven

Figure 4.4 *When fescue roughs go to seed and change color, they can provide stunning framing for golf holes like this backdrop of a putting green (left). However, these areas are not free of maintenance and can hinder the speed of play if installed too close to landing areas (right).*

rotary mower, flail mower, or farm-type sickle bar mower at a height of at least 6 inches. Needless piles and/or clumps of clippings should be removed. From time to time, herbicides may need to be applied to control the weeds.

NATURALIZED ROUGH AREAS

During the 1970s, Paul Voykin, a superintendent from the Chicago area, started preaching the gospel of: "Overgrooming is overspending." Paul was at the forefront of superintendents who recognized that large areas of a golf course that were out of play could be naturalized and planted with native wildflowers, thus saving time and labor that might otherwise have been devoted to cutting the grass on such areas. Today, many superintendents have adopted this method and have added black-eyed Susans, coneflowers, columbines, cornflowers, coreopsis, milkweed, and other species in accordance with the hardiness zone and have sanitized their naturalized areas by removing weeds (Figure 4.5). Golf courses have been recognized by providing habitat and stopovers for many insect pollinators like honey bees, moths, wasps, and butterflies. Some superintendents have even learned to keep bees on their courses and sell the honey to the membership to further promote future pollinator projects.

Figure 4.5 *Golf courses have been recognized as safe havens for many different plants and wildlife. A stand of milkweed in an out-of-play area provides food and shelter for important pollinators like the Monarch butterfly.*

The first steps to establishing a naturalized area with wildflowers require fertile soil, moisture, and occasional mulching to preserve the moisture. Maintaining a naturalized rough area will require a controlled burn of the vegetation at least once every three years during the spring. This burn is a necessary process that will help to regenerate the plants, similar to the way it happens in nature when lightning strikes. This type of burn may be regulated by several governmental agencies and may also require various permits. Maintaining wildflowers requires as much attention as any other plant material.

It is not necessary to overseed with grass or to plant wildflowers in order to create naturalized areas. When out-of-play areas are left to their own devices and are no longer cut, they will automatically revert to their native state. We have seen this happen, time and time again, but the superintendent must be patient when embracing this method. It may take several seasons for the desirable species to become established and dominant, and during that time some selective trimming may be necessary to achieve the desired results. Often, time is not a luxury to convert these areas to their naturalized state and superintendents must take a more proactive approach by planting seed and plugs of native plants. A common practice is to plug small plants on the exterior of the area and use seed in the middle to establish naturalized areas.

Another option some superintendents have employed is to combine their naturalized areas with tree nurseries. This idea has merit, as long as it is understood that small trees need encouragement. In their initial stages, trees should be mulched around their base, protected from rodents and rabbits, and provided with nutrients that are necessary for growth. In the end, only the healthiest trees will survive in this natural environment. As the trees grow larger, they can be transplanted for use on the golf course property. If a nursery is part of the natural area, care must be taken to transplant the trees before they are too large. There is always a risk that trees will take over the naturalized areas. To avoid this situation, sapling trees should be removed before they become established. The costs for developing a naturalized area will depend on the size, scope, and variety of the plantings that are desired by management. When developing a naturalized area, it is important that superintendents research proper plant material with local experts. Superintendents concur that naturalized areas are often more expensive to maintain than the primary roughs. It appears that beauty has a price.

SUMMARY

There are times when superintendents have wonderful opportunities to leave living legacies. Letting the grass grow in out-of-play areas and planting trees and wildflowers are examples. Such havens of tranquility, where birds make nests, rabbits scurry, and bees buzz are proof of the superintendent's role as an environmentalist.

A rough may mean different things to different people, and golfers and superintendents rarely agree on what actually describes the rough. To the golfer the rough is a meaningful punishment for errant shots. For the superintendent the rough provides an opportunity to frame the fairways on the course in a natural way. A rough is never static. It changes with the seasons, it changes over the years with the encroachment of natural growth, and it also changes as a result of humans' interference with nature. Whatever form or shape a rough takes, it provides character and contrast on a golf course. If a rough provides a challenge as well, then most players will also be happy.

5

Bunkers and Their Maintenance

During a typical round of golf, there are only a few shots that are actually played from the bunkers. However, golfers are the most critical about the condition of the course when it comes to the sand in the bunkers. When golfers fail to execute a perfect shot from a sand bunker, it is rarely seen as the fault of the person swinging the club. The blame invariably lies with the sand in the bunker. The sand is too hard or too soft, too fluffy or too dry, too coarse or too fine – or even more so, the common complaint is the sand lacks consistency. Sand and bunkers are very controversial, and when being discussed can make otherwise rational persons become quite unreasonable.

Bunkers are an essential part of golf for the following reasons:

- They add challenge to the game.
- They frame and define golf holes.
- They provide contrast and accent.
- At times, both sand and grass bunkers serve to catch wayward shots.

TYPES OF BUNKERS

Walter Woods, the legendary links supervisor at St. Andrews, Scotland, in a letter, contributed this information about bunkers in his native country:

No one knows when bunkers came into play, and like many things in the old days, just evolved by trial and error. We do know that golf originated on the east coast of Scotland on the sandy windswept coast from Aberdeen right down to St. Andrews and round to Edinburgh. This is where golf as we know it began, and the golfers would play on roughly mown fairways through hollows and mounds from tee to green. Most of this land supported nothing else but rabbits and sheep, and the golfers soon discovered that some areas in the lee of the hollow protected the sheep from the wind, and soon the whole depression was so severely worn that it was better to turf the banks and make the sand uniform to make it a fair hazard for everyone. As the years passed, more bunkers came into play, particularly at the greenside, for it was discovered that they did create more interest and demanded more accuracy.

Owing to the introduction of the rubber gutta percha golf ball, which made golf easier and more predictable and most importantly, less expensive, golf soon became popular first of all in England, then Europe and Asia, followed by North America. Scottish professionals were in demand to become golf course architects, having a head start in golf course design. Bunkers provided one area where strategy could be provided and used to create interest into the concept of parkland golf courses.

Revetted Bunkers at St. Andrews, Scotland

St. Andrews was the forerunner of bunker building, and the easiest way to build the bunkers was to copy the construction of walls that were erected by the stonemasons. Starting at the bottom, a solid foundation is made to the shape of the inside of the bunker. A layer of turf is then laid onto the compacted sand. This process is continued upward by laying the next layer slightly back from the previous layer, which dictates the angle and prevents the face from being vertical. The more one sets the next layer of turf back from the previous layer, the greater angles one makes. At all times, one must backfill with sand and keep the turf and the sand compacted. Once the revetted turf is up to the desired height, it is topped with a collar of turf. The steeper the face, the longer the slope of sand should be to allow the ball to roll away from the face or edge.

Revetted faces using turf last for about three to four years but can be made to last longer if good maintenance is practiced with brushing, watering with a hose, and adding a wetting agent. Apprentice greenkeepers are taught this skill at an early age and just like golf, this has been introduced all over the world (Figure 5.1).

Golfers walking or climbing out of the bunker can wear down the turf wall. It can be patched by creating a foundation at the worn part and then building upward and fitting the layers of the side into the existing turf. Revetting bunker faces is labor intensive and can only be of value

Figure 5.1 *Revetted bunker design provide a unique challenge to the most skilled superintendent often requiring periodic rebuilds of their telltale face.*

where mounds do not provide an acceptable alternative. Links land is one area where revetted faces can be beneficial, mainly to prevent sand from blowing away. If a large amount of revetted bunker faces is required, it will be necessary to have a large turf nursery. The thicker the turf, the quicker the face can be built. The thick turf with its fibrous roots provides a block effect that conveys a dramatic finished look.

The design of revetted bunkers has been copied by architects in North America. Sometimes just a few bunkers are done in this manner to give a particular course a Scottish flavor. Some superintendents use artificial turf to create the revetted layer extending the life of the specialized face and the need for periodic replacement.

Sand Bunkers

Trees or water can take the place of bunkers effectively, but when a property lacks either one or both, then sand bunkers are often the only desirable alternative. Golf course architects use their creative talents to shape mounds alongside fairways and then accentuate these features by including sand-filled hollows and flashes. In that manner, they try to duplicate what the sheep and the winds did naturally in Scotland many years ago.

In olden times, it has been alleged that the location of the fairway bunkers on golf courses were often determined by the abundance of divots in certain locations. As an alternative to repairing the divots constantly, greenkeepers would simply dig out an area to create a grassy hollow or a bunker.

With much forethought, bunkers are positioned near the green, adding difficulty and challenging the golfer in their attempt to reach the putting surface. The design of the bunker should not encompass the green to the extent that it is difficult to exit the green after the hole has been completed. Surrounding the green with too much sand can create irregular traffic flow and unnecessary damage to the turf (Figure 5.2).

Many golfers fear making their shots out of the bunker, and these scary thoughts often lead to pitiful shots and higher scores. Escaping from bunkers or being able to avoid them altogether is one part of what makes golf such an interesting and addictive game. Meanwhile, golf course superintendents have to deal with the realities of maintaining sand bunkers, which is often a much more difficult task than just growing grass.

The Sand in Bunkers

An acceptable bunker sand is hard to find and rarely available locally. White silica sand is the favorite with many superintendents and golfers alike.

Figure 5.2 *Too much sand, perhaps? Some bunkers are so large and still require continual maintenance. A power rake begins the process of raking a bunker during the morning hours.*

The sand particles are uniform in size and angular, rather than rounded, which makes for a firm surface. Its brilliant white color makes the bunkers stand out on the golf course (Figure 5.3). When the sand is still new, it can be dazzling and almost blinding to the golfers who have the misfortune of finding themselves in such bunkers. Some architects and superintendents will choose a more subdued color that is softer on the eyes and also blends in better with the existing shades of the surrounding landscape.

Architects all over the world soon realized that bunkers improved the visual effect of what was once flat boring ground and transformed the land by installing picturesque bunkers (Figure 5.4). American architects took advantage of this and were soon constructing large bold bunkers filled with white silica sand that provided a more modern approach to golf course design.

Superintendents should analyze why a change of sand is necessary before making the decision to switch sand. The sand may not be the reason that the bunker is in poor condition; these adverse conditions may be a result of improper drainage or the bunker design. It should be determined what is necessary to make the bunker acceptable, before rebuilding or adding new sand. If new sand is added in a bunker, it should be compacted with a mechanical tamper before the bunker is put into play. Wetting the new sand also helps stabilization. It takes time for sand to settle, and fresh sand should not be added prior to a tournament.

Figure 5.3 *Brilliant white color sand bunkers stand out against the surrounding turf.*

Figure 5.4 *Spectacular sand bunkers created by Mother Nature herself at Sand Hills Golf Club in Mullen, Nebraska, change each year with blowing winds and rainfall.*

The particle size of sand is extremely important. Fine sand blows away in the wind. Coarse sand often leaves scratch marks on golfers' clubs, and sand blasted out of the bunker unto the green can dull the blades of the mowers. Sand that is characterized by round-faced particles tends to create unstable ground, making shots somewhat more difficult for golfers. When the sand particles are angular, they will compact more easily and provide stable footing. Such sand may easily become too hard because of compaction and will require routine raking.

Describing the perfect sand in terms of particle size leaves many factors out of the equation, but it is generally agreed that a major portion of the granules should be 0.25–1.00 mm. Mason sand that is cleaned, modified, and washed and has virtually no clay or silt is often the best available local sand to use and it allows an excess of 20 inches (51 cm) per hour infiltration rate. Sands that contain a high percentage of clay and silt will drain slower and turn the bunker into a bathtub after a rainfall. A penetrometer is used to evaluate ball lie in a bunker. Sands that have a high tendency to bury the ball on impact are not desirable and are considered soft. Penetrometer values of 2.4–2.8 (kg/cm^2) provide the most desirable and consistent ball lies. Particle shape of the sand can dictate the way a ball interacts with the surface as well. Analyzing the particle size, measuring the infiltration rate, and evaluating the playability of the sand should always be accomplished prior to installing new sand.

A superintendent charged with choosing a certain type of sand for use is well advised to check with fellow superintendents from courses in a wide surrounding area and do a thorough study of available materials. Professionals will seek outside advice for the benefit of the golfers. Once the available materials are found, a decision can then be made by the superintendent and a committee to select which sand is best for the situation. Before making a final decision, filling a practice bunker with a few selected sands and allowing golfers to practice from each of them will assist in the selection process of which one of the sands is most playable (Figure 5.5). Finding the most suitable sand is sometimes difficult, but once a source has been discovered, it is advisable to keep a pile in storage.

Golfers have asserted that they prefer firmer sand in fairway bunkers than in greenside bunkers. The reason for this may be that a hybrid club can be used from the firmer fairway sand, but a wedge is the preferred club to use from a lighter, looser sand in a greenside bunker, thus making it a challenge for the contemporary superintendent to fill the needs of all golfers with a suitable sand that is appropriate at these different locations.

Figure 5.5 *A practice bunker filled with different sands. (Photo by Wyatt Byrd, Biltmore Country Club, Barrington, IL)*

Reasons Why Sand Bunkers Should Be Renovated

When one or more of the situations in the following list occurs, it may become necessary to renovate bunkers:

- The sand has become contaminated with clay, silt, or stones.
- The sand lacks uniformity and depth from one bunker to another.
- The particle size of the sand is either too small or too large causing poor (plugged) lies.
- Golfers desire white instead of gray sand.
- The bunker drains poorly or not at all.
- The original shape of the bunker has been lost under the management of several superintendents over a period of years.
- The water is flowing into the bunker from surrounding areas causing the sand to washout after heavy rainfall events.
- The liner is not working properly.

Bunkers deteriorate and fail over time. Drainage systems get clogged or crushed, liners deteriorate over time, sand gets contaminated from dust and pollen in the air, leaf litter, and grass clippings. Sand is even lost through wind erosion, especially in the winter months. The lifespan of a newly installed bunker is only eight years.

When the site is selected for the bunker to be rebuilt, an awareness of the surrounding features, flow of slopes, and landscape will be essential so that the bunker face also blends into these surroundings. On many occasions, on fairway or greenside bunkers, the face can be shown to provide strategy and balance to the golf hole. Sand selection is also important. It should be able to compact sufficiently and yet allow the top two inches to be slightly softer. Whatever reason(s) may drive the renovation process, it is best to employ an experienced golf course architect at a very early stage. Once the plans have been approved and the money allocated, a competent golf course construction company should be contracted to carry out the work. At all times the superintendent should play an important part in the process of making the final decision for the selection of the sand's particle size and color, as well as supervising the installation of the sand in the bunker (Figure 5.6). After all, when the work is completed by both the architect and the contractor, the superintendent is left to look after the renovated bunkers for many years to come.

Pot Bunkers

Pot bunkers, though seldom considered, are probably one of the most interesting and often challenging bunkers on any golf course. Though

Figure 5.6 *New sand is deposited in a bunker via a conveyor belt from a material handler, saving labor and reducing damage to surrounding turf.*

the pot bunker may encompass just a few square yards in total area, when properly constructed, the bunker will capture far more balls for its size than one could imagine. The surrounding land slopes toward the crater and golf balls easily become entrapped by the bunker and are reluctantly freed with only an expert shot. An unfortunate golfer who finds his or her ball up against the face may have to play sideways, or even backward, to get out of the bunker. We have all seen golfers' frustration as they try to free their ball from the pot bunker, only to fail time and time again. How agonizing it must be to fail so miserably and finally just throw the ball onto the green in disgust! Greenkeepers are only too familiar with the anguish of golfers voicing their irritation with these bunkers – and on occasion also experience the same misfortunes while playing the game.

The face of a pot bunker is occasionally constructed like a sod wall, with layers of sod piled on top of each other and held in place with metal bars and wires. Such sides are hand-trimmed with Weed Eaters and at times even with scissors. The bunker should appear to be saucer-shaped with sand drawn to the edges so that golf balls will roll away from the edge.

Pot bunkers are invariably so small that they cannot be maintained with mechanical rakes but must be looked after manually. Because of their size, they quickly become foot-marked and need constant care by the greens crew.

Grass Bunkers

There are areas on the course where grass bunkers can provide a unique aesthetic look while offering a different challenge to the golfer. As the name implies, these bunkers are filled with grass instead of sand. Nevertheless, such bunkers are still very much a hazard because they present the golfers with a variety of uphill and downhill lies, as well as frequently longer-than normal rough-height grass. Grass bunkers require less maintenance, but just like sand bunkers, need to be well drained and possibly constructed with a catch basin in the lowest spot.

Waste Bunkers

Large areas of unraked sand intermixed with clumps of grass, shrubbery, and small trees have been included in some architectural golf course design plans. These areas are at times used to define a dogleg on a hole. Waste bunkers are not hazards as defined by the rules of golf, and golfers are allowed to ground their golf clubs in a waste bunker. Waste bunkers are seldom raked on a regular basis, and difficult lies are commonplace in such bunkers. It is a fallacy to believe that waste bunkers are maintenance-free. Attention needs to be given to all the vegetation inside the bunkers, including trimming the trees and shrubs, tending to the ornamental grasses that are frequently planted, and smoothing the sand periodically. If weeds become a problem, they must be sprayed or removed. Waste bunkers are generally quite flat and often lower than the surrounding lands and, therefore, require proper drainage. When necessary, tile line similar to that used in regular bunkers should be installed preferably at the time of construction.

BUNKER DRAINAGE

The various shapes of bunkers influence the collection and retention of water. Necessary provisions need to be made so that the collected water drains properly. Elaborate gridiron tiling systems under greens are commonplace, and most superintendents have accepted the same type of equally extensive drainage systems for bunkers. One single tile line through the center of a bunker is insufficient under most conditions, and most golf course architects will specify a herringbone design of drain tile with adequate lateral lines to take away normal rainwater and even a heavy downpour of storm water. The header of the herringbone should empty into a catch basin just outside the bunker, and from there be connected to a drainage main or taken into the rough (Figure 5.7a). A cleanout should

Figure 5.7a *The renovation of an existing bunker. Channels are dug for drain tile and pea gravel is piled to fill in the trenches and line the base of the bunker in preparation for a polymer spray.*

be installed at the opposite end of the catch basin, providing access to the system for cleaning out the main tile line should it become filled with sand. Using a hose with pressured water at the cleanout opening will allow the greens crew to flush out the main tile line.

In years past, superintendents experimented with filter cloth stockings installed around the drainage tiles. The premise was the stockings would prevent the bunker sand from entering into and clogging the tile. Others found that the stockings block the movement of water, or at least slow it down. For best results, we believe that the tile should be surrounded in pea gravel that is round and smooth. On new bunkers, the 4-inch tile should be laid in a trench that is partially filled with pea gravel, and is about 5–6 inches wide. The top of the tile should be at least 8 inches below the bottom of the bunker. This helps to prevent frost from bringing the tile to the surface in frigid zones. Throughout the installation, grade levels should be taken to make certain that there is gradual decline in the tile so that water drains. Making small adjustments in the height of the pea gravel at the bottom of the trench will ensure proper flow. When the base is satisfactory, install either perforated, flexible plastic tile or rigid construction-type tile with holes in the walls. Either type should be of

4-inch diameter. Cover the tile with more pea gravel, making make sure that both the tile and pea gravel are below the base of the bunker. In some instances, you may want to put a layer of coarse sand, which is called a choker layer, over the top of the pea gravel before the final layer of sand is put in place. The addition of the coarse sand will help prevent damage to the golfer's expensive sand wedges by avoiding scratching and denting that is caused by hitting directly into the pea gravel. There is understandable concern that no matter how careful the installation, some of the pea gravel will get mixed up with the bunker sand. For that reason alone, one should consider backfilling over the tile with coarse sand to circumvent the pea gravel mixing with the bunker sand. Superintendents and architects are keen to try new drainage methods and the trend now is to use a smaller 2-inch diameter perforated drainpipe. In this method, narrower trenches are cut into the base of the bunker utilizing a trencher with the digging teeth turned inward. The narrow pipe is then laid directly into the trench and covered with bunker sand.

BUNKER LINERS

Bunker liners can prevent the materials in the base of a bunker from contaminating the bunker sand. Contamination can sometimes occur when the water is allowed to flow into the bunkers or the bunker design has faces that are steeper than the angle that can be maintained to prevent the sand from slumping. Such flashes often look spectacular and make the bunkers visible from afar, but they can be a maintenance headache for the grounds crew. Without bunker liners, any sudden downpour, summer storm, or prolonged rainfall can wash the sand from the steep faces, causing the base underneath to erode and mix with the sand. Shoveling the sand or pushing the sand back up the slope with a bunker rake is a painstaking task and over time can result in increased labor costs and diminished playing conditions.

Bunker liners can be classified into several categories: filter fabrics, spray-on polymer products (Figure 5.7b), high-lofted nonwovens, and even porous aggregates. Bunker liners are installed throughout the base of the bunker and on the flashes between the sand and the subgrade. This method permits the water to flow down through the mat without disturbing either the sand or the base material.

There have been many advancements in bunker construction and renovation since our last update. Porous bunker liners constructed from concrete or aggregates in combination with new polymers have been a welcome advancement to keeping bunkers playable after heavy rains. The concrete or aggregate has taken the place of the pea gravel bed directly

Figure 5.7b *Better Billy Bunker polymer is applied to a layer of gravel to hold it in place and create a liner for the sand.*

underneath the sand and serves several purposes. They help to hold the sand in place after a rainfall event, they prevent sand from moving downward in the drainage system and keep the sand cleaner from unwanted particles moving upward. Drainage is still an important factor in a properly functioning bunker and still needs to be installed under these new liners.

In extreme northern climates, ground frost may cause severe heaving in the subgrade. This natural action may free stones from the subgrade and bring them to the surface of the bunkers. This is an unwelcome surprise in the spring. Superintendents have an obligation to remove objectionable materials from the bunkers. The use of bunker liners may be an excellent tool to prevent this type of contamination.

Bunker liners help prevent washouts and reduce the amount of sand that moves on bunker faces. It is important to regularly check the depth of the sand to prevent the bunker liner from being damaged. A depth of 4–5 inches of sand is adequate for new bunkers. It is helpful to obtain a water curve analysis from an accredited soil testing lab that can calculate how deep the sand should be inside the bunker. This will ensure the consistency of the sand and provide your players with an ideal moisture level throughout the bunker while also protecting your bunker liners.

Motorized bunker rakes that still have their cultivator tines attached have a tendency to dig in along the sides as well as the bottom of the bunkers, and they have been known to tear into fabric bunker liners with disastrous results. For these reasons, superintendents should be cautious when using motorized rakes and always monitor bunker sand depths to provide optimal playing conditions. Always research the advantages and cost of each product before considering which if any option may be best for the course.

RAKING THE BUNKER

The regular routine of golf course maintenance includes raking the bunkers. Prior to the invention of the mechanical bunker rake, caring for bunkers on an 18-hole course could be a monotonous chore taking the efforts of several staff members the better part of a day. A superintendent from Georgia was the first to invent a motorized bunker rake. Never mind that the contraption looked like a moon buggy. It was a prototype and soon copied by all the major golf course equipment manufacturers. Raking bunkers was changed forever. Bunker designs were no longer restricted and architects immediately set out to create large and impressive fields of sand that accentuated the playing areas and made for target golf at its best.

The job of raking bunkers is usually reserved for members of the greens staff that have been trained to operate the mechanical bunker rake with expertise. Raking bunkers is just as important as other assignments and must be done with the same degree of perfection that is applied to all other tasks. To rake bunkers competently and efficiently requires an energetic person who can get on and off the machine with ease. The person in charge of raking should be ahead of the golfers and alert to their whereabouts. If raking the bunker while golfers are approaching, they must be able to get out of their way quickly and stay out of the way of the players.

On older golf courses with traditional bunkers, there may not be enough space for the bunker machines to maneuver and, in such cases, hand-raking is the only alternative. The bunkers at Oakmont of USGA fame in Pittsburgh were hand-raked with hay rakes for many years. These antique instruments left characteristically deep grooves – many golfers despised them, and others thought they lent charm to this famous course.

To prevent plugged lies in high-flashed bunker faces, some super-intendents roll the sand smooth on the flashing and rake only the flat area of the sand (Figure 5.8). This encourages balls to roll back down into the flat bottom of the bunker. Golfers, caddies, and maintenance staff should all be trained to enter bunkers from the low side and never climb up the flashed areas, pushing sand down and creating huge footprint craters for the next group that comes through.

Figure 5.8 *Hand-raking bunkers takes a lot of time and provides the best results. A new practice is to compact and roll the slopes of the sand and rake the flat areas to prevent golf balls from plugging in the bunker faces.*

Golfers are usually so absorbed in their game that they either forget to rake the sand or do a haphazard job. At the same time, golfers should be encouraged to rake bunkers with two hands on the rake so as to achieve a more acceptable result. If the bunkers have been machine-raked in the morning, superintendents who know the shortcomings of their players should consider sending out staff in the afternoon to touch up the bunkers by hand-raking.

The selection of rakes to maintain the bunker is important. Old fashioned hay rakes were often chosen that had wooden, evenly spaced teeth; its large width enabled the individual who was raking to complete the work fast and efficiently. These old-fashioned wooden rakes have been phased out and are usually replaced with fiberglass rakes that are available in a variety of sizes. Many superintendents have found that the long-handled, large-headed fiberglass rakes, which are easier to reach into the bunker, are preferred by the golfers. Some golf clubs provide small bunker repair rakes, which are often thrown about with no regard for the players that follow. Where to place the rake is often discussed. Some say outside the bunker and others say inside. Logically speaking, it would be better to place the rake inside and away from the line of play, to prevent golf balls from being deflected. Some courses provide rakes on the golf cart, thus keeping the rakes from being placed in or around the bunker.

Steps to Rake a Bunker Properly

1. Place the hand rakes outside the bunker, while inspecting and removing debris.
2. If using a mechanical bunker rake, operate at half throttle through the center, making a gentle turn at the end, and continue with the same process.
3. Stay away from the bunker's edge by at least a foot. Touching the grass or the soil with the rake will contaminate the sand.
4. When the entire bunker has been raked, exit carefully, making sure not to drag any sand onto the surrounds.
5. Hand-rake the edges upward, and make sure that any marks left at the exit are obliterated. Any ruts in the bunker should be removed by hand-raking.
6. Replace the hand rakes inside the bunkers (or the area that is designated for rakes), and also check for damaged handles and tines.

EDGING THE BUNKER

On finely manicured golf courses, the bunkers are characterized by a sharp, distinctive edge. This is the result of meticulous work by proficient greenkeepers. If left unattended, the grass surrounding the bunkers would quickly grow into the sand, causing the bunker to lose its shape and definition. Golfers would have difficulty determining whether their golf balls were inside or outside the bunker, and because different rules apply, there could be problems with interpretations and with fellow players.

For the longest time, superintendents had their staff hand-edge bunkers several times during the golfing season. Power edgers with oscillating blades then came into use, and more recently used are the power trimmers with reciprocating teeth. A sharply defined edge is created with little effort, and now the work can be completed quickly.

The location of the bunker line cannot always be determined with certainty. Unless edging is done routinely, it is possible for the bunker's outline to be lost. If not maintained regularly, bunkers can quickly lose their original shape. In this situation, before any serious edging is contemplated, the superintendent should outline the bunker with a paint gun. After the bunker has been edged, the pieces of sod and strings of rhizomes must be removed from the bunker. The sand on the greenside should be raked back up, leaving a lip at the grass level. On the backside of the bunker, the sand should be raked to form a soft, rounded edge that will encourage playable lies. When edging fairway bunkers, a lip is not necessary in most cases and the sand should be raked to the grass level.

Golf courses that have limited staff or the proper machinery can try to address the edging situation by different means. Though it will not have the same appearance, it may be more cost effective and less time consuming. We are referring to a process that involves spraying the edge of a bunker with nonselective herbicide that effectively stops the grass from growing into the sand. There is another important benefit – by eliminating the use of the mechanical edger, we are also eliminating the chance that the surrounding soil will accidentally mix with the bunker sand. The herbicide must be applied carefully in a narrow band; otherwise, it will look unsightly.

SUMMARY

There has been an ongoing debate about placing the rakes either inside the bunkers on the sand or outside the bunkers on the grass. Rules officials have had a difficult time making up their minds about where the rakes belong. Now it seems that the majority of courses place the rakes on the sand where they can be easily seen by the golfers.

A regular routine of raking and edging the bunkers, trimming the surrounds, and making sure that the hand rakes are sufficient in number and in good repair are among the factors that help create a favorable impression of the golf course to regular golfers and visitors alike. Although greenkeeping is primarily an endeavor of trimming the grass, maintaining the bunkers is equally important. As previously indicated, the measure of a greenkeeper's competency is often determined by the way the bunkers are maintained. Maintain bunkers from a playability standpoint and golfers playing your course will appreciate your work.

When bunkers begin to fail (drain slowly, need sand, or need renovation), it is time for the superintendent to act. Do not wait until the bunkers become a negative topic of conversation around the clubhouse. Start the process of repairing, renovating, or refreshing the bunkers by seeing what other superintendents in your area are doing to keep these areas in tip-top shape.

6

Water

GREEN GRASS AND WATER

All living things depend on water. Without water, there would be no life. Water provides the vital life source for growing healthy green grass. In those few words lies a basic element of greenkeeping: Green grass depends on a water supply. Superintendents learn early in their careers that they must have water to grow grass, and in the days of watering with rubber hoses, that lesson was brought home through hard work and long hours by a watering crew. Anyone who has done a night shift on the watering crew knows about groping in the dark for pipe fittings, lugging water-filled hoses, and taking a nap in the pump house between sprinkler changes. The job required a strong back as well as a fearless mind. There were always frightening shadows in the dark and inexplicable sounds that sent shivers up the spine of the most stouthearted waterman. The first glow of dawn was a welcome sight, and the company of fellow greensworkers arriving for the day shift was warmly appreciated.

Fortunately, gone are the days of the hardworking and fearless watermen who thankfully performed their duties under the cover of darkness. The development of automatic sprinklers was a welcome sight for those who were responsible for maintaining quality turf. The superintendent is in charge of the watering operation and the advent of automatic sprinklers brought with it a whole new philosophy toward watering. Manual watering, by necessity, had encouraged drenching an area until it was thoroughly soaked, and once the saturated area had dried out, it was watered again. This method of watering was thought to encourage root growth because it was necessary for plants to extend their roots deeper in-between watering to obtain the precious liquid needed for their survival. Now that watering has become automated, it

Figure 6.1 *Superintendents can apply water today with pinpoint accuracy, providing the turf with only the water it needs to grow and be healthy. Moisture meters are used to tell when the turf will need a sip of water.*

also has become possible to water the entire course nightly, including the greens, tees, fairways, and on occasion the rough. Usually this is just a light watering, perhaps one or two turns of the sprinkler, but water just the same.

Programming the automatic sprinklers was an easy task in comparison to scheduling manual nightly watering. However, it was easy to turn on too many sprinklers for too long a period, which at some courses led to overwatering and sloppy wet turf. Superintendents had to learn how to water all over again and how to manage their watering systems for the benefit of the grass and the golfers.

WHEN WET IS TOO WET

A problem can occur if there is a malfunctioning fairway sprinkler, causing an area to be saturated, or when the system does not shut down when it is scheduled. Imagine an irrigation head spewing 50 gallons per minute or more over a circle with an 80-foot radius for six hours. That amounts to the equivalent of a 2-inch rainfall, and the mishap will result in a wet spot for at least a day. A malfunctioning greenside sprinkler, with much less output and smaller coverage, can still cause excessive wetness on the green. Overly wet greens are almost impossible to manicure, and golfers will more than likely leave extensive deep ball marks. The same applies to soggy fairways, which lessens the roll of the ball.

There are many adverse situations caused by excessive water. When a malfunctioning sprinkler causes excessive wetness, the affected area should be roped off and taken out of play. When rain is the culprit, golf cart traffic may have to be restricted to certain areas or path only if continuous cart path systems are in place. If there is an excessive amount of rain, the entire golf course might need to be closed. Soil scientists will testify that it is best not to walk or drive on supersaturated soils. This compression on supersaturated soils will cause the soil structure to lose its natural composition and become quite squishy, much like a mud cake in a child's hand. When the soil dries, it loses structure and there may be a lack of pore space, which can be a detriment to the plants' healthy root growth. Therefore, the excess water must either be allowed to drain naturally or be removed manually with a squeegee or a pump, so that oxygen can once again enter the root zone.

Excessive freestanding water can become quite warm in the heat of summer and may actually scald the turf. Superintendents should be aware of this phenomenon and make every effort to disperse this water as quickly as possible by opening existing drains, dispersing large quantities of water with a pump, or in smaller puddles, pushing the water out of the saturated areas with a squeegee turf roller.

WHEN WILTING GRASS NEEDS WATER

Recognizing the latter stages of wilting turf is one of the most important and difficult skills that aspiring superintendents should learn from their mentors. Competent assistants need to recognize the different stages and colors that send an alarm that the grass is beginning to wilt. This near-fatal process can happen very quickly. The greens look perfect in the morning, having been freshly cut with a distinctive checkerboard appearance. The early morning breeze is light and refreshing, and as the day approaches the noon hour, the winds quickly change, becoming strong and dry. As the temperature rises, the humidity falls, and by midafternoon the grass plants are losing more water through the leaves than they can take up through the roots. The plants quickly lose their turgidity and characteristically turn a purplish blue. Footprints from golfers on turf at this stage show as depressed grass that fails to spring back. Operators should refrain from cutting, fertilizing, topdressing, or verticutting when such stressful conditions prevail, or else the demise of the grass plants is certain.

Syringing

Wilting grass can be brought back to health by the simple expedient of syringing – a very light application of water, administered either by hose and nozzle or by the syringe cycle of the automatic watering system. Either way, the idea is to apply a small amount of water to the wilting grass plant. The water will improve the moisture level in the plant, and it will survive. This method is very successful and has been proven to work well. When syringing, the application of too much water can be detrimental. It can result in a soggy upper layer of the root zone in the turf, with all the harmful side effects that were mentioned earlier.

Syringing the greens is very important (Figure 6.2), but other areas may also require water. The aprons or collars will often start wilting even before the greens, and these sensitive strips need to be syringed during the course of a very dry day. Aprons can show signs of wilt before the greens, because the turf on aprons require more water, there is more leaf tissue and shoot growth to support. One should also keep in mind that aprons are subjected to mowers making turns leading to compaction, and golfers blasting sand out of greenside bunkers causes drying of the turf. In both cases, the apron or collar will need repair or extra maintenance. If aprons are lost repeatedly, they should probably be replaced with a better-quality soil mix and superior turf.

Figure 6.2 *In spite of the popularity of computer-controlled irrigation systems, hand syringing remains a common practice at many courses.*

On hot days during the summer, the high knolls on fairways may also need to be watered by syringing. A superintendent with many years of experience at a course will become very acquainted with the familiar areas that quickly show signs of stress. Such areas are singled out and often receive extra water at the crack of dawn in anticipation of a stressful day. This is practical greenkeeping, resulting in success where others fail.

TIP: A keen eye will recognize all the signs of wilting turf like footprinting and turf that begins to change color (purpling) from stress.

WHEN TO WATER

During a drought, there are certain areas on every golf course, such as the back of a green or a high tee, that show the first signs of stress and need immediate watering. Another sure sign of the need to water happens when the turf on the top of a French drain (see Chapter 12) starts to turn blue or shows signs of wilting. Veteran superintendents will immediately recognize these signs and will be looking for them. Their appearance rings a bell and triggers a reaction; now is the time to start an irrigation cycle. We suggest a nighttime watering with a lesser amount than may be required, and then playing catch-up with additional watering in the morning with the help of daylight. This method prevents overwatering, and in fact, keeps the entire golf course on the dry side and very playable.

Experience and sound judgment – along with weather stations, soil moisture sensors, and other intricate instrumentation – are necessary in making the decision of when to water (Figure 6.1). Using a soil moisture sensor to monitor the soil moisture can improve irrigation scheduling by measuring the existing volumetric water content of the soil anywhere in the field. These meters are lightweight and display measurement on an LCD screen. Overwatering can be avoided, and now it is not necessary that all grasses on the golf course be lush and green as long as there is ample moisture in the soil. Golfers tend to accept some areas that are browning off and greens that are firm, if these areas are still suitable for play. Greens that are pockmarked with ball marks are not always the result of golfers failing to repair their ball marks but the direct result of overwatering or wet greens. The same applies to fairways that are soggy underfoot and permit no roll of the ball.

LOCALIZED DRY SPOTS

Sand is now the only material that is commonly used for topdressing a green. A light sprinkling of sand is easy to apply and even easier to work into the turf. However, all this sand can have a serious side effect: localized dry spots (LDS). Over time, almost all greens that have been topdressed with sand, or built from a homogenous sand mix, develop brown areas of wilted grass that can range in size from 1 to 3 feet in diameter. No matter how long of a time the sprinklers are left on, the soil cannot absorb water under these dry spots. This hydrophobic condition is believed to be caused by a fungus that lives on the sand, and its mycelium, or fungal root system, shuts off the pore spaces and prevents water from entering the soil. Superintendents should be aware that when the organic matter content in soil mix rises above 3 percent, pore spaces between the particles of soil are shut off, which will then inhibit the movement of water and nutrients.

Aerating the localized dry spots (LDS) can temporarily alleviate the problem. Another method of treating LDS is the process of forking, which involves the use of a pitchfork to poke holes into the dry spots and then drenching the holes with a wetting agent or surfactant. There are several choices of surfactants that are now available. Many combine iron, liquid nitrogen, and biostimulants to control LDS. Wetting agents were introduced to break down the viscosity of water and improve water movement. Wetting agents make water droplets smaller and actually make water wetter, so that the water can penetrate into even the smallest of pore spaces and provide relief to thirsty plants. Greens treated with wetting agents are characteristically without dew in the morning, at least for the first few days after application. Wetting agents have much the same effect on grass and soil as rinsing agents have in dishwashers. Both break down the water into a thinner liquid. In a dishwasher, this results in no spots on the glasses, and in the soil the grass roots are able to drink with little effort. In fact, rinsing agents and wetting agents consist of very similar chemicals.

Rarely is the problem cured completely, apart from a prolonged rain, and even more so if it's followed by a cool period. Remarkably, the old-style push-up green rarely suffers from LDS, an indication that progress has a price.

THE PERCHED WATER TABLE

The late Dr. Bill Daniel from Purdue University is thought to have been the inventor and undoubtedly was the promoter of the perched water table in green construction. Dr. Daniel visualized a layer of sand atop a layer of gravel and a bed of tile. Water in the sand layer would reach field capacity and then flush through the gravel into the drainage tile. Greens built in that fashion could not be overwatered, and drained almost perfectly. In his lifetime, Dr. Daniel witnessed many greens and sports fields being built according to his specifications. Even some of these turf areas with perched water tables showed signs of localized dry spots during extreme weather conditions.

THE WATERING SYSTEM

The lifeline of any golf course is its watering system. Once that is understood, one will then also comprehend how critical water is for the survival of the grass. The intricate system of underground pipes, tubes, and conduits must be in perfect working order at all times for water to be applied when and where needed. When the system fails for any reason, its repair becomes a priority of the utmost order. Repairing pipe leaks, sprinklers, and electrical lines has become a highly specialized technical occupation. Most golf courses now employ someone to take responsibility of the watering system. That person needs to fully understand the operation of the pump house and must have the combined skills of an electrician and a plumber. The irrigation technician should realize that the job may possibly entail working in mud and water. For safety purposes, the area being worked on should be screened to protect the technician, especially when the work site is in the line of fire of flying golf balls.

What an Irrigation Technician Should Know

An irrigation technician should be knowledgeable with the following functions and duties:

- The operation of the pump house
- The location of all isolation valves and how to shut them off in the event there is an irrigation problem or a line bursts
- How to make pipe and electrical repairs
- How to use a voltmeter for checking voltage or ohm readings
- The principles of friction loss and the purpose of thrust blocks
- Sprinkler operation and water distribution patterns
- Water and air pressure fluctuations
- The principles of water hammer
- How to winterize the water system in northern climates and the startup procedure to recharge the system in the spring
- The use of irrigation computers and other handheld (radios, phones) to schedule and control the system

The Pump House

The irrigation system is the lifeline of the golf course, and the pump house is the central core of the system. The importance of the pump house cannot be overemphasized. A typical pump house on an 18-hole golf course may have several pumps with a total capacity of 1,000 gpm or even more. Most pump houses are now fully automated and fully pressurized at all times. The pump house is a sophisticated, complex building that houses many various controls, pumps, motors, fertigation supplies, and other products that are basic components of the irrigation system. The initial cost of an adequate pump house is a major expense. The necessity of maintaining the pump house in good operating order is, therefore, obvious. A chart posted in the pump house with a routine maintenance schedule will help to keep the pump house maintained properly and avoid potential problems with the watering system on the golf course.

Identifying and Repairing Leaks

The first step in repairing a breakage in the watering system is to determine the nature of the break. Is it the pipe, the swing joint, or the sprinkler that is leaking? Once the cause has been determined, close the isolation valve(s) that control the affected area – or, if necessary, shut down the pump.

Excavation

Place a piece of plywood near the area to be excavated. Cut the sod and remove it carefully with a long-handled sod knife. If repairing a swing joint or sprinkler, dig a square or rectangular hole, or if repairing a pipe, dig a trench, being careful not to cut the electrical wires (Figure 6.3). Make sure that the opening is large enough to provide adequate room to maneuver while making the repair. The excavated material should be placed on the plywood.

Repairing the Leak

After pumping the water out of the area, locate the leak. If the swing joint is at fault, the problem is most often a broken nipple. Replace it, and seal the threaded connections by wrapping one or two layers of Teflon tape around the threads of the pipe. Too many layers of Teflon tape on the pipe

Figure 6.3 *Irrigation repair holes become larger as the problem is repaired. Keeping the area clean will help to replace the soil and turf once the repair is made.*

thread can cause leaks or breaks. If the system has old galvanized fittings, it may be the cause of leaky swing joints and should be replaced with polyvinyl chloride (PVC) fittings.

Sometimes the cause of a leak is a cracked sprinkler body. This is often the case in northern climates after a harsh winter. If a sprinkler is to be replaced, releveling the new sprinkler is absolutely necessary. Tilted sprinkler heads cause uneven water precipitation patterns and waste water.

TIP: Leveling irrigation heads to the grade of the surface will increase water efficiency by 15–20 percent.

The most difficult repairs are those necessitated by broken pipe leaks, because they usually involve a section of pipe that needs to be removed. A longer excavating trench is required to make the repair. Pipe leak repairs are usually more time-consuming to complete. Use a sharp saw to make a clean, straight cut to remove a section of the pipe, then bevel the edges of the cut with a rasp or a file. Insert a new section of pipe using gasket repair couplings at both ends.

Many different tools are used to make repairs to the irrigation system. The following is a list of all the tools and items that should be available to excavate the site and repair the leak:

- Shovels, including a standard and a trenching shovel
- A long-handled sod knife
- A fine-toothed general-purpose saw or battery operated reciprocating saw with a quality saw blade
- A carpenter's hammer and a small 5-pound sledge hammer
- A pipe wrench and a set of vise grips suitable for metal pipe or PVC
- A set of screwdrivers
- General-purpose pliers and one pair of snap ring pliers
- Valve-insert tools for various makes of sprinkler heads
- Suction pump or a bailing bucket
- Plywood, to keep the job site clean
- Towels or rags to clean the area in need of repair
- Safety items such as screens, stakes, ropes and caution tape
- GUR (Ground Under Repair) signs, to keep the golfers happy

Most of these items should be carried on a small maintenance vehicle. All repair technicians should carry a two-way radio or a mobile phone so that they can quickly inquire and respond to the situation at hand.

Backfilling

Once the repair has been completed and the water pressure tested, the excavation should be backfilled with the original soil to within 6 to 12 inches of the surface, while being packed down with the technician's feet or a tamping tool. In the root zone area, backfilling with a modified soil mix is recommended. Soaking the repair site with water will also compact the soil. This helps to prevent settling. Replace the sod as levelly as possible, tamp it down firmly, and finally, fill the cracks with topdressing materials.

Winterizing the System

As winter approaches in the regions where the soil freezes below the irrigation line, the pipe lines and the pump house will require winterization.

The first step is to connect an air compressor to the main pipe and pressurize the system with air. Once a static pressure of about 50–75 psi has been attained, the sprinklers can be cycled, much as if one was syringing, and the pressurized water will be blown out through the sprinklers. Caution should be taken while pressurizing the system because air pressure in the waterlines can fluctuate dramatically and become very explosive and dangerous. Occasionally, the pressure in the system can cause water hammer strong enough to split the pipes. After the pipes have been pressurized, water may settle to low sections. To ensure that all of the water in the system has been removed, many superintendents will completely shut down the system and then will repeat the process.

Blowing out a water system is a tedious job requiring much patience. One must make sure that all water is removed from the pipes and that only a thin mist comes from the sprinklers (Figure 6.4). A common method is to open heads at the furthest point from the compressor until the air pushes the water out of the system. Then heads should be opened in order, back to the compressor. It may be necessary to move the air compressor around to the extremities of the system, thus making sure that all water lines are thoroughly blown out.

Winterizing the pump house involves making sure all the pumps have been drained; if necessary, antifreeze can be added into the pumps. Electric controls should be set in the off position and electricity to the pump house must be shut off by either locking the main switch and/or

Figure 6.4 *Using an air compressor to blow out the watering system is a yearly ritual on northern courses every fall.*
(Photo Courtesy of Wyatt Byrd, Golf Course Superintendent Biltmore Country Club, Barrington, IL.)

removing the fuses at the power source. The building needs to be secure to avoid unwelcome guests. The irrigation control boxes on the golf course (satellites) should be inspected and sealed for the winter months.

Recharging the System after Shutdown

In the spring or after an emergency shutdown of the system, certain precautions should be followed when restarting the system. After shutdown, the lines will be filled mostly with unpressurized air. During the recharging process, water is pumped back into the system and the lines fill with compressed air, which can be very dangerous. The irrigation pipes or valve heads of the system that are now pressurized can burst, and there is a potential danger for anyone who is working on the system, similar to those mentioned earlier when winterizing the system. The preferred and safest method is to allow only a small amount of water to flow into the irrigation system at a time, while at the same time opening valves and irrigation heads to relieve pressure at different points throughout the system. Most important, relieving pressure at the far ends of the system is essential where there will be the largest concentration of trapped air.

THE WATER SOURCE

Irrigation water may be drawn from many different sources, such as rivers, lakes, wells, and even municipal water mains. The source of the water is very important. It will be the determining factor on what water for irrigation is accessible, and the quantities that are available. Some courses are fortunate to be able to pump an ample supply of water directly from a river, or a holding pond that is fed by their own private well. Others are at the mercy of a municipal water system that charges high per-gallon costs and may restrict the amount of water that can be used daily. Some courses have started to use effluent water, known as "recycled" water. State regulations must be followed, and the effluent water must be treated properly before its use on the golf course. Although the use of effluent water may not be noticeable on the course, posted signs should be used to warn golfers about contact with the water.

   In the heat of summer, some courses need as much as a million gallons a day, but most use much less. Computer-controlled automatic irrigation systems have made watering more efficient, and by uniformly using less water, they have also improved course conditions. Many superintendents use either hand-held moisture meters or buried meters that provide readings via cellular networks to help ascertain when the grass plants need water. These devices have dramatically helped superintendents and those watering to apply the correct amount of water, ensuring the best playing conditions.

The quality of the water is very important. Aerating the water by means of fountains will help retard the development of algae. Aquatic weed control by means of approved chemicals is governed by state statutes, and in many areas the necessary permit is required. Sprinkler heads, valves, and other components often have sensitive parts that can malfunction when the water contains silt or other impediments. If untreated water is a problem, filtration devices will need to be installed to screen out the pollutants. At the same time, beneficial additives can be added to the water that will make the precious liquid even more important to the plants. There are a number of products that can be injected into the irrigation system, such as adding fertilizer through the water system (also known as fertigation), adding wetting agents, adding acid, and even introducing bacterial cultures through the water system to the grass plants as a means of disease prevention. In all cases, superior water quality is essential to make these systems work to their optimum. Water tests should be conducted annually and at different times of the year, because water quality may fluctuate and affect the growing conditions of fine turf.

SUMMARY

Applying water has become incredibly sophisticated in recent years, and the methodology will continue to advance because water is such a precious resource. Managing the water system is an important aspect of the duties performed by the superintendent. An experienced irrigation technician is essential for troubleshooting, checking the sprinkler head coverage, maintaining the pump house, and other related irrigation system responsibilities.

Golfers do not often understand the importance of the irrigation system, because most of the working parts are underground and not visible, and are usually functioning during the evening hours. For the same reason, it is frequently difficult for superintendents to obtain the necessary capital expenditures to maintain and improve the watering system.

Superintendents should walk the course frequently to make sure that water is being properly applied and to experience the physical condition of the soil and its water content under their feet.

TIP: Superintendents should schedule irrigation heads to run in visible areas when golfers may arrive on the course every once in a while, so they see this asset in action. The 18th fairway or tee may be a set to turn off last in the morning or those located along the boundaries of the course as members drive into the club.

7

Fertilizers

Grass plants, like any living organism, require nutrition to sustain life and grow. In the simplest terms, grass plants get their nutrition in the form of elements through their root system from the soil and to a lesser extent above ground through the special openings in the leaf. Superintendents provide these essential elements in the form of fertilizer to grow healthy turf plants. There are many different types of fertilizers from many different sources with many different characteristics. Understanding plant fertility and the relationship with the soil is a very important process for a superintendent to know. Classes and courses provide key principles in plant nutrition and soil chemistry that are a must for any golf course superintendent who wishes to grow fine turf.

DIFFERENT TYPES OF FERTILIZERS

Some fertilizers are manufactured in plants, some are simply mined. Others are generated from decaying plants, animal waste or other organic byproducts. No matter the source, turf plants require essential nutrients or elements that fertilizers provide.

Most mixed fertilizers contain all three major nutritional elements – nitrogen (N), phosphorous* (P) (which is now regulated in some states), and potassium (K) – in various proportions. Nitrogen encourages growth and color, phosphorous is needed for the roots, and potassium gives strength to the plants. If applied improperly all three can potentially injure the grass. Nitrogen is the chief culprit and should always be handled with respect.

---

*It should be noted that the use of phosphorous is being regulated, and in some states the use of commercial fertilizer, including phosphorus, has been regulated or banned altogether.

As a general rule, mixed granular fertilizers should be watered in thoroughly after every application. Fertilizer today can be divided into three grades or sizes, which include greens grade fertilizers, midsize fertilizers, and large granular fertilizers and are composed of the following:

- Greens-grade fertilizer is a mix that can include nitrogen, phosphorus, and potassium (potash). Greens require a higher-quality fertilizer with minimal growth rate.
- Midsize fertilizers are usually used on tees and fairways, where it is generally more important to maintain high-quality turf and encourage recovery from divots and wear and tear.
- Large granular fertilizers because of their size are effective for some fairway applications and most often are applied in the rough. These fertilizers are generally less costly.

SYNTHETIC ORGANICS

Urea formaldehyde and its many polymer cousins are useful and important components of fertilizer programs. Like the true organics, these products don't burn. The nitrogen and other nutrients that make up these formulations are released at a very slow rate over the duration of the growing season, resulting in a consistently low growth rate of the grass. Many mixed fertilizers now contain at least some of these synthetic organic products.

Fertilizer granulation was a problem when the different elements would come in different size granules that resulted in uneven applications. Modern fertilizers are characterized by uniform particle sizes, in which each particle contains the formulation that is written on the bag. Such materials can be applied with greater accuracy and at reduced rates and still ensure that every plant will receive the specified nutrients it requires.

Sulfur-coated urea (SCU), urea-formaldehyde (UF), and isobutylidene diurea (IBDU) are all synthetic sources of nitrogen for organic fertilizers and all are often used in blended inorganic fertilizers.

Sulfur-coated urea is a pellet of urea nitrogen enshrouded in a skin of sulfur. The idea is that the sulfur skin will crack or dissolve, and in the process the nitrogen will become available to the plant's root system.

Urea-formaldehyde is a slow-release source of nitrogen and breaks down more rapidly in warm weather than during the cooler months.

Isobutylidene diurea releases nitrogen by a reaction with water. It is most effective during cool seasons since nitrogen is not affected by temperature.

Manufacturers maintain that all these synthetics can be applied without fear of burning the plants, and should be "watered in" for best results. The best policy is to be safe, rather than sorry, and to at least wash these materials off the grass blades. Subsequent irrigation cycles or natural rainfall will ensure that the fertilizer granules filter down into the soil. As stated earlier (see Chapter 1), baskets should be left off the mowers if there are fertilizer granules that have been recently applied and are mixed in with the clippings, ensuring that the fertilizer remains in the appropriate area.

LIQUID FERTILIZERS

Combinations of concentrated liquid fertilizers that require mixing with an appropriate balance of water make it possible for superintendents to apply nutrients through the sprayer or even through the irrigation system. The water/fertilizer combination is applied to the plant as a mist or a light artificial rain, and some of the foliar feeding actually enters the plant and is absorbed through the grass blades. The remaining fluid moves down to the soil and the plant roots. The grass responds very quickly, and results are visible in a day or two. When using a sprayer, it is essential that it has a computerized mechanism to apply the fertilizer correctly to the designated areas.

Superintendents prefer different methods to feed their turf and there are numerous combinations of liquid fertilizer, depending on the location and situation that are acceptable for feeding grass. Many apply the liquid form on the greens (and other areas) to precisely control the growth rate of the plants throughout the season. It's common for superintendents to apply granular products in the spring and fall on putting greens and to all other areas of play when needed. With the help of highly accurate sprayers and operators, pinpoint fertilizer applications are the future of turf.

IRON

When turf turns to a yellow shade, many superintendents will spray small amounts of iron on the plants to rejuvenate color. Some apply it on the greens, tees, and fairways; others apply iron from fence to fence as part of the preparation for televised golf. Iron applied as a spray is absorbed through the leaf blades, enters the plant's veins, and turns it green within hours. The dark green color will last from a few days to a week. Iron provides color without the surge of growth that is produced by a nitrogen fertilizer. Iron is not a component of chlorophyll but is required for the production of chlorophyll. Iron is part of the makeup of enzymes that assists in photosynthesis, the process by which all plants use sunlight for energy to convert carbon dioxide into carbohydrates (food) while releasing water vapors and oxygen. Mixtures that contain iron, nitrogen, and other nutrients should always be tested in experimental areas first, and only after the effects of the spray have been observed and found to be satisfactory should the "cocktail" mixes be applied to greens, tees, or fairways.

Applying too much iron is a frightening experience. The application of excessive amounts of iron can be detrimental to the appearance of the plants; the instructions on the packaging must be followed precisely. A miscalculation of the rate to be applied can result in the turf turning to a strange dark gray color. Watering at that time will not help; the iron is already absorbed by the plant and the damage has been done. Fortunately, the strange dark color of the turf is only visually unappealing. The turf will lose its dark color in stages and will be back to normal in a few days. When applied properly, the grass will turn a richer, deeper blue-green color. The addition of iron to the turf is what makes Kentucky Blue Grass "blue."

FERTILIZERS THAT BURN

Mixed fertilizers contain various proportions of the three major nutritional elements – nitrogen, phosphorous, and potassium – and all three can burn grass and should be handled with respect. Compounds such as ammonium sulfate and urea act identically, and when the granules are applied to the grass surface, they attract moisture from the atmosphere (and grass plant) and literally dissolve in their own sweat. They are powerful solutions that can easily burn the grass and should also be used with caution. Experienced superintendents know how to handle water-soluble fertilizers, but novices in the field should become carefully acquainted with these products. Many mixed fertilizer formulations contain at least some water-soluble components. As a general rule, the less expensive the fertilizer, the more likely it is to be water-soluble and the greater the chance that it will burn.

FERTILIZERS THAT DON'T BURN

The original nonburning fertilizers were mostly organic in nature and origin. The most well-known organic of all is Milorganite, a byproduct of Milwaukee sewage sludge. Organics are low in nitrogen. Milorganite contains just 6 lb. of actual nitrogen per hundredweight, and none of it is water soluble. For that reason, Milorganite, and many similar products, can be applied with impunity. Spilling a bag of organic fertilizer is not a disaster – just simply sweep up the granules. There will be no fertilizer burn, but in a few weeks the grass will be exceedingly green and lush. Occasionally, organic fertilizers are fortified with additional nitrogen, which then increases their burn potential. The success of Milorganite has led many other companies to copy the product. Sustane, a byproduct of the poultry industry, has recently become widely accepted.

Some organic fertilizers also tend to depress fungus disease infestation. Besides the major elements, the organics often contain sulfur, iron, and many minor and trace elements that seem to have a positive effect on the plant's metabolism and its ability to resist diseases. In areas where fungicidal applications are severely restricted, organic fertilizers deserve to be part of the nutritional program. Organic fertilizers need to be broken down by microbes in the soil into plant-usable forms. This process is in direct correlation to the activity level of the microbes; they are most active when the soil is warm and has adequate moisture.

Many golfers object to the smell that occurs just after an organic fertilizer application. Considering their origin, it is not surprising that both Milorganite and Sustane are guilty in this respect. Superintendents may well take the sensibilities of their customers into account and schedule their fertilizer applications with the golfers in mind. To simply give up on organics because of the smell is to miss out on some great fertilizers whose many benefits far outweigh this one small drawback.

APPLYING FERTILIZERS

As a general rule, it is good to water in granular fertilizers after their application. After the fertilizer has been applied in the morning, footprints around the cup (Figure 7.1) and between the tee markers can

Figure 7.1 *Some fertilizers are prone to footprinting after application. You can tell from this picture where a golfer was working on making putts from the two footprints left. Though unsightly, this discoloration does not hurt the turf and is not seen in a day or two.*

sometimes be seen by the end of the day. Applying fertilizers during cool weather lessens the possibility of burning. By covering the hopper of a spreader, one can apply fertilizer when it rains and enjoy the benefit of washing the nutrients into the soil immediately. A sensible program, then, should consist of applying a granular fertilizer that may burn during the cool or shoulder seasons and nonburning fertilizer during the heat of the summer.

When applying fertilizers to small areas, such as tees and greens, a walk-behind cyclone-type spreader is usually quite adequate. Before starting, check out the spreader and make sure that it operates properly. Many of the small cyclone spreaders are not as reliable as one might expect. Test the spreading pattern on cement or an asphalt floor. Make sure the fertilizer spreads evenly, and measure the width of the application. Now is a good time to calibrate the rate of application. Measure the area that has been applied and sweep up and weigh the material that has been used. From these two figures, the rate of application can be determined.

For example, if 20 lb. of material has been applied to 1,500 sq. ft., the rate of application per 1,000 sq. ft. is 20 divided by 1.5, or 13 lb. per 1,000 sq. ft. If the average green on the golf course measures 4,000 sq. ft., the calibrated setting would require a 50 lb. bag per green. Should the green be fertilized in two different directions (recommended practice), half of the calculated total amount should be applied in each direction.

For larger areas such as fairways and roughs, one may use a tractor with a power take-off (PTO)–driven spreader with a large-capacity hopper. These large machines are best calibrated in the rough, to avoid causing mishaps on the precious fairway turf. Read the instructions carefully for the suggested setting and rate of application, which is printed on the bag. However, some machines may vary slightly in distribution. In this case, a more accurate calculation may be derived by measuring out an area, filling the hopper with a 50 lb. bag of fertilizer, and selecting an appropriate tractor speed. After the 50 lb. bag is depleted, measure the covered area and calculate the number of bags needed to cover the acreage that will be fertilized. Calculations similar to the preceding one should provide a rate of pounds of material per acre of turf.

Rate of application in lb. per acre = lb. of material divided by area covered in acres

Today there is a new trend of applying fertilizer to large areas. Many fertilizer distributors now have trucks that have large fertilizer hoppers, flotation tires, and GPS technology (Figure 7.2). These machines have computer technology that is used to apply a custom application by calculating the quantities of fertilizer that are appropriate for specific areas. This process has many advantages, which include eliminating the need for storage space for large

Figure 7.2 *GPS-guided spreaders with onboard scales accurately dispense dry fertilizers and other products.*

quantities of fertilizer, allowing time for staff to work on other assignments, and the fertilizer application is completed quickly and efficiently.

As was mentioned before, the best way to apply fertilizer with a cyclone spreader is in two different directions, guaranteeing complete and accurate coverage. Experienced operators can make use of the mower patterns on tees and greens to ensure sufficient overlap, thereby avoiding the need to cross-fertilize and saving time. The aprons, collars, and approaches are generally fertilized at the same time as the greens. On tees, one may fertilize just the tee top but not the sides, because fertilizing the sides merely promotes excessive growth and the need for extra cutting.

When using a tractor-driven spreader, the suggested approach is to spread from tee to green down the center of the fairway and then make an extra pass along each side. Extra passes may be needed, depending on the contour and width of the fairway. Most spreaders are now of the cyclone type, but occasionally one may observe a drop-type spreader that has a hopper, allowing the material to fall onto a baffle board and then sliding down onto the grass. Drop-type spreaders, because of their design, can easily lead to inconsistent application patterns. For this reason, these drop-type spreaders are now used rarely and only for selective applications. The use of GPS-guided spreaders, innovative designs, and other spreader technology has improved considerably and will continue to do so.

MANAGING FERTILIZER SPILLS

When a fertilizer spill does occur, instant action is required. Use a lightweight, square-mouthed shovel to pick up as much of the spilled material as possible without bruising the grass. As tempting as it may be, do not use a broom to sweep up the material. The bristles of the broom can break open the leaf blades, making it possible for the fertilizer to be absorbed by the plants and injure the grass. Be ready with a hose, and after careful removal of the spilled fertilizer, wash off the remainder of the fertilizer with water pressure. Using a portable vacuum cleaner to remove the spilled fertilizer is a good idea. A power broom or blower can be used to disperse the spilled material. Even after this process, the grasses may burn or have increased growth. If a burn occurs, it can be repaired with a sod cutter and new turf. One option is to cut the sod at the time of the spill, carefully remove the fertilizer, place the cut sod back, and drench the area with water.

SOIL SAMPLING

Periodic soil sampling is a well-advised practice to monitor the soil nutrients. Decisions made on plant nourishment should be based on knowing what is already present in the root zone. A private soil laboratory or a government agency will specify how samples should be taken, and their resulting report should be the basis for a fertilizer program. Private soil laboratories will send a representative out to visit the site and take samples for testing from the greens, tees, and fairways on the golf course. The representative will then return with an interpretation of the soil samples based on a report that has been submitted by the lab technician who is an expert in the knowledge of soil and fertilizer chemistry. Although testing can be expensive, these costs for accurate tests are warranted.

Often, the soils laboratories tend to stress the importance of pH and, indeed, a range between 6.5 and 7.0 is probably best for optimum grass growth. These ranges are seldom the case, and excellent golf turf can be grown above and below these parameters. If necessary, lime can be added to the soil to quickly raise the pH, and to lower the pH sulfur can be applied annually, with results that are considerably slower. However, grass adapts quickly to a variety of conditions, and rarely is pH the most critical factor.

Testing the nutritional content of the leaf tissue is yet another means of finding out what the grass plant needs for sustenance. Sending samples to a certified lab will provide accurate results, and tissue-testing kits are also available. However, the time expended checking and reading in-house testing kits might be better spent on more pertinent duties such as managing the crew and making sure that the assignments are completed.

Experienced superintendents can tell at a glance when turf needs feeding. They recognize when color is fading and when tillering is slowing. They know how, when, and what materials are needed to make turf respond with vigor. This knowledge comes from the day-to-day working experiences and visual observations that take place during many seasons on the golf course. Combine this experience with modern technology and academic training, and the result is consistently superior conditions.

TIP: When in doubt, test two separate samples of soil from the same location to ensure accurate results of nutrients in the soil of the area in question. As in all testing, results can vary.

PREPARING A FERTILIZER PROGRAM

A plan to feed the grass must be in place at the start of the growing season. Such a plan should be carefully prepared and be based on soil testing and the nutritional requirements of the grass plant for a specific climatic zone. Older, well-established turf requires less fertilizer than turf on a newly constructed golf course. The game of golf is more pleasurable when played on lean turf than on lush, succulent grass. Lean turf is equated with healthy turf. More often than not, less is better, and moderation should be practiced not only when it comes to feeding the plant but in all facets of golf course management.

A fertilizer program should state the specific areas to be fertilized, the number and timing of applications required, the quantity, and type of fertilizer to be applied. Remember that grass plants experience an inner urge to grow vigorously, and after a period of dormancy need very little fertilization. At other times, the grass needs nutritional supplements to boost its growth. Knowing when and what to apply is based on judgment, experience, and careful study of the plant and its environment.

Based on the plan and the budget of the golf course, the materials can be purchased all at once or when needed. Purchasing surplus fertilizer that is not needed for immediate use at discount prices is only cost-effective if the fertilizer can be stored properly. Granular fertilizer should be stored in a dry place on pallets, and liquid fertilizer is often stored in the chemical building. Granular fertilizer that is bagged and shrink-wrapped can become moist, making it difficult to apply.

SUMMARY

Turfgrass nutrition is an extremely complex subject that requires a thorough understanding of soil chemistry, grass plant physiology, and the best materials available to apply. Most superintendents are now college graduates of either two- or four-year programs and are well prepared to understand fertilizers, their optimum rates, and times of application. It's a good practice to have soil tests completed by independent turf consultants or labs. Too many superintendents employ those selling fertilizer to take and interpret their soil tests. Superintendents should use their knowledge and experience to develop their own programs, taking into account plant needs and matching them with available products. Perhaps testing a "new" fertilizer on a trial area or nursery green is the best way to see how the product will react, allowing a comparison to areas that are fertilized with different products, or comparisons to areas that are not fertilized at all.

It is wise to seek help when uncertain, but the final decision rests with the superintendent. A well-trained and knowledgeable superintendent is the best-qualified person to make the final decision, and it should be done with a degree of frugality, resulting in the best program at the most economical price for the employer.

8

Topdressing

The practice of topdressing is the process of applying a thin layer of soil-like materials to the top surface of the turf. The process will have an immediate and positive impact on the health of the grass by invigorating and smoothing the grass areas of the greens, tees, or fairways. Topdressing with straight sand, or sand and peat, or even a mixture of sand, soil, and peat, will encourage the grass to respond almost immediately. Stability of the turf is promoted by the topdressing particles filtering down between the grass blades. The thin layer of topdressing provides a cushion around the grass plants, offering a welcome reprieve from the pounding feet of the golfers and the cutting and rolling of the mowers. Topdressing that is watered in increases the strength of the turf, and topdressing that is composed of materials with nutrients will improve the health and color of the turf. When such a sward is cut with a sharp mower, it looks smooth and putts to perfection. In fact, it is impossible to create a perfect putting surface without the benefit of timely topdressings. The purpose of topdressing is to keep turf healthy, and to smooth the surface of pitch marks, aerification holes, old hole plugs, scars, and other blemishes. Topdressing can also help to control thatch as well, but it is a fallacy to believe that one can bury thatch with heavy topdressings.

WHAT KIND OF MATERIAL?

In years past, greenkeepers often used various types of compost for topdressing. Since compost is rich in humus it provided the extra benefits of a natural fertilizer. Most compost needed to be screened prior to application, the coarser particles were removed, and the rest was suitable to filter into grass mat.

Today's choice of topdressing material on greens or tees on newly established golf courses is usually predetermined – always use the same components of the root zone mix that were used in the original construction. When the original components are unknown, soil analysis is used to make sure topdressing materials are compatible with the existing soil and soil structure. Superintendents rightly fear the buildup of layers of differing topdressing materials in the soil profile. Layers of different materials can be detrimental to both root growth and water movement in the soil. Successive regimes of different superintendents who all had their favorite mixtures can be documented by analyzing the core sample of a green.

The height of cut of the grass is another factor that must be taken into consideration. Greens that are cut very short require frequent light topdressing. Greens that are planted with ultra-dwarf varieties of Bermuda grass and newer bentgrass cultivars are often topdressed with dried sand that is applied lightly with a walk-behind cyclone spreader on a weekly or semimonthly basis. Topdressing material that is applied on bentgrass putting greens needs to be fine so that it will sink in between the grass blades, so as not to interfere when putting.

Heavy topdressing is a relative term: How heavy is too heavy? Smothering the grass with too much topdressing can be detrimental. After topdressing, the grass blades should still be clearly visible so that the growth processes can continue and the plants will not suffocate. Topdressing that is applied more than ⅛ inch (3.2 mm) is too much and will smother the grass. It is better to make frequent light applications than to apply one heavy dose. In northern climates, a thick application of topdressing near the end of the golfing season and as part of a winter injury preventative program has proven to be very effective.

SAND VERSUS SOIL MIXES

Straight sand as a topdressing material has been widely accepted by many turfgrass managers. There are several advantages:

1. Washed and kiln dried sand is clean and easy to apply.
2. Golfers can putt after a light application.
3. Sand can quickly be worked into the existing turf.
4. Sand levels the putting surface.
5. Watering sand in can be done quickly.
6. Play is usually not interrupted when using straight sand as topdressing.

Greens topdressed with sand on a regular basis frequently develop localized dry spots (LDS): small areas ranging from a few inches to a foot or more, where the water will not penetrate and the grass cannot survive. Repeated aerations help to puncture the layer of sand and the soil underneath. Sand is a very abrasive material that easily injures the grass blades, especially when a steel mat or a brush is dragged across a sand-covered green. The combination of the sand and the matting action may cause injury to the grass, especially when the turf is under moisture stress. The symptoms are akin to wilt, and a timely syringe cycle will help to save the grass.

Repeated dressings that consist entirely of sand will build up as a layer on top of the greens profile. Topdressing with sand is so easy and quick, superintendents tend to do it too often, and as a result, after a few years, the layer of sand can become an inch or two thick. If precautions are not taken, the layer of pure sand can play havoc in the root zone. The grass roots can have difficulty growing through the buildup of sand, and the sand can impede the vertical movement of water through the soil, unless preventive turfgrass cultural practices are followed in conjunction with the applications.

Sand used for topdressing should be readily available and accessible for a topdressing machine. When large quantities of sand are used, it is best to avoid waste and mess, by keeping the sand out of the elements and wind and stored in a silo type unit (Figure 8.1). The storage units are sealed and will keep the sand clean, dry, and weed free.

Figure 8.1 *Sand silos keep kiln dried sand dry and allow the operator to fill up the hopper on the topdresser quickly.*

TIP: Remember that sand has different characteristics and quality when selecting a sand to be used for topdressing.

THE PROGRESSION OF CHANGE IN TOPDRESSING MIX

Mixing topdressing material was traditionally part of the art of greenkeeping, learned through experience under the supervision of the head greenkeeper. Various proportions of sand, soil, and peat were mixed and shoveled through a shredder or over a screen. During the mixing process bone meal, ammonium sulfate, and mixed fertilizers were often added to the mixture. The old-time greenkeepers would occasionally take a handful of the material, finger it lovingly in the palm of their hand, and then squeeze the mix. If the ball of earth that was formed in his hand crumbled easily, he was satisfied and the magic mix was approved for application. Old-timers guarded the secrets of their mixes carefully, unwilling to share this hard-earned knowledge with their fellow greenkeepers.

Over the years, the mixing process became a little more sophisticated. Loaders were used to shovel the various materials into high-capacity shredders, replacing the method of hand-shoveling the material up a slanted screen. Currently, the process has become even more refined and formulated blends can be purchased from companies that distribute specialized sands and various topdressing materials. The major constituent of the topdressing mix is sand and one must remember that all sand is not the same. Careful attention should be given to ensure the sand that is selected has the desired physical properties. A physical as well as a chemical analysis should be obtained before making the selection of the topdressing materials.

TOPDRESSING GREENS—PAST AND PRESENT

For a long time, topdressing was spread by shovel onto putting greens. It had to be spread carefully with a fanning motion to avoid lumping. Workers used square-mouthed aluminum or other lightweight shovels that made it possible to take a sizable amount of material from the back of a truck or wheelbarrow. With a long, sweeping motion, an experienced worker could spread the dressing to perfection. It would feather out as it left the shovel and would never leave lumps. This method of applying topdressing was difficult to learn and very time-consuming. Modern topdressing machinery quickly replaced the old-time greenkeeper and his shovel. Machinery could apply the topdressing at an even thickness and uniformly over the entire green. The new machines resembled a small version of the farm manure spreaders and were equipped with a rotating brush, the bristles of which propelled the topdressing particles into the turf.

An offshoot of the fertilizer spreader involved a cone-shaped hopper with an oscillating applicator that propelled the topdressing material onto the putting surface. This model of spreader made it possible to apply sand in a very thin layer to an entire green in a matter of minutes. Currently, the use of a cyclone spreader allows for even distribution of the sand topdressing, and the material can be applied quickly and easily (Figure 8.2). Topdressing all the greens on an 18-hole course could be completed in just a few hours.

Cutting the greens prior to sand top-dressing or dragging them with a hose is beneficial because it will help the greens to dry faster. Applying the sand or the topdressing material to a dry green will help to make the greens playable more rapidly for golfers. Repeating the topdressing process and brushing the green is helpful in controlling the grain. Also, spiking or verticutting prior to topdressing will ease the movement of the sand down into the turf.

Once the sand is applied, the sand is left to dry, and then brushed into the turf with either a steel mat or brushes. In many cases, a utility cart

Figure 8.2 *Applying sand topdressing is quick and easy with a cyclone spreader.*

Figure 8.3 *Brushing topdressing material into the grass mat makes for smoother greens.*

is used to drag the mat or the brushes (Figure 8.3). If the utility cart is traveling at an excessive speed, the brushes can bounce, which will result with undesirable waves or ripples on the putting surface. As with most other maintenance equipment, it is best to throttle down and travel at low speed.

The topdressing material should be watered in either immediately after it has been applied or during the nightly irrigation cycle. Once the turf has dried after the irrigation cycle, the final step in the process is to cut the green, and in most cases this will be completed in the morning. Using a mower with smooth or solid rollers is preferred because grooved rollers and groomers have a tendency to kick up the topdressing particles making a messy surface, instead of pressing the particles down into the turf. The abrasive action of the sand on the cutting cylinders will require that the mowers be sharpened frequently. Setting aside an old mower, especially for the topdressing operation, will spare the regular units.

When scheduling the application of topdressing, the following should be considered:

- Is the timing of the application such that the golfers will object?
- Is the weather too wet or too dry?
- Is the temperature too hot or too cold?

- Will application on the days before the weekend be intrusive?
- Is there enough staff available to complete the topdressing process?

Intelligent superintendents will consider all the factors and make an educated decision. This may be the day that a few of the daily maintenance duties (such as raking the bunkers or divoting the fairways) are skipped. An application of topdressing will smooth the surface of all the greens and ultimately improve putting. Always remember a near perfect green is the top priority in the overall maintenance program.

There are situations where it may be unnecessary to topdress the entire green. Some greens may have sections or spots that are heavily used and show wear before the entire green is scheduled for topdressing. Observant greenkeepers will recognize the problem and quickly topdress the specific areas. If the affected area is small in size, it is often easier to omit the high-tech equipment by taking a bucket full of topdressing material and hand sprinkling it over the area or fanning a shovel loaded with top-dressing material onto the area. Then using a Levelawn or the back of an aluminum rake, gently rub the material into the turf.

TOPDRESSING TEES

Because tees tend to be cut somewhat higher than greens, thatch can develop more readily. The regular topdressing of tees is applied for several reasons: to repair the divot scars, to create a level and firm surface, and to prevent the buildup of thatch.

Removing any dew by mowing or dragging or other means prior to topdressing is beneficial because it helps the tees to dry faster. Applying the topdressing material to a dry turf will help render the tee suitable for play almost immediately.

In northern areas, overseeding before topdressing is beneficial because the topdressing helps to protect the seed. Do not miss such glorious opportunities to apply seed just prior to its being covered with a thin layer of topdressing material. Seed spread before topdressing has a better chance of germinating and growing into healthy plants. The rate of seeding should be at least 1 lb. of bentgrass, or 5 lb. of rye or bluegrass seed per 1,000 sq. ft.

Care must be taken when topdressing tees to preserve the flat surface that is greatly appreciated by golfers. There is a tendency, particularly on long, narrow tees, to topdress only the center, where most of the play and consequent damage occurs. This is a common and costly mistake, because repeated applications of topdressing to the center of the tee area will eventually form a mound, and will later need to be regraded and returfed to renew a smooth and level teeing surface.

Unlike greens, topdressing tees can be done almost anytime, even if there is an occasional group of players, but remember to just keep a clean space for teeing the ball between the markers.

> TIP: Apply topdressing material to tees on a dry, sunny day. It will dry quickly and can be worked into the turf almost immediately after application.

TOPDRESSING FAIRWAYS

Applying topdressing to all the fairways of an 18-hole golf course is a vast undertaking. Although large quantities of topdressing materials are needed, modern machinery has made the application process easier. When fairways are topdressed straight sand is most often used. Since a large amount of sand is required, it may take several truckloads to cover all the fairways. Topdressing with sand on fairways is common on many courses. Not only is the sand topdressing helping to firm up fairways, it also significantly improves the firmness of the ones that are otherwise soft and soggy. Landing areas on fairways that may become severely scarred by divots should be identified and could be topdressed several times during the golfing season. Since fairways are usually established on native soils, adding sand usually does not lead to the establishment of localized dry spots (LDS). Similar to the results of topdressing greens and tees, topdressed fairways become smoother, healthier, and are less prone to develop thatch.

Recent innovations in topdressing machinery have made it possible to apply minuscule amounts of material to fairways by dusting the fairways with a light coat of topdressing. If fairways are uneven or bumpy because of improper grading, machine-applied sand topdressing may help to alleviate the condition by leveling and smoothing out the undulations. Correcting the poor quality condition of the site may take repeated topdressing applications to improve the area completely.

> TIP: Prior to starting a fairway topdressing program, check out other courses in your area with an established fairway topdressing program. The golf shot from a topdressed fairway can produce a tighter lie, requiring a different golf shot that is not always desirable by all players.

TOPDRESSING SOD

After sod is laid and rolled, it may be necessary to fill in the cracks between the rolls of sod and other indentations such as footprints with a topdressing mix that is suitable for the newly sodded area. Some prefer to wait to apply topdressing once the sod has taken root; others apply topdressing immediately after the laying and rolling of sod. Topdressing sod is usually limited to small areas on the tees, greens, and fairways. The topdressing should be worked in with a Levelawn or the back of an aluminum rake. Avoid the use of a steel drag mat that could tear up the edges of the sod. The topdressing material should be watered into the cracks so as to push the material down into the area where it will smooth and level the sod.

DIVOTING

The turf on tees is often damaged by golfers making divots while taking several practice swings with their metal woods and irons, and when they actually hit the ball. This is especially true on par 3 holes that can quickly become scarred with divots, and unless such tees are repaired regularly, they suffer permanent damage.

In addition to regular topdressing applications to tees, there is often a need to fill divot scars on tees with sand, soil, and other additives (Figure 8.4). This marvelous mixture of several different ingredients is the

Figure 8.4 *An early evening divot party hosted by a superintendent is a great way for members to help care for the course and the superintendent to spend time with the membership. Superintendents provide the divot mix and refreshments to members as they stroll the course, filling divots along the way.*

essence of growth and regeneration. A divot mix may contain any or all of the following materials:

Sand

+ / or Peat

+ / or Compost

+ / or Seed

+ / or Fertilizer

= DIVOT MIX

The sand can be topdressing sand, bunker sand, or other suitable sands. For good measure, many superintendents add an organic component such as peat moss or compost. For seed, be sure to use the same species or variety that is currently growing on the area that is being filled. Do not apply a divot mix containing rye grass on a bentgrass tee, and vice versa. A tuft of rye grass will look out of place on a bentgrass tee. A fertilizer that is ideal for the divot mix should contain phosphorus if available. Although many superintendents blend their own special brand of divot mix, a ready-for-use material can also be purchased from suppliers.

> TIP: Superintendents will often use sand that is dyed green or dark organic materials in their divot mixes. The dark colors can help the seed to germinate more quickly during cooler temperatures by using the warmth of the sun to warm the seed.

On some courses, the par 3 tees have containers filled with divot mix so players can fill in the divot that was made from their shot. Divot mix may also be provided in containers on golf carts. In areas where Bermuda is the primary species of grass that is grown on the tees or fairways, a container filled with straight sand, that is sometimes colored, is typically preferred for filling in the divots. In other parts of the country, where superintendents use bent or bluegrass on the tees and fairways, the preferred divot mixture may be composed of various amounts of sand, compost, and peat that are mixed with or without seed. The fear among superintendents is that if the container of mix on the golf cart has seed added to the divot mix, the seeded divot mixture could inadvertently be applied by golfers to an area that has a different species of grass. When the divot mix is being applied by one of the crew members, it should have seed added to the mix because they should be familiar with the appropriate mixture to apply into the divots.

When possible, divots should be filled with mix or repaired. On northern courses with bent and bluegrass fairways, the divots, especially in the landing areas, can easily be repaired by the greens staff with divot mix, and often the golfers can assist by replacing the divot. On southern courses, the divots are usually not replaced because the Bermuda grass rejuvenates quickly back into the turf. On most courses, the filling and repairing of divots has become part of practical golf course maintenance. Replace or fill the divot? One must communicate to the staff and the golfers what the process is, especially if it changes over the course of the season.

SUMMARY

Topdressing grassed playing areas is an important part of turfgrass management. Topdressing can revitalize, level, and smooth grassed areas, particularly putting greens. Proper topdressing applications can help to maintain putting greens in an optimum condition. Remember that an overapplication of topdressing material, especially during stress periods, can be detrimental to the health of grass. Ugly divot scars on tees and fairways mar the beauty of a golf course. Golfers can help to fill and repair divots, but superintendents must take steps to fill the gap.

9

Aerating, Verticutting, and Venting

Aeration or cultivation of turf is the most assured way of relieving the problem of compaction. Compaction is the physical pushing of soil particles together, squeezing out room between them for water, air, and plant roots. Compaction occurs from the use of the site from foot and golf cart traffic, mower and equipment traffic – even heavy rainfall compresses the soil. In many cases, compaction is unavoidable and a direct consequence of play. The health of turfgrass is compromised in compacted soils. Physical root space is limited, there is less air and water for the plants to use as the plant health declines in compacted soils. As soon as superintendents recognize the symptoms, action should be taken, and aerating the turf ought to be considered. Aeriation of the soil is done by many different methods; all relieve compaction by loosening the soil particles that have been pressed together.

Core aeration is the most disruptive form of aeration to play because circular channels or cylinders are punched or drilled into the soil beneath the turf. The depth and diameter of the hole can be adjusted to the amount of compaction present. Cores can be removed with hollow tines. Solid tines do not remove cores but still leave holes. Either way, this process is usually completed in the spring and/or fall when play is slow and the healing is least impactful to play.

Venting or spiking is a modified and less disruptive version of core aerating. They involve making a shallow puncture in the surface of the grass mat and into the soil. They are less drastic and hardly interferes with putting.

Verticutting involves slicing the surface, at times deep into the mat and the soil below. Verticutting improves turfgrass health and can reduce thatch and grain. As mentioned earlier (see Chapter 8), verticutting prior to topdressing will ease the movement of the sand down into the turf.

All three – aerating, venting, and verticutting – are cultivating practices that improve both the playing surface and the soil, and are especially beneficial if the superintendent recognizes the need to improve the health of the grassed areas.

AERATING GREENS

The words *aerating* and *coring* are often used interchangeably, since both words refer to the same process. *Coring* is a generic term, whereas *aerating* is derived from the name of the first coring machine, which was known as the aerifier and was invented by Tom Mascaro shortly after World War II. Aerating also refers to the process of circulating water in ponds by means of a fountain. Air and oxygen are introduced into the water or the soil when aerated.

Not all greens are created equal, and some need aerating more often than others. Small greens, because they receive more foot traffic in a concentrated area become compacted quicker than large greens. Whereas average greens (over 5,000 sq. ft. or 450 sq. m) may need to be cored only once annually. Small greens that are subject to more compaction in a small area may require aeration treatment two or three times during the season. Under rare circumstances, large, sprawling greens may be omitted from the aeration program. Similar to topdressing, aerating the entire green is not always necessary. Seek out the popular cupping areas, walk-off areas or areas of heavy mower traffic and plan extra aerating treatments for those portions of the green. Take note that the popular cupping areas on greens compact quickly and often become infested with *Poa annua*. *Poa annua* in many cases is considered a weed or unwanted plant in a stand of finely manicured turfgrass. *Poa annua* is an annual grass that competes very well with desired species because it is able to adapt and grow in very difficult growing conditions – compacted soils is one of them.

When greens become compacted, the beneficial grasses, such as bent and Bermuda and Paspalum, are the first to decline and make way for *Poa annua*. The most important and effective prevention is timely aerating. Every possible measure must be taken, including timely aerating to prevent the encroachment of *Poa annua*. This bears repeating: The only turf that will grow on compacted soil is *Poa annua*. In fact, when *Poa annua* rears its ugly head, the most likely cause is compacted soil.

Scheduling

Aerating the greens should be scheduled at least once during the growing season. The preferred time should be one that inconveniences the least number of golfers and is still optimal from an agronomic viewpoint. Since many factors need to be considered, the best time to aerate should be determined by the superintendent:

- Aerating in the early spring can help speed recovery from winter injury.
- Aerating in late summer will help the greens recover quicker.
- Aerating in the early fall can help alleviate compaction after a busy golf season.
- Aerating twice, once in the early spring and once in the early fall, can help winter recovery and help alleviate compaction.

At some golf courses, play is suspended for a few days or even a week during the summer so that all the playing areas can be completed at once. Some courses will close one nine at a time, others will do a few holes a day. Some will start the aerification process in the evening and continue through part of the night. The method selected is usually one that can quickly be completed and does not interfere with play. If the equipment is owned, the cost savings to have an ongoing aeration program may be one of the deciding factors on when and how often to aerate. Golfers dislike aerating or any other process that disturbs the putting surface; they need to be warned well in advance when aerating will take place. Use all of the following methods to warn golfers of pending surface disturbance:

- Post notices on bulletin boards, both in the clubhouse and on the golf course.
- Make announcements in the club newsletter and the calendar of events.
- Use email or other social media outlets to alert golfers.
- Include a brief explanation about the benefits of aerating.
- Inform the golf professional and the pro shop staff as well as the greens staff, so that they can respond to golfers' questions intelligently.
- Be visible when aerating is in progress, and lend a willing ear to golfers' concerns and criticisms.

TIP: Here's a bit of trivia to inform golfers if they start to get a little testy about how the small holes on the green have ruined their round. According to an article by the GCSAA, consider the fact that PGA Tour legend Tom Watson shot a sizzling record 58 at his then-home course, Kansas City Country Club; just days after the greens had been aerified.

Aerating a green, a tee, or a fairway is like performing major surgery on the turf's grass plants. Aerating pulls loose the grass with its roots from the turf and often initially causes the remaining turf grass plants' metabolic systems to go into shock. At times, there will be a temporary setback instead of an expected improvement to the turf. This happens especially when the turf is weak from the beginning. Therefore, it is best to aerate a green when the turf is strong and healthy and actively growing to ensure plant recovery. When turfgrasses are under severe stress, aerating may only compound the problem and weaken the turf further. When compaction is established as the cause of the stress, aerating a sick, weakened green with anemic turf should only be attempted as a last resort, especially during periods of high environmental stress. Aeration should never be thought of as a cure-all for all maladies that befall grass during the course of a growing season. Be aware of the false phrase, "When all else fails, aerate."

On northern golf courses, aeration occurs naturally during the winter season. The freezing and thawing of the soil profile loosens tight soils and makes room for air and oxygen to pass through the pore spaces. When aeration is implemented during the spring, the cultivating action of the aerator tines will help to stimulate growth by opening the surface of the turf (Figure 9.1). Applying seed and fertilizer on the green after aeration will also promote plant growth – but remember that seed does not germinate when soil temperatures are less than 50°F (10°C). Superintendents should determine which greens need to be aerated, and how often, at the beginning of the season and should schedule this operation as part of the overall maintenance program.

Benefits of Aerating

The following are some of the many benefits of aerating turf (Figure 9.4):

1. Relieves compaction
2. Opens the surface of the turf
3. Facilitates entry of water and air into the root zone
4. Helps to control thatch
5. When topdressing is applied after aerating, the soil profile is easily modified

TIP: Always be accessible to the golfers during the process, and communicate the benefits of the aerification for the turf and playability.

Figure 9.1 *Greens aeration is an important management tool that stimulates growth and speeds recovery. Here greens are topdressed with sand and then aerified with solid tines. (Photo Courtesy of Wyatt Byrd, Golf Course Superintendent Biltmore Country Club, Barrington, IL.)*

On the Negative Side

Aerating turf can also have some negative effects including the following:

1. Aerating disturbs the putting surface.
2. Recovery of the putting surface, when not attended to properly, can be very slow.
3. Aerating should encourage the growth of the grass, and if not maintained properly, may slow the speed of the green.
4. Aerating during the heat of summer can be risky and result in turf loss.
5. Aerating with oversize tines can slow down the recovery of the putting green surface.

Selecting the Proper Tine, Tine Diameter, and Spacing

Tines come in different diameters and lengths and the spacing between them can be varied to address different degrees and depths of compaction, soil types and surface disruption. Tines can also be hollow to allow the removal of the core or solid to displace the soil underground. There are many different combinations of tine type, diameter, and depth, and it is up to the superintendent to find the best combination for the purpose at hand. In general, the larger the diameter of the tine and depth of hole created, the greater disruption to the playing surface, but the most compaction relieved. The opposite holds true as well, the smaller the tine size, the less impact to the turf and the least amount of compaction that is relieved. Larger tines can be spaced further apart (up to 6 inches, or 15 cm), whereas smaller tines can be spaced at 1 inch (2.2 cm) apart.

Smaller solid or hollow tines (often called needle or micro tines) are used in the middle of the growing season on putting greens to break up the top crust of soil to allow water to reach the root system more effectively and not disrupt play. Conversely, ⅝- to ¾-inch hollow tines may be used on putting greens in the fall to remove cores followed by topdressing to alleviate compaction and amend the soil with the addition of a more porous sand into the aerification holes.

It is a good practice to vary the depth of aerification over the years to avoid creating a hard pan layer. This layer can occur if one depth is continually used for every aerification process and may prevent rooting to occur below it. Superintendents will routinely rotate solid, larger, and longer diameter tines every other year into their aerification program to help break up the soil profile to differing depths.

Hollow tine coring is a method of aeration that extracts a core of soil from the turf. The core may vary in size from a ¼-inch to 1 inch in diameter. The length of the core or the depth of the resulting hole also varies, from ½ inch to more than 1 foot. The number of holes per square foot varies greatly: The smaller the tine, the closer the spacing. Larger tines may be spaced as much as 6 inches (15 cm) apart. The choice of tine sizing depends on the purpose of the application. Use mini- or pencil tines when overseeding greens to be assured that disruption is minimal.

When trying to improve a serious hardpan layer condition or relieve compaction (a layer of soil that is impervious to water), or drainage problem, use the largest size tines available. The most common aerating application is to relieve compaction in the soil profile and also to control thatch. When aerating for compaction, tines ranging in size from $^3/_{16}$ inch to ¾ inch in diameter should be used, penetrating 5–15 inches deep and spaced 2–3 inches apart. When aerating to dethatch a putting green surface, a small tine ¼ inch in diameter should be used, and the surface should only be penetrated to the depth of the thatch – generally 1–1½ inches, and spaced no further than 3 inches apart.

Filling in the Holes

When hollow tines are used the cores of soil, organic matter and some grass plants are removed from the soil profile. If the soil from the green that is being aerated is desirable, the pulled cores can be pulverized by verticutting and then used as topdressing and worked back into the green. If the soil is less than desirable, the cores should be removed and hauled away (Figure 9.2). A Flymo, blowers, or handheld brooms can also be used to help disperse the sand into the aerated holes, when sand is used as topdressing. In either case, the aerator holes need to be refilled right to the top of the holes, making the putting surface smooth.

Additional topdressing applied to the top of the pulled cores, combined with brushing or matting, is another method used to fill in the aerated holes and helps to restore the putting surface to its former

Figure 9.2 *When hollow tines are used and the soils under the surface are less than desirable, aerification cores are removed from the surface before filling the holes with sand.*

(Photo Courtesy of Wyatt Byrd, Golf Course Superintendent Biltmore Country Club, Barrington, IL.)

condition (Figure 9.3). At times, a light rolling after aerating can be beneficial to help level and smooth the surface of the green. Golfers can become irritated when the aerating practices are not completed properly causing putting to become erratic.

TIP: Superintendents should plan for the quickest healing of the putting surfaces following aerification by carefully limiting growth regulation and maximizing fertility peaks.

Time to Tiny Tine and Overseed

When there is an area on the green that is approximately 100–300 sq. ft. that has become worn and weak because of stress, it becomes a source of aggravation for the superintendent. This worn and weakened area spoils the nearly perfect appearance of the green. The area should be aerated with mini-tines at 1-inch-square spacings to a depth not exceeding 1 inch. The tiny cores of soil and vegetative material are brought to surface and

Figure 9.3 *Walk-behind blowers and push brooms are used to work the sand into the aerification holes, making sure to completely fill the holes.*
(Photo Courtesy of Wyatt Byrd, Golf Course Superintendent Biltmore Country Club, Barrington, IL.)

left to dry. Meanwhile, bring out a drop seeder and apply a mix of organic fertilizer and grass seed cultivar that is best suited for the green. The seeds will fall vertically, causing many of them to fall into the tiny holes. Some will fall all the way to the bottom; others will attach to the sidewall of the hole. Now take our favorite greenkeeping tool, the Levelawn, and crush the cores, pulverizing every last one. The core mass will quickly disappear, and the crushed material can be spread on the weakened area and used as a topdressing. Some of the ground-up earth will find its way into the tine holes, where it becomes part of the growing medium. After completing the operation, the area needs to be cleaned up. The treated area can be cut with a greens mower and lightly syringed. Keep the cup away from the aerated area for at least a week, or until the area has recovered.

Meanwhile down below, in its tiny compartment, the seed has been exposed to moisture, heat, and light and in just a few days the magical germination process has taken place. The seeds burst from their shells and send roots down and grass blades upward. Since all of this takes place in its very own growth chamber, the biological processes are not impeded by foot or mower traffic. The grass quickly becomes established as a small tuft and becomes part of the greensward.

How do we know this? Because we have seen it happen by getting down on our hands and knees and, with the help of a magnifying lens, have observed the results of the germinated seed that has pushed up miniscule blades of grass that start to emerge out of the tiny tine hole. We highly recommend using tiny tines when aerating the greens for seeding and introducing new grass cultivars into an existing turf. The use of tiny tines and seeding has been proven to be a quick and effective method of correcting stressful areas on a green.

Shatter Core Aeration

There are times when superintendents have substituted solid steel tines for hollow tines. This type of aeration is also known as *shatter core aeration*. These tines are forced into a green and literally shatter the soil profile as they enter through the surface. Holes are created as the aerator advances, and later these holes should be filled with topdressing. Many believe that repeated use of solid tines at the same depth contributes to compaction and creates a hardpan layer just below the surface of the green that impedes the movement of both air and water. To avoid compaction and hardpan layers during repeated shatter core aeration, the use of tines with various diameters and depths should be implemented. Shatter core aeration should only be used as part of a total aeration program because it has short-term benefits.

The Hydroject

The Toro Company introduced a machine that uses water injection, known as the Hydroject. In order to use this machine, there must be access to water via a hose and quick coupler that is connected to a water supply that feeds the machine. This self-propelled machine spouts streams of pressurized water into the soil without disturbing the surface. The pressurized stream creates channels within the soil profile through which air and water can move. The result is remarkable on compacted greens: There is immediate relief for the struggling grass plants as a result of the process. It was thought at first that the Hydroject would replace core aeration, since it apparently had all the benefits of regular core aeration without the disruptive surface agitation. Although many superintendents use the Hydroject regularly and have made it part of their aeration programs, it has not replaced standard core aeration.

The DryJect

The DryJect machine is similar to the Hydroject machine in that they both inject water, but the DryJect machine can also inject 250 percent more topdressing material than traditional applications with the water injection. The machine can aerate and topdress in one pass and eliminates the need for the crew to drag or remove cores. Various types of dry materials can be injected to modify soil while aerating and large amounts of dry sand can be incorporated into the upper root zone with high-pressure water. The putting surface can be quickly smoothed and ready for play. When added to the maintenance program, it can reduce the need for core aerification. This equipment and service is available through authorized contractors.

The Vertidrain

The vertidrain is an aerating machine used for root management and for the relief of soil compaction. The machine was invented in the Netherlands and used primarily on sports fields to improve vertical water movement through the soil. The Dutch soon discovered that their new machine was ideally suited to break up the layers of compacted soil on the push-up greens. The benefits of the machine were quickly recognized elsewhere in the developed world, and the machine is now being manufactured worldwide, including in North America. These machines today can have humongous tines that can penetrate 12–16 inches into the soil, rock back and forth at their greatest depth, and literally shake up the surrounding soil. The machine can be modified with several different tine sizes and spacing. There are machines light enough that can be used for application on greens and heavy enough for other areas. This aggressive aerating process is most beneficial in the spring when the conditions are best for the turf to quickly heal. Many superintendents now use the vertidrain on fairways and in the roughs as well as on the greens and tees.

Drill and Fill

The Drill and Fill is a machine consisting of a series of drills mounted on a metal frame, which can be raised and lowered into the soil. The drills bore vertical holes into the green or tee and remove soil at the same time. These holes are up to 12 inches deep on 6 inch centers. Each hole is refilled with sand or another suitable material that was loaded in the hopper (Figure 9.4). After a clean-up operation the green can be played upon almost immediately. This method of aeration is used by superintendents who want to drastically modify and improve the growing medium on greens. It is ideal for use on putting greens with poor internal drainage.

Air2G2

The Air2G2 is a machine that injects pressurized air through probes that are inserted into the soil. The probes are inserted into the ground to a depth of 6 inches and the first blast of air is released; then the probes are pushed to a depth of 12 inches and the second blast of air is injected into the soil. The injected air relieves soil compaction with very little disruption to the putting surface. A handheld probe can be used for smaller areas that suffer from the negative effects of compaction.

Aerating Tees

As mentioned in a previous chapter, tees can become scarred quickly during the playing season. Even though the location of the tee markers is often changed, the turf on tees takes a continual beating, especially if the tees are of insufficient size. A regular aeration program for tees is a must. Aerating tees once a season may be enough on some courses, but if there is a considerable number of rounds played aerating more frequently may be necessary. Aeration of tees should be a preventative measure. A tee should be aerated and reseeded before the turf becomes completely worn. If the turf on a tee becomes completely worn out, aeration will not restore its cover; sodding will be the only alternative.

Figure 9.4 *The sand-filled shafts from aerification provide pathways for roots, water, and nutrients for the plant and can help to break up layering of soils that can inhibit plant growth.*
(Photo Courtesy of Wyatt Byrd, Golf Course Superintendent Biltmore Country Club, Barrington, IL.)

The most common size tine to use on tees is ½ inch; however, some tees are best aerated with even smaller tines. Larger tines should be used if the soil needs to be modified, in which case the cores should be removed and the aerator holes filled with desirable topdressing. In other cases, the cores can be pulverized and the crushed material can be spread on the tee used as topdressing.

Superintendents may realize that small portions of the tees that are worn can be aerated and kept out of play until the process can be completed in a short time, the task then becomes manageable.

Core Disposal

Cores that are not pulverized and worked back into the soil as topdressing are often collected and removed from the area. These cores are a welcome addition to a compost pile that can serve other purposes on the golf course property when mixed with other suitable landscape waste.

When an aerated area of turf has an acceptable soil composition, there is no need to remove the cores. The cores can be pulverized on the spot and the remaining material can be used as topdressing. Cores that are removed from small areas can be broken up and worked into the existing turf with an aluminum rake or Levelawn. On areas that are larger, a verticut mower works well for pulverizing the cores. Running over an aerated area with a verticut mower back and forth and in two different directions is usually all it takes to make the cores disintegrate. Dragging a steel mat or power brush will help to level and filter the remains of the cores into the aerated holes. The fluff-like material that remains is a vegetative mix that was once the roots, rhizomes, and the grass blades of the grass plant. These leftovers can be blown into a pile with a leaf blower, hauled away, and then added to the compost pile. The tee should be mowed followed by an irrigation cycle. The project is now complete, the healthy growing process has begun, and soon the tee area will be restored.

Aerating Fairways

Fairways encompass a large area and aerating the fairways is a considerable responsibility for the golf course superintendent. The magnitude of the project to aerate the fairways should not be discouraging, but planned out and accomplished each season.

The scheduling of fairway aerification takes on many forms and is often dictated by staffing, weather, and equipment availability. Some fortunate superintendents are able to close off nine holes while they aerate the fairways leaving the other nine holes available for play. Others are able to close the entire course for one or two days to accomplish the task or even a few days more if they are able to aerify greens, tees, and fairways concurrently. Some superintendents will aerify one fairway at a time, keeping the course open for play during the process.

The aerating process can be accelerated by various methods. Contemporary equipment is more efficient and less time consuming than the machinery of just a few years ago. Adding extra units, either by borrowing or renting, will help to speed up the operation. Some golf courses will employ outside aerification contractors to help with part or all of the process. Working longer hours without the interference of golfers, even beginning in the early evening, can help to get the work done in a timely manner. It is up to the superintendent to maximize the compaction relief with tine depth and spacing, and to minimize disruption of play, taking into account weather, staffing, equipment, and other logistics that impact the process.

Once a fairway has been aerated, it needs to be groomed. The cores can be removed, but usually they are pulverized with a verticutter or a steel drag mat and worked in as topdressing. Another method of removing the cores can be accomplished by using a core processor. The core processor sweeps, processes, and dispenses aeration cores in one pass and is attached behind a tractor drawn aerator. When using the core processor, it may be necessary to drag the fairway with a steel mat to work the residual topdressing into the core holes. Another method of grooming the aerated fairway is to blow off the residue with a powerful blower. Cutting the fairway without the catchers attached to the mower puts the finishing touches on the challenging and time consuming job.

The weather may have an effect on successfully completing the aerating operation. It must be dry enough so that the cores do not clog the verticutting machine heads or bog down the steel mat, unless using the core processor machine that can function in many different weather and soil conditions. A sunny day with a slight bit of wind, some warmth and low humidity, provides the ideal condition for aerating. A word of advice: Do not wait for perfect conditions to start the process, those conditions rarely occur. Rather, anticipate ideal conditions and start the project.

Once fairways have been aerated, superintendents will note a quick improvement in the water absorption rate during and after the irrigation cycle. The multitude of aerator holes encourages the absorption of the water and helps to provide air and water to the roots. The plants will soon show improvement and start to grow vigorously.

Although aeration is an exceptional process that can be used to rejuvenate damaged turf, it is not a cure-all. Caution should be taken when aerating areas of the fairways with sparse turf, turf under stress, and turf with minuscule root systems. After aerating the stressed areas, the weak turf must be treated with special care, which might include some or all of the following: seeding, topdressing, syringing, and roping the area off to prevent foot and vehicular traffic, giving the stressed area every possible chance to recover.

Aerating Bits and Pieces

There are areas in the rough as well as areas near bunkers, green surrounds, and fringes that are worn from concentrated traffic that can benefit from aeration. Observant superintendents recognize such areas quickly during their daily tour of the golf course. In all such cases, the traffic should be diverted and the compacted area aerated, seeded, fertilized, topdressed, and watered to help restore life and playability.

An unfortunate consequence of aerating can occur after the holes are opened, causing the grass to desiccate along the edges. This misfortune may happen during the summer, when drying winds make the grass wilt, or during the winter, when the aeration process was completed too close to the winter freeze (a questionable practice at best).

Aerating cultivates the soil while only slightly disturbing the surface. It allows water and air to move through the soil to the root system of the plant. It opens the soils and provides physical space for the root system to grow, exposing the plants to more nutrients found in the soil. This renewed vigor of the root system is apparent by the health and related growth of the turf plant on the surface. It is important for the golf course superintendent to manage the soils' fertility to maintain healthy turf grass, as aerating does not improve the inherent fertility of the soil. Aeration combined with timely and judicious fertilizer applications will result in a healthy turf cover.

TIP: Whenever one aerates or opens up the soil areas of weak or sparsely covered turf areas, grass seed should be sown to promote new plants and turf cover.

VERTICUTTING

The verticutting process consists of a mower that uses a series of vertically operated metal blades that are driven perpendicular through the thatch on the green and sometimes into the surface of the soil. In the process, parts of the grass blade, crown, rhizomes, and stolons are cut and are brought to the surface. The width and spacing and cutting depth of the blades determine the intensity and the amount of plant material that is brought to the surface. The primary purpose of verticutting is to reduce thatch and encourage the upright growth of leaf blades that have begun to grow horizontal to the soil surface, also known as grain (Figure 9.5). Verticutting can be vigorous process that should not be attempted when the grass plant is under stress. The best time to aggressively verticut varies from region to region; however, occasional verticutting is beneficial for all turfgrass species. During the growing season, a very light (where the blades almost "tickle" the plant) verticutting grooms the grass and improves putting with very little disturbance. Superintendents in southern regions often verticut their Bermuda greens prior to overseeding with northern grasses for winter golf and again at time of transition to native Bermuda turf. The new ultra-dwarf varieties of bent and Bermuda grasses are both very vigorous growers and require frequent verticutting.

TIP: If one is unsure of how aggressive to be when setting up a verticutting unit, make trial runs over a putting green nursery and see how the turf responds.

Figure 9.5 *Verticutting a golf course fairway using a Wiedenmann Tri Gang Verticutter.*
(Photo Courtesy of Wyatt Byrd, Golf Course Superintendent Biltmore Country Club,
Barrington, IL.)

VENTING

Periodically during the height of play, a superintendent will vent the soil by piercing the upper crust of the turf/soil interface. The crust often develops in the course of a growing season from play, rainfall, irrigation, and mowing. The crust hurts the turf by inhibiting water and air movement into the upper root zone. Superintendents will use different machines to vent the soil. If the area is small enough, a pitchfork can be employed. Venting is less disruptive to play than other aerification methods and is a favorite process among superintendents to help keep the turf plants healthy during the middle of the playing season.

A spiker is a machine that consists of a rotating disc with sharp tines that is used to vent soils. When used on a putting green it creates many shallow holes less than ½ inch deep. Spiking in two directions is a best practice, providing a short-lasting fix that allows the turf plants some relief and does not impact ball roll after a mowing or rolling. Like aerating, spiking can be combined with overseeding. The tiny seeds can gain a foothold in the small holes left by the spiker, and then can germinate and eventually become part of the grass mat.

SUMMARY

When soil becomes compacted, the soil must be aerated. There are no shortcuts or painless remedies. There is a price for postponing the inevitable, especially if there is damage from summer stress or winter injury. Greens, tees, and fairways must be aerated on a regular basis and incorporated into a well-thought-out program. Aeration is the single best cultural practice a superintendent can employ to ensure healthy turf each year. Healthy turf is the result of hard work based on a plan, and that plan always includes aeration.

10
Spraying

Between the microscopic nematodes feasting on grass roots and wild boars digging up turf lie the gamut of pests that confront turf managers in the pursuit of maintaining finely manicured playing surfaces. Like the nematodes, fungi, bacteria, and viruses cannot be seen by the naked eye. Others, such as raccoons, skunks, geese, beetles, and larvae can be seen with the naked eye but can be destructive to turf in their own right as some dig for grubs, worms, or seeds while others feed on turf roots. There are many other pests of turfgrass, and usually only harmful when there are enough of them to do irreparable damage to turf.

Besides the members of the animal kingdom, there are many plant species that compete with turf for space, water, nutrients, and sunlight. When left unchecked, weeds can become another problem within the turf. Each pest has a limit before a threshold is reached and action must be taken by the superintendent to ensure the turfgrass plant is not impacted. The first step in battling pests is to grow healthy turfgrass plants by utilizing proper nutrients, amounts of water, and properly timed and defined cultural practices. When the conditions (often environmental) are favored by the pest and all other strategies have been employed, superintendents may have to use their expertise in judicious use of pesticides to give the turf back its advantage so it may grow and thrive.

All superintendents should be familiar with how to operate a variety of sprayers, whether using a backpack sprayer, a tractor-drawn sprayer, or a self-contained computer-controlled sprayer with a shrouded boom. One needs to know which product or combination of products will be the most effective anecdote for preventing or curing the diagnosed pest. The turf manager needs to be familiar with the appropriate rate, quantity, and method to apply products effectively and safely. Will a small backpack sprayer with two gallons of mixture suffice to control the pest? Perhaps the superintendent must employ a 200-gallon sprayer with GPS and individual nozzle control to make a precision application. No matter the method used, the pest must be identified and then controlled using adequate and the safest measures possible. The application of turfgrass chemicals and pesticides is a science in itself; thankfully, there are vast resources and information available for the safe and effective use of turf products.

> TIP: When spraying, create a check area by placing a piece of plywood or like material on the turf to make sure the products used are effective, this is especially helpful when trying new items.

Superintendents should avoid mixing many products into a single tank or application. Some products are not compatible with others and do not readily mix, clogging pumps, hoses and nozzles. Some combinations of products can be too much for the turf to handle at once and will be detrimental instead of helpful to the turf. Whatever the case, spray applications to turf is always advancing with time and technology as products are safer, rates are less, and application equipment is guided by computer and GPS (global positioning systems). Drones are even making their way into the realm of spraying from the air by an operator in an office behind a computer screen. Our intent is to focus on the practical and commonsense approach regarding the application of pesticides and other ministrations that promote healthy grass plants.

TESTING THE EQUIPMENT

Sprayers come in many different sizes. The smallest hold one to two gallons of mixture to the largest used for fairways and rough that may hold 300 gallons of solution. No matter the size of the sprayer, it is imperative that they are checked frequently. The easiest and safest method to check for proper spray patterns, turn on/shut off, and coverage is to fill the reservoir with water only and test the unit in the parking lot. Any improperly functioning component will be quickly seen and can be repaired. This is also a great time and place to train employees new to the task of spraying in a safe and easy place to maneuver. The small handheld or backpack sprayers are handy for spot treatments, especially around trees, fence lines and other areas where a large sprayer is difficult to operate. Licensed (where required) operators should be well trained on the larger sprayers, whether they are mounted in the back of a utility vehicle, pulled behind a tractor, or a self-contained unit. The products applied in these sprayers are expensive, and often the process is time consuming and sensitive.

It is important to have responsible and conscientious employees taking care of this critical task.

> TIP: When taking delivery of a new sprayer, read the manual, require training from the distributor, and make sure your equipment technician is trained so they understand its operation and use.

CALIBRATION

Calibration of a sprayer is a combination of ground speed, pump pressure, and nozzle size to properly apply the products at the labeled application rate. It is a fairly simple process that starts with an adequate ground speed to complete the job expediently. Next, the pressure of the pump is calculated with the nozzle type, size, number, and spacing to match the ground speed. The best speed is somewhere around 5–6 mph, depending on the terrain of the course.

For example, if the boom is 20 feet wide, one needs to travel more than linear 2,000 feet to cover an area of approximately 1 acre. Common sense is using a more practical method of traveling the distance of 500 feet four times. To check the sprayer, drive two stakes in the rough, exactly 500 feet apart. Fill the sprayer with water to the brim and spray the area between the stakes four times. At completion, measure how much water is needed to refill the sprayer to its former level. If it takes 30 gallons, then we know that the sprayer will apply 30 gallons of liquid to each acre. If the sprayer is equipped with a 300-gallon tank, we also know that we can cover 10 acres with one tank filled to the top at the selected speed.

Modern sprayers are equipped with computer controls that monitor the application rates at varying speeds. The details of the rate of application, the boom width, and the speed of the vehicle are entered into the computer and calibrated. A computer-controlled sprayer applies exactly the same amount of liquid to every square foot of turf (Figure 10.1). GPS using satellites in space are now used on sprayers to track where they have sprayed. In addition, maps can be entered into the controls that automatically turn off and on booms while the operator just drives the unit over the area. These guided and computer-operated sprayers function in precise methods, applying products with greater accuracy, less overspray, and reduced amounts. Precise maps can be used to track pest outbreaks and control procedures defined from them. In addition, savings can be gained by the reduction of product used and the labor of the employee by streamlining the spraying process. The use of computers and GPS greatly simplifies the calibration process; however, today's superintendents should still know how to derive the basic calculations.

Figure 10.1 *Computer-controlled sprayers apply the same amount of liquid to every square foot of turf that is mapped by GPS.*

RULES AND REGULATIONS

All pesticide applicators are currently regulated by country and federal governments and licensed by state or local governments. The requirements vary from state to state, and one must be licensed in their own state to apply pesticides and/or be under the direct supervision of someone who is licensed. The licensing process educates and instructs applicators usually through an intensive program that can include but not be limited to the cause of various diseases, effects of pesticides, safety regulations, environmental guidelines, and also the current rules for application. Most of the rules and regulations involve a commonsense approach to spraying operations. Here we share information that we have acquired through personal experience in a practical and logical format:

1. Read and understand the label. Though much of it appears to be legalese to protect the manufacturer from liability, the label is the document that legally binds the user with the governing bodies to only use the product as set forth within it. The label has been developed to provide you all the information needed to control the pest and is the best source of information for the product. For example, the product may have certain exclusions for specific plants

or there may be some allergy information that may affect golfers and applicators. Personal Protective Equipment (PPE) is defined for the applicator as well as the best way to store unused product. It is best to read all the instructions the day before, so the spray application can be started first thing in the morning.

2. Be thoroughly familiar with the product that is being applied. One needs to be acquainted with new pesticides including herbicides, fungicides, or insecticides before using the product. It is advisable to try a new product on a test area such as the nursery, rough, or driving range target greens. Only after a new product has been tested satisfactorily should it be applied on a problem area.

3. When trying a new product for the first time, consider using the lowest dose on the label. It has been our experience that this dose will provide adequate means of control even if the interval of control is decreased. One can always make a second application if it is needed; however, once the product is applied, it is impossible to put it back in its container.

4. Applying pesticides that are no longer registered or using a product that is not labeled for use is illegal and may result in serious penalties for the operator and the owner(s) of the golf course.

5. Avoid mixing pesticides to save time and labor. Few people would mix a weed killer with an insecticide, but some may try adding a fungicide to an insecticide. Although some pesticides are compatible in a tank mix, some are not, and it is better to be safe than sorry.

6. Adding a defoaming agent while the tank is being filled will prevent an overflow with big blobs of foam.

7. When filling the tank, fill half the tank with water, then add the product while the agitator is rotating before topping off the tank. Pesticide containers that are empty should be triple-rinsed and the residual returned to the spray tank. The containers should be sliced and crushed before being properly discarded or recycled.

8. The best time to spray is at the crack of dawn when wind is usually absent or minimal. When there is dew on the grass, markings on the grass in areas that have been sprayed are visible. It is best to spray in front of play or schedule sprays when the course will be closed due to an afternoon event. Consider partially filling the tank with water the night before, gaining a head start for the early morning.

9. There are many devices that leave a mark in the grass to help the operator decide what areas have been sprayed. The simplest, but perhaps the most outdated, method is using a small piece of chain at the end of the boom that is dragged over the grass leaving a trail. Consider using a foam marker to identify the areas that have been sprayed rather than dye that does not look good on white golf shoes, yardage plates and sprinkler heads.

10. When the job is finished and the tank is empty, it is cleanup time. Rinse the tank with water and drain the remaining solution into the rinse pad, recycling container or apply the rinsate to an area of rough. Many areas require a rinse pad for chemical disposal and permits are required from the state or locality. Check all nozzles and screens and put the equipment away so that it will be ready to go the next time it is needed.

11. A written report documenting the spray application is absolutely essential. This report is one of the most important pieces of record keeping in the superintendent's journal. The report should include date and time, weather conditions, the names and quantities of the materials, where it was purchased and its registration and lot numbers, the area sprayed, and the name of the applicator; the sprayer settings should also be recorded. The pest that is being treated and the extent of the injury should be described as well. In fact, the more information included, the more value the document has for future reference.

DECISION TIME: WHEN TO SPRAY AND WHEN TO WAIT

An important part of a superintendent's duties includes checking the golf course in its entirety on a regular basis. During the growing season, one must constantly be on the lookout for signs and symptoms of disease, especially on the tees, fairways, and greens. On every golf course, there are greens that are always the first to show visible signs of concern because of their location, lack of air movement, or shade, and are invariably the first places for disease and/or pest infestation. Your first inclination may be to check these greens, but sometimes the area in the back of a tee, that is located in the midst of a group of trees or a low-lying area on a fairway, will show the first signs of disease. Observant superintendents know from experience where these areas are located, and they base their decisions about when to spray on what is happening in these indicator areas.

The most common disease on golf courses is Dollar spot, which occurs most often during humid weather with warm days and cool nights. It has an appearance of yellow-green blotches on the grass blades and forms in patches that are 2–5 inches in diameter; the disease affects only the blades of the leaf. If grasses are observed in the morning when there is dew present, a white cobweb-like growth of the fungus (mycelium) can be seen. All turf grasses are susceptible to Dollar spot and are more susceptible when they are nutrient-deficient and the soil is dry and humidity is high.

When the first signs of Dollar spot show in their usual locations and the weather conditions are favorable for the onset of the disease, a prudent superintendent will apply a fungicide immediately to the area before the forecasted conditions make it easy for the Dollar spot to run rampant.

Similarly, Pythium blight is one of the most destructive turfgrass diseases and is often observed in low areas or swales. Pythium blight is known to be able to destroy large areas of turf within a 24-hour period when conditions are favorable for the spread of the disease. The disease can be recognized by water-soaked leafy patches that can be 4 inches in diameter. In high humidity in the morning hours, the growth can take on a cottony appearance and spread quickly. High humidity and hot daytime temperatures around 85–95°F and high humidity in the evening with temperatures around 70°F or higher should be a warning sign that Pythium blight will attack. When these conditions occur, it may wise to stay on the property and monitor developments. If necessary apply a preventative fungicide on greens, tees, and fairways or spot spray vulnerable areas, especially when hot and humid days and warm nights are in the forecast.

All workers who are on the course daily, under the guidance of the superintendent, should be trained to watch for signs of disease and pest invasion. The decision to spray is never taken lightly. The actual blanket application of a pesticide to all greens, tees, or fairways may be preceded by treating localized areas. At times, spot-spraying may nip the problem in the bud. The decision to bring out the sprayer is based on observation, scientific evidence, and long-time experience. Neighboring superintendents are a great resource for advice and thoughts on the decision to spray. Social media is another great resource to see what others are seeing in the geographic area, especially paying attention to weather patterns that are tell-tale signs of what is approaching your course. Check other online resources that provide computer modeling for disease encroachment based on growing degree days (GDD) and other measurable factors needed for diseases to strike.

Many superintendents know that healthy turf is far less likely to be infected and, therefore, they believe it is in their best interest to grow healthy grass. They know that maintaining vigorous turf will help to reduce weeds that can be hosts for pests and insects, and the weeds compete with turfgrass for nutrients and moisture (Figure 10.2).

There have been superintendents that were concerned about the environment, and they practiced their grass-growing skills to the highest levels. These superintendents introduced an integrated plant management plan into their maintenance program long before Integrated Pest Management (IPM) became a buzzword. IPM has now become a

Figure 10.2 *Pesticides and plant protectants are a small part of growing healthy stands of turfgrass.*

maintenance and pest-control philosophy. Superintendents should adhere to the three stages of IPM, prevention, observation, and intervention, and include this policy in their approach to turf management.

TIPS:

- Regularly scout the golf course for pests and other problems.
- Determine the specific cause of a pest and contain it by adjusting cultural practices.
- Establish a criterion for when a pesticide application is an option.
- Spray only as a last-ditch effort when all else has failed.
- Always try to spray an environmentally safe product.
- Verticutting reduces thatch and increases the effectiveness of pesticides, thus reducing the amount needed.
- Keeping reels sharp reduces mechanical damage to turf and, therefore, susceptibility to pest damage.
- The pH greatly affects the efficiency of pesticides.
- When applying pesticides avoid waterways (Figure 10.3).
- Include the principles of IPM as part of a regular employee-training program.

Figure 10.3 *Algae and aquatic weeds are a common problem, especially on shallow ponds. Manual removal avoids the use of costly pesticides. Water aeration is another option.*

FATAL MISTAKES

Unfortunately, sometimes errors occur during the process of pesticide application that result in dead greens, and at times several or even all the greens on a golf course have been killed by an overdose, the wrong pesticide, or a lethal combination of pesticides.

- Soluble fertilizers mixed with pesticides should never be applied until such a mix has been tested in a trial area or the nursery.
- A problem green with thin grass cover that requires treatment should always be sprayed with a pesticide that has been used before and has worked satisfactorily.
- Always figure out the disease that is attacking the turf and then develop a plan to treat the problem.
- Double-check calculations when determining amounts of products to add to the tank mix. If something doesn't seem right, it probably isn't.
- Grass can die as a result of accidents caused by human error as well as spraying inappropriately. Sometimes doing nothing is the best thing to do.

- Spraying when the wind is blowing can cause the spray to drift causing uneven distribution of product or worse yet off target and onto neighboring areas.
- Inadequately cleaning the sprayer after use and leaving unused product in the tank could create a deadly mix the next time the sprayer is used if incompatible products are added.
- Don't forget to check and clean filters and nozzles.
- Watch what and where you spray. All of these can be harmful:
  - Spraying the wrong pesticide on an area
  - Spraying pesticide on the wrong area
  - Spraying the wrong pesticide on the wrong area

EDUCATION

The spectrum of plant damage and diseases caused by fungi or insects is very complex, and combating them requires obtaining a continuing stream of information from universities, colleges, and research centers. When combined with nutritional deficiencies, environmental stresses, and water quality issues and the continual introduction of new products, it is readily apparent that superintendents need to constantly update their knowledge of pesticides and their application.

The introduction of soil surfactants, biostimulants, and growth regulators compound the knowledge needed to maintain turf to the highest standards. Turf managers need to continually seek information on these products and their interactions to find where they fit within their turf management program. A successful superintendent will nurture a wide network of fellow superintendents, attend educational seminars, pay attention to current research findings, and engage with the industry to stay on top of this ever-changing realm of turf management. The slow period of a golfing season or the off-season are ideal times to go back to school to keep up to date and learn about new products and ideas in the world of turf.

TIP: An easy way to stay abreast of new products and their uses is to use your lunch break. Take the time to browse online one new product or process for a few minutes each day. There is always more to learn.

SUMMARY

Turfgrass diseases have become more prevalent as golf course superintendents balance turf health, environmental conditions, and the playability of the grasses they manage. New and greater restrictions limit the choices of available products superintendents have to control many turfgrass pests. Superintendents, now more than ever, are needed to grow strong, healthy grass that can withstand the onslaught of disease.

In some parts of the world, pesticides, chemicals, and even fertilizers are not permitted to be applied on golf course turf. Limitations and regulations began in a few European countries. Some states and local jurisdictions have followed suit in North America and have banned or limited the use of pesticides on lawns, parks, and golf courses. Through legislation, many restrictions have become part of the environmental programs that are mandatory in many parts of the world. This has made the art and science of greenkeeping a greater challenge, and we continue to adapt to our changing world. Practical greenkeeping methods are a proven basis for the healthy turf plants and can reduce the use and quantity of turf chemicals.

11

Seeding, Sodding, and Sprigging

Golf is meant to be played on grass, and the quality of the grass determines the reputation of the superintendent. There are very few courses around the world where bare earth is acceptable. Every concerned superintendent strives to cover all grassed areas of the greens, fairways, tees, and even the rough with high-quality turf. This is never an easy task. Establishing a quality turf by means of seeding, sodding, or sprigging requires both skill and knowledge. Once the plant has taken root, the never-ending job begins. The new grass plant needs constant encouragement and nourishment to develop into healthy, strong turf.

SEEDING

Seeding is the most cost-efficient method of establishing nearly all turf. Since seeding does not add a layer of foreign soil (vs. sodding) to the surface the superintendent often prefers this method for planting new grasses. There are some drawbacks to seeding, and most important is the narrow window for almost perfect conditions to complete all phases of the seeding process, as well as the necessity for the soil temperatures to be above 50°F for the seeds to germinate. Seeding with superior bentgrass cultivars have developed greens that grow more vigorously, are disease resistant, and can be cut at a lower height and outcompete weed infiltration. These superior plants have virtually eliminated the practice of planting bentgrass stolons. However, the practice of sprigging (see sprigging in this chapter) rather than seeding is the preferred method for the establishment of most of the Bermuda grasses.

Warm soils and adequate moisture are vital for seeds to germinate. Once a seed absorbs water, its hull is broken, allowing the tiny roots to develop and reach into the soil for nourishment. Unless the earth is warm (in most cases above 50°F), very little takes place inside the seed.

Cool season grasses are best planted in the fall and spring. Turf experts consider early fall the best time to plant because the soil moisture from the heavy dews and seasonal rains provide conditions that are favorable. In addition, competitive weed activity diminishes greatly during this time of the year. Once established, the plants have a greater chance of survival if conditions should turn unfavorable for growth. Spring is considered the next best time for successful planting once the soil temperatures have consistently reached 50°F.

Warm season grasses are best planted from late spring to early summer. High soil temperatures that are around 70°F (daytime air temperature around 80°F) and rainfall during this time allow for faster germination of the seedlings. Planting warm season grasses in the fall when the soil temperature is too cool can result with weeds germinating, plants going dormant, and the risk of damage to the seedlings from an early frost.

TIP: Research, investigate and use the newest and most advanced turf cultivars on the market when renovating or seeding new areas. It is not often a superintendent is able to start with new grasses. Buying and installing the best available will pay dividends down the road using less inputs to sustain healthy turf.

Minimum Soil Temperature Requirements for Seed Germination

Cool Season Grasses		Warm Season Grasses	
Perennial rye grasses	50°F	Bermuda grasses	65°F
Bentgrasses	60°F	Zoysia grasses	70°F
Bluegrasses	55–60°F		

In the early spring, seed can be planted while the soil is cold; however, the seed will lie dormant until the soil temperature rises. A method to accelerate the process entails covering seeded areas with a geotextile fabric to keep the seedbed warm especially when overnight temperatures drop. During the warmth of the day, heat builds up under the cover and the blanket must be removed. Cautious supervising of the growing medium by covering and uncovering the seedbed will accelerate the germination process by several days. To achieve success, constant attention to nursing the small grass plants until maturity is required. A deft superintendent is able to push the turf balancing covers, proper nutrition, adequate water and, if needed, fungicides to protect the seedlings from opportunistic fungi that spawn under the same conditions and feed on the new grass roots.

Seed Sizes and Germination

Seeds come in a variety of sizes, and the smallest seeds are those of the various bentgrass cultivars. The minuscule size of the bentgrass seed makes the individual seed almost invisible. Although a handful of bentgrass seed feels light as a feather, under favorable growing conditions millions of seeds will produce millions of grass plants. Bentgrass germinates in 5–10 days. Under ideal conditions, when the area is covered with dew, a haze of green can be detected early in the morning of the fifth day. Not all seeds germinate at the same time. Over a period of several days, more and more seedlings will emerge from under the earth, becoming blades of grass and collectively forming a greensward.

Tall fescue seeds are much larger than the bluegrass seeds. Most cultivars of bluegrass take 14–28 days to germinate (some newer cultivars will germinate in as little as 7 days) and twice that long to form an appreciable grass mat, while the fescues will germinate in 10–21 days. The perennial rye germinates quickly, within 5–14 days. It has been known to sprout a blade in just 3 days, and a visible cover within a week. On the other hand, annual rye grass seed is the largest in size of all the common lawn grasses. Since rye grass grows so quickly, birds have less chance to eat all the seed before the grass takes root.

Seeding Rates

The following seeding rates are for the application of seed to properly prepared bare earth. When rates are exceeded, seedlings can become thin and frail, and disease may occur in the newly seeded area.

	lb. /1,000 sq. ft.	*lb. /acre*
Bentgrasses	1–2	40–80
Improved bluegrasses	3–5	120–200
Improved fescue grasses	6–8	240–320
Perennial rye grasses	5–7	200–280

Scorching Turf and Seeding

The "scorched earth" technique is a method of preparing the soil for seeding. Scorching the earth is accomplished by spraying the turf with nonselective herbicide, which kills all the treated grass in a matter of days. The decaying grass plants create a mat that is then scarified and seeded into, and in a few weeks the old turf that has been killed is now replaced with a suitable species of grass. This is precisely how *Poa annua* infested fairways are converted to bentgrass fairways on golf courses in the northern climatic zone.

Overseeding with a Slit Seeder

The most frequently used machine for overseeding is a slit seeder. It is a machine that creates a narrow groove in the soil into which the seed falls and helps to jumpstart the germination process. Young plants often have difficulty competing with the dominant turf of actively growing grass. If the existent turf is sparse, the new seed has a much better chance to compete and to become established. Whatever process is used for overseeding, the seeds must be spread into the soil and the soil containing the seeds must stay moist. Don't overlook using a starter fertilizer at this time to provide adequate nutrients for the young plants.

Winter Overseeding of Bermuda Turf

Southern grasses are not very tolerant of cold temperatures, and it is an accepted fact that when nighttime temperatures drop below 50°F for any period of time, the grass will go dormant and turn brown. Superintendents overseed their southern turf on greens, tees, fairways, and even roughs, with large quantities of bent, rye, fescue, and *Poa trivialis* grass seed. The process is unique, and it requires great skill and judgment to obtain satisfactory results. Since timing is critical and golfing schedules often interfere, results may vary from one year to another.

Several weeks prior to the scheduled overseeding, superintendents cut back on fertilizer programs and so reduce the vigor of the Bermuda turf at a time when falling temperatures also reduce plant growth. In order to prepare the seedbed further, extensive verticutting is carried out, which opens the turf mat so that seed can filter down to the soil level. At the same time, the height of cut is raised to provide a canopy for the seed. On low-budget courses, greens are overseeded with rye grass, and so are the fairways and the tees. At high-end resort courses and private country clubs, the seed of choice for greens is bentgrass, often augmented with a small quantity of *Poa trivialis*.

Overseeding Rates for Southern Turf

Bentgrass on greens and tees	1–3 lb./1,000 sq. ft.
Poa trivialis on greens	10 lb./1,000 sq. ft.
Rye grass on greens and tees	20–40 lb./1,000 sq. ft.
Rye grass on fairways	200–750 lb./acre

Seed size and seeding rates are related: the smaller the seed, the greater number of seeds there are per pound. The number of individual seeds per square foot of soil needs to be adequate to achieve complete and thorough coverage of the area to be seeded. There is a danger, particularly with the fine-seeded bentgrasses, in applying too much seed. An extremely thick stand can easily give rise to disease, such as "damping-off" caused by the *Pythium* and *Rhizoctonia* fungus species. The mycelia of these fungi will quickly wipe out a large stand of newly germinated grass seed. As soon as they have been identified, they should be treated with an appropriate fungicide.

Overseeding and Interseeding on Southern Turf

Perennial rye grass is the primary variety used for overseeding. For best results, the perennial rye grass will consist of a double or triple blend of different cultivars of rye seeds. In some southern regions, newer varieties of rye grasses have been developed and are used because they fade sooner, allowing the Bermuda grass to compete during the transition period. Some golf courses overseed the rough as well as the fairways; others leave the rough to its own devices, which means that, at least for much of the winter, it is mostly brown and often makes for an attractive contrast with the lush green fairways.

After greens are overseeded, topdressing is often applied and is watered intermittently to encourage germination. The two-week period following overseeding can be frustrating for golfers because the greens tend to be excessively moist and very slow. Once the seed germinates and the plants become established, conditions return to normal as superintendents reduce watering and lower the height of cut.

The process for overseeding fairways is very similar but not as intensive. Seed can be broadcast by a cyclone spreader, but the outer edge is seeded with a drop-type spreader to make for a distinctive line of contrast. Following the seed application, the fairways are drag-matted or brushed to work the seed into the turf mat.

If the overseeding process is time consuming and tricky, the spring transition back to Bermuda turf is equally difficult. Perennial rye plants have a tendency to be very healthy and can often cause a negative impact on the emergence of the Bermuda grass during the transition period, and because seeding rates are higher, the transition from rye grass back to Bermuda grass becomes more challenging. As soon as air and soil temperatures rise, the northern grasses must make way for southern grasses. That means the height of cut is lowered and fertilizer is applied to pop the Bermuda grass out of its dormancy. If the rye grass is permitted to flourish well into spring, it is often at the expense of the Bermuda grass with disastrous results.

In southern Florida, in a line from Fort Lauderdale to Naples, where the temperatures do not get cold enough for the turf to go completely brown, the Bermuda turf stays green very consistently and overseeding is only done on 15–25 percent of the golf courses. The goal is to have a blend of ryegrass and Bermuda grass with neither one being dominant in the winter months, providing a cushion for the players rather than providing color. This method of overseeding is often referred to in the south as "interseeding." From there on north, the decision to overseed is often a gamble. A superintendent may guess right one year and be a hero; the next year the superintendent could be a villain and lose his or her job.

Another method that many southern golf courses have adopted in recent years it to dye or paint the dormant Bermuda grass, especially fairways, tees, and approaches. Many will still overseed the putting surfaces, but opt to spray paint the other areas of turf for the winter months. Not only is the dye cheaper than seed, this process minimizes the amount of maintenance as dyed turf does not need to be cut.

Preparing a New Seedbed

Debris, rocks, and stones must all be removed from the area that is being prepared for a new seedbed. Usually, such items are hand-raked into piles and carted away. Mechanical stone pickers are useful when a large amount of stone and debris must be removed. Nothing must be left to interfere with the growth of the grass and required maintenance practices. For the germination process to begin, the seeds must make contact with the soil, allowing the sprouting roots to embed themselves among the soil particles and to extract nourishment from the growing medium. Therefore, the seedbed must consist of a layer of enriched and fine-textured soil. This can be attained by rototilling the area to be seeded, then firming and leveling with a landscaping device such as a seedbed or specialty roller that is capable of breaking up large clods and leaving in its path a bed of fine topsoil.

Also, other landscaping tools such as the Gill or the Viking seeder can be attached to a three-point hitch system found on most tractors and can do a commendable job of fine-grading the area to be seeded, sodded, or sprigged. Any of these methods are acceptable when working on large seedbed areas.

Other methods for preparing seedbeds, which are mainly used when working on small areas, include dragging a steel I-beam, a piece of chain-link fence, a steel mat, or even just the power rake used for sand bunkers. For even smaller areas such as greens, where prescribed contours have been carefully designed by architects, working with caution is absolutely essential and hand-raking may be the only alternative.

Fertilizing the Seedbed

New seed planted in a seedbed requires different fertilizers than established grass. A soil analysis should be taken to make certain that the appropriate nutrition is present in the soil to nurture the germination of the seeds. Once the soil in the seedbed is prepared, a starter mix of fertilizer containing a mix of nitrogen, phosphorus, and potassium should be mixed into the growing medium. In order for the seeds to grow, the seedbed must contain phosphorus for germination and potassium, which encourages root growth. Once the plant has rooted, fertilizer mix with higher rates of nitrogen can be applied. If the starter fertilizer was inadvertently omitted from being mixed into the growing medium before seeding, the fertilizer can be added to the finished grade at a different rate. There may be a justifiable fear that too much fertilizer will burn the root hairs as the grass germinates.

TIP: Overfertilizing with too much nitrogen may cause seeds to try to grow too fast. Fertilizer with higher nitrogen rates should be added only after the plant has rooted.

Seed Application Methods

Larger seeds, such as rye and fescue, may be applied by means of a cyclone spreader. An over-the-shoulder spreader with a wide shoulder strap that has a hand crank used for spreading the seed is handy, especially in small and hard-to-reach areas.

A drop-type spreader works best when planting smaller bentgrass seeds. Small bentgrass seeds can be easily spread by mixing the seeds with sand or organic fertilizers such as Milorganite or Sustane as a carrier. This method increases the bulk of the material, while achieving uniform coverage.

When using a cyclone, shoulder, or drop spreader, always apply the seed by overlapping in two different directions to ensure uniformity. Since wind is an important factor, the best time to seed is a time during the day when there is little or no wind. A brisk breeze can easily blow away the seed from the intended area. After the seed has been applied, the soil should be lightly raked, rolled, and moistened to create optimum growing conditions and a smooth surface.

For larger areas, use a tractor-drawn "Brillion" or cultipacker seeder. These seeders consist of a hopper that releases seeds and a corrugated steel drum-like packer that rolls on the soil pressing the seed and covering it with a fine layer of soil. The weight of the packer forces the moisture currently in the soil to the surface, thus assisting the germination process. As with other applications, the area needs to be kept moist until the seeds germinate.

A hydroseeder (a machine that uses a planting process that sprays slurry consisting of grass seed and mulch) should be considered for use on steep and uneven terrain. The slurry mix can consist of various ingredients including fertilizer, tackifiers (that aid in the bonding ability of mulch), green dyes, and other additives. As the name implies, the method involves water that is sprayed under pressure to apply a seed and slurry mix to bare hillsides or other areas to be seeded. The slurry tends to form a crust over the soil, which helps prevent erosion and speeds up germination. Recently, newly constructed golf courses have used the hydroseeding process on the entire course, including greens, tees, fairways, and rough with great success. Hydroseeding is much less expensive than sodding, is very efficient, and produces turf quickly.

Mulching

Covering seed with mulching products creates a barrier to hold in moisture during germination, reduces the need for constant watering, and prevents seed and soil erosion. Straw was the main mulch that was used for many years. The old-fashioned method of using a pitchfork was the practical way of spreading the bales of straw. This method has given way to the use of straw rolls that are interwoven with plastic strands that keep the straw in place (Figure 11.1). This type of straw blanket is particularly effective on steep hills. Today, these blankets are made from other biodegradable products and are attached to the soil with biodegradable anchoring staples that can degrade within a year. These blankets provide a wonderful cover, keep surface water movement to a minimum, and speed germination. The use of a cover can provide the additional time that may be needed for successful seeding. In northern climates, the blankets provide warmth and moisture, and the time frame for seeding can be extended by as much as

Figure 11.1 *Seedlings emerge through a straw mulch blanket in a fall seeding. The blanket holds the soil in place and helps to keep the seed bed moist.*

a month in the fall. The soil moisture and heat are preserved under these cozy covers, allowing the seed to germinate quickly, and soon the seedling will grow through the straw mesh.

Penn Mulch is a biodegradable product that is green in color and can improve the look of the area being seeded. The mulch comes in pellet form that consists of water-absorbing paper and polymer pellets that contain fertilizer. Since this product biodegrades naturally, it is safe to apply by hand or by a spreader.

TIP: Mulch should not be so heavy that it entirely covers the seeded area and smothers the seedlings.

Watering Seed

Newly seeded areas need to be lightly watered just enough to keep things damp on a regular basis. Once the seeds have soaked up water, the seeds must not be allowed to dry before they germinate. Under normal conditions, watering lightly two to three times a day should keep the seedbed moist. However, too much water at a time can cause puddling or runoff. Automatic underground sprinklers can be set with precision, but they need to be checked during each irrigation cycle, making sure that underwatering or overwatering is not occurring. The objective is to keep the soil damp while the tiny grass plants are sprouting their roots. Once the grass plants are established, they must be kept moist to grow actively and form a mat of dense turf.

> TIP: Be careful not to overwater the young seedlings. It may induce a *Pythium* or *Rhizoctonia solani* infestation, which are two fungi that can kill seedlings before or after they germinate. If there is a question on how deep to water, pull a new grass plant and see how deep the root has grown. This will tell you how much water to apply – any deeper and it is a waste.

Establishing bentgrass on high-sand-content greens can be difficult. The sand dries out so quickly that it needs to be watered frequently, often as much as once an hour, especially during the heat of the day. Even after the seed has germinated, it needs constant attention or the grass plants will wither and die. During the entire process of growing the bentgrass on the sand greens, a member of the crew under the watchful eye of the superintendent must be alert and observant to the moisture conditions, ensuring success and preventing disasters.

Fertilizing New Turf

New turf has an inborn desire to grow, but this process must be stimulated with extra nutrition and requires at least twice as much fertilizer as established grass. Applying fertilizer by means of heavy equipment can be damaging to newly growing turf because of the absence of a wear-resistant mat. When fertilizing entire golf courses, superintendents will often apply liquid fertilizer via the automated sprinklers to avoid rutting that is caused by vehicles.

After Seeding – The First Cut

Time for the first cutting takes place when the seeds have germinated, the grass plants are actively growing, and a thick cover has formed. Rolling the turf lightly prior to cutting is beneficial. This action presses the plants into the soil and promotes firm root contact that will prevent damage caused by the shearing action of the mower. Wait a day or two after the grass plants have been pressed down by rolling, and the grass will bounce back again and be ready for cutting.

> TIP: If a cover with plastic netting was used to protect the seed, the plastic portion of the netting should be removed to avoid potential problems when cutting the new turf for the first time with a reel mower.

The most important step is to check that the blades are exceedingly sharp on whatever mower is being used. If the blades on the mower are dull, they can tear the tops of the grass plants or even worse, pull the whole plant out of the soil. On a newly seeded green or tee, a greens mower may be used, but it should be raised to its upper limit. In all cases, the clippings should be removed. Gobs of grass left in haphazard heaps will kill the turf underneath and cause unsightly dead spots. Amazingly, after the first cut, the rate of growth of the new stand increases rapidly, and with successive cuttings, a healthy sward soon becomes established.

If the cover of grass is imperfect because of washouts or poor germination, corrective action is required. Small areas with sparse growth can be spot-seeded by applying seed that is combined with a mix of materials (that are the same as those applied to the original seedbed) to the affected area much like a divot mix. If the washout areas are deep, sodding may be the only means of correcting the problem and preventing it from becoming more serious. Action should be taken very quickly. Repairs must be made so that the success of the project is not impeded by indecision.

New seedlings grow inexhaustibly and, subsequently, absorb large amounts of nutrients from the soil. These nutrients in the soil must be replenished; therefore a follow-up fertilizer program is essential. During their infancy the grass plants that are lacking the required nutrients will quickly turn yellow or purple, depending on whether they need nitrogen or potassium. Regular applications of balanced fertilizer are essential to overcome these deficiencies. It must be understood that the nutritional requirements of new turf are at least twice as high as those of established stands. Growing in new turf to maturity has now become a recognized art, and a small group of "grow in" superintendents make their living traveling from new course to new course, growing in the young turf to maturity and preparing it for play.

SODDING

Preparing the soil for sodding is very similar to preparing it for seeding. The area to be sodded needs to be cleared of debris, making sure that nothing interferes with the roots of the sod being able to penetrate into the soil. Rototilling the soil, fertilizing, firming, leveling, and again checking for debris are a must before the sod is laid. Sod should be fresh, preferably cut just the day before delivery, and laid by the next day. A roll of sod can cover a lot of sins, but if the soil underneath is not prepared properly, it may come back to haunt a person. Stones and rocks will find their way to the surface and eventually pop up through the sod, damaging the mowers as well as the golfers' clubs.

The surfaces of tees and greens that are to be sodded must be perfectly smooth and firm, almost a bit hard, so that there is no footprinting when the sod is laid. Prior to laying the sod, the fertilizer should have been tilled into the soil mix. If this step was inadvertently omitted, fertilizer can be applied on the finished grade. Planks or sheets of plywood are often used when sodding greens or tees. The workers can now walk on the wood planks instead of the grass or the soil to prevent footprints. One way to start the project is to lay the first row of sod down the middle of the tee or green in a straight line, and lay the next row of sod butting up tightly against the first row, staggering the ends similar to bricks in a wall.

Some superintendents outline the green using landscape paint applied with a paint gun. Another way to obtain a perfectly smooth naturally flowing line is to use a heavy hose. Place the hose in the preferred outline forming a natural contour that has been designed by the architect for the tee or green. Once the outline has been determined, use a sharp sod knife to cut the edge of the sod (Figure 11.1). If the apron or collar is to be sodded as well, the sod rolls can now be unrolled around the outside edge of the green to the desired width.

Sodding Bits and Pieces

The following are a few tips to lay sod and help encourage survival:

- Prior to laying sod during the heat of summer, consider syringing the dry earth. A little bit of moisture on the surface of the soil before the sod is laid will promote root formation and help to prevent the sod from drying out or wilting.
- Rolling sod after it has been laid is essential. The weight of the roller draws moisture to the surface and makes sure that the sod comes into firm contact with the soil. Air pockets will be eliminated by repeated rolling.
- Sodding slopes, bunker faces, or surrounds of tees requires special care. On steep slopes, lay the sod perpendicular to the slope and in an alternating brick-like pattern. Laying the sod so that it goes around the hill in rows will prevent erosion and water runoff. The sod should be attached to the soil with biodegradable staples. On severe slopes, consider using wooden pegs or biodegradable stakes, and hammer these into the soil to a depth of 6–10 inches.

Once the sod has rooted, the wooden pegs may be removed. The biodegradable staples or stakes will disappear with time.

- When sodding around the face of the bunker a strip of sod should be laid along the edge of the sand. Continue to lay the sod out and away from the edge of the bunker. The same holds true for sodding around the edge of tees; lay a strip of sod around the outside perimeter of the teeing area and continue laying the remaining rolls of sod up against this strip, using staples if necessary in areas that have a slope to keep the sod in place.
- Sod that is grown on a sand mix usually drains well. This mix should meet USGA specifications for applications over sand-based root zones. One of the primary applications for this type of sod is for use on sand-based greens.
- Some sod producers can provide their product in Big Rolls. The Big Rolls come in a variety of widths and lengths, ranging from 2–4 feet wide and, depending on the equipment, used can be laid in lengths over 100 feet. The smaller Big Rolls can be laid by using a special attachment that fits on tractors or forklifts. Specialized machinery is required to lay the large, heavier Big Rolls (Figure 11.2). The advantages of using these large rolls are that

Figure 11.2 *A machine used to install big roll sod on a golf course fairway.*

areas can be covered quicker, using less manpower, and having fewer seams to knit together. A new machine called the SideKick is now utilized to lay thick cut Big Rolls with virtually no seams returning the areas to play as soon as the sod is installed. A tee can be installed in a day and be open for play the next.

- Washed sod, as the name implies, has had the soil washed away from the roots, leaving behind a mass of roots topped with green grass that can be laid on its intended surface. The advantage is that foreign soil is not imported into the soil mix allowing the sod to knit to the soil quickly. The lightness of the washed sod reduces the weight, making shipping possible to almost anywhere in the world.
- Aeration can also be helpful to promote bonding between the sod and soil. Washed sod in particular seems to benefit from several aerations early in its establishment.
- Whether sod arrives on pallets, skids, or in rolls, it should be laid immediately, especially during periods of high temperatures. On a hot day, sod left on a pallet can yellow quickly. The rolls of sod, tightly packed together, create a condition that is anaerobic and produces heat, which in turn will kill the grass. In cool temperatures, sod can be stored for longer periods.

Watering Sod

During the first week or so, newly laid sod requires heavy watering, keeping the sod moist but not saturated. The grass mat must be kept alive by keeping it moist so that the water will pass through the grass mat and encourage the roots to firmly grow in the soil. Apply too much and you will have created a messy quagmire; too little water can cause the sod to wilt or perhaps die. Particular attention should be paid to watering the seams of the sod; this prevents the edges of the sod from curling up giving it an unhealthy appearance. Sometimes after a rain, sod that appears dead may only be dormant and will return to its green color. The best way to keep the new sod moist is by watering daily. Check for the development of tiny white root hairs by lifting a corner of the sod and checking for moisture between the soil and the grass mat. Once they appear, they will quickly find their way into the soil and provide anchorage for the new turf. Unrolled sod may temporarily be stored on a plastic tarp and the sod must be watered regularly. A mass of roots will develop where the soil meets the plastic tarp. The sod can be left in this manner for several days, depending on the weather conditions, and later used to complete a construction project. The sod that has been stored on the plastic tarp will have roots that are particularly anxious to renew their contact with the soil. Such sod, when watered, becomes firmly attached to the soil in just a few days.

> TIP: When watering newly laid sod, soak the sod until the soil underneath it becomes wet. Pulling up a corner of a piece and looking underneath is the best way to know you've put down enough water.

SPRIGGING

The process of distributing small cut-up portions of stolons over a seedbed for the purpose of establishing turf is known as sprigging. Stolons are the above ground stems that contain growing points called nodes from which roots and shoots can emerge. At one time new greens in the northern climatic zone were routinely sprigging in preference to seeding, but with the advent of superior cultivars of bentgrass and their availability in the seed form, this practice has largely been eliminated in the north. However, sprigging is still used extensively in the southern climatic zone with Paspalum and Bermuda species of turf on tees, greens, and fairways. Sprigs, or parts of stolons with one or two nodes, can be produced at a turf nursery and shipped to golf courses in refrigerated containers.

Sprigs are usually broadcast by hand by several workers, and when the green or tee is entirely covered, the sprigs are packed into the soil with a roller or with the studded tires of a small lawn tractor or bunker rake. The sprinklers are turned on next, and in two to three weeks' time, the sprigs will develop roots and leaf tops and begin to look like a green or a tee. Topdressing begins when the sprigs have rooted and continues at regular intervals until the green is ready for play.

Bermuda Sprigs

The quantities of sprigs used can be phenomenal when planting Bermuda grass. On greens and tees the application rate may be as high as 20–35 bushels per 1,000 sq. ft. The total area of fairways is too big for hand-sprigging, and mechanical spriggers are employed that spread and push sprigs into soil. It takes more than 450–475 bushels of Bermuda sprigs per acre to plant a fairway and when planting takes place later in the season it may be necessary to plant 1,000 bushels of sprigs per acre. When planting large quantities of Bermuda sprigs, use a slicer type machine to cut sprigs into the soil and slice three to four different directions for optimum results.

Paspalum Sprigs

Paspalum is native to parts of South America. The warm season perennial grass grows in tropical areas throughout the world. Paspulum sprigs should always be considered in warm climates especially where golf courses are close to the ocean, where saltwater and spray is a problem, and water usage is restricted. Paspalum can tolerate recycled water also known as gray or effluent water. It requires less nitrogen than other grasses and is shade and drought tolerant. When planting Paspalum it is recommended that sprigging rates be 200–600 bushels per acre. Planting procedures are the same as those of Bermuda sprigs.

> TIP: Contacting a superintendent who is familiar with Paspalum or attending one of the GCSAA (Golf Course Superintendents Association of America) seminars for more information about planting may be advantageous when selecting a species of Paspalum.

Watering Sprigs

As soon as the sprigs are planted, herbicide can be applied and watering should begin. Sprigs can die in a few hours if left exposed to the air. The soil should be saturated during the first watering and continue to water lightly every hour during the day for a couple of weeks. Weather conditions will dictate the timing of the watering applications.

After Sprigging – The First Cut

Be gentle on the first cut, because the new grass is very delicate, and never contemplate performing this important operation in the morning when the grass is wet. There is merit in rolling the young turf with a roller that presses the shoots firmly into the ground. When the height of the turf approaches 0.5 inch, the time is right for the first cut. Waiting too long may cause the grass to grow too tall and too thick. Cutting the grass at a later growth stage can have an adverse effect and shock the plants.

A walk-behind mower set at height of 0.5 inch can be used for the first cut on the greens, using a lower height of cut may catch and pull the newly

Figure 11.3 *Superintendents will sometimes use aerification cores to match the makeup existing turf when expanding areas as pictured here in this fairway expansion project. Cores were pulled from the existing fairway and used as sprigs to create the new fairway area.*

planted sprigs out of the soil. Newly established Bermuda fairways may be cut with regular mowers suited for that purpose, but at no lower than a height of 0.5 inch and preferably a tad higher. In all cases, it is important to remove the clippings. Clumps of mown grass left haphazardly may smother some of the grass mat.

Newly sprigged turf areas should gradually be brought down to their desired height. If this process is unjustifiably accelerated, the new turf may suffer a setback, and if the process is too slow, there may be a thatch buildup. The height of cut can be lowered at a rate of 0.0625 inch every week until the desirable height is reached.

DECIDING WHEN NEW TURF IS READY FOR USE

There are many deciding factors to consider before making the decision to start using the new turf, but most important is if the new grass is strong and healthy enough for play. With each successive cutting, the grass will thicken and form a dense mat. On greens and tees, the establishment of the turf is greatly assisted by frequent topdressings. On the larger fairways, topdressing may be more cumbersome, although equipment is now available to topdress widespread areas quickly. During the first growing season, the height can be lowered a bit with each successive cutting until it eventually reaches the desired setting. This is certainly the case on greens, and perhaps on tees. Fairway turf should be taken down fairly quickly to prevent the development of thatch.

A new or rebuilt green on an established course that has been seeded is subject to the pressures of impatient golfers to be prematurely put into play. Saying no to the insistent golfers in these situations is very difficult, and the assistance and support of the greens chairman or other person of authority who is ultimately responsible for the management of turf will be helpful in making this tough and unpopular decision. This is a situation where the mettle of a superintendent will be put to the test. Such new greens will look and feel perfect, but they can be destroyed in a matter of just a few weeks or even days. The turf needs to mature before it can withstand the hardship of golfers' feet and the regimen of regular maintenance. In such situations, new golf courses have an advantage. The number of players on new courses is generally low at first and gradually builds up over a period of months or even years, as a result giving the turf a better chance to mature. On an existing golf course, with 200–300 golfers per day, when a rebuilt green is put into play there is a sudden shock to the turf from no play at all to constant foot traffic all day long.

A new green needs time to mature. Not just the turf on top but the time needs to pass for a moderate amount of mat to develop. The mat is comprised of decaying plants, thatch and soil that provides cushioning and provides a smooth foundation for the plant. Superintendents should be aware that a new green may need to be treated differently for quite some time. Often the turf around the cup wears out more quickly on a new green than it does on existing greens. Sometimes it can be helpful on busy days to change the cup more than once to avoid wear and tear on the new turf. New greens should be inspected frequently, and all little imperfections should be remedied immediately. New greens should be pampered until they are established.

Once the decision has been made to open the new green, one needs to realize that a new green amongst 17 established greens will present unique situations. The new green will putt and play differently for quite some time. Pitch shots will play differently, and the putting speed, whether real or imaginary, will seem out of sync with the rest of the greens. This is understandable, because in all likelihood the soil underneath the turf is different from that of the other greens. It will take time for the roots to anchor, and continual maintenance – including watering, topdressing, and fertilizing of the new green – will help the green to play and give the perception of the existing greens.

SUMMARY

The miracle of new grass covering bare earth is a phenomenon that is very satisfying. Satisfaction comes from reaping the rewards of hard work and seeing the landscape develop.

Seeding, sodding, and sprigging present opportunities to apply the skills and knowledge of practical greenkeeping. The actual ability to make things grow is a unique and special gift. Hard work and dedication are translated into a flourishing greensward that is perceived by a layperson as wondrous or even awesome, and perceived by the instructed as the fruit of one's labor.

12

Drainage

The greatest environmental factor that affects the playability of a golf course is the amount of moisture present in the soil. A course that is too wet plays longer, balls do not roll as far, sometimes plug, the sand is heavy and putting greens are slower. Most golfers prefer to play on a course that is covered with healthy turf, with firm footing, balls that roll, and greens that are smooth and putt true. The majority of golf courses built in the last 50 years have been constructed on the less desirable tracts of land, often low, wet areas where water naturally flows toward. Many of the older courses were constructed around water features, including creeks, rivers, and basins. These natural ground features provided interesting and visually appealing layouts for many golf holes but still contain wet and heavy soils. Golf courses constructed on high ground or seaside (links style) do not have problems with an abundance of water because it flows through to lower ground.

Healthy turf is grown as dry as possible. When a turf is overwatered, it becomes too lush, prone to injury from traffic, susceptible to disease, and often has a shallow root system. Superintendents who grow the finest turf in the world understand this relationship between water, turf health, and playability. Superintendents need to be able to provide water for the plants to live and grow, but they also need to be able to take the water away. This is accomplished through an underground system commonly referred to as drainage.

Golf should be played on firm fairways and greens, and on lowland this can be achieved by the installation of a network of tiles, culverts, and catch basins that facilitate the rapid removal of excess water. It is a system that cannot be overlooked and is one that constantly needs amending, expansion, and maintenance. The installation and care of drainage can extend the golfing season by reducing or eliminating the need for course closures from heavy rain events. It can increase the number of days that golf carts can be used on courses without restrictions and, most importantly, can support the growth of healthy turf.

SURFACE DRAINAGE

When water runs unimpeded across grass-covered land, there is a natural slope between the high and low areas that is known as surface drainage or sheet flow. A 1 percent gradient or slope (1 foot vertical for every 100 feet horizontal) is the minimum needed for the free movement of surface water to drain. In most cases, steeper grades are more desirable for water to move quickly.

Surface drainage is often hindered by faulty golf course construction and/or the settling of soils after they've been disturbed. Many golf courses were built on farmland where existing plow furrows were not graded properly during construction. Low areas, hollows, or pockets often formed and were the result of areas that were improperly filled or graded, or just settled over time to provide adequate surface drainage. Turf grown in these low areas suffer from tight or compacted soils and lack of gas exchange, causing shallow roots. These low-lying areas often resulted in dead grass. Superintendents should be observant of the conditions and take the appropriate remedial action. Fairways that have areas with severe undulations should be regraded. If the turf is of acceptable quality, it can be lifted, the soil smoothed with a landscaping device, and the sod relaid. On larger areas, the process becomes more cumbersome and may require the expertise of a golf course architect and a skilled shaping contractor. In either case, the end result should be a smooth fairway that permits adequate surface runoff.

Some older golf courses have these low areas on tees and even greens. These "bird baths" must be repaired, and usually corrections can be made during the slow season when there is less play. The work should be completed in a timely fashion, probably in just a few days.

SUBSURFACE DRAINAGE

Areas that appear to have good surface drainage can hold water beneath the turf, causing the surface to become wet and soggy. Water that accumulates in the soil builds up above field capacity (the measure of water in the soil immediately after gravity removes what it can) and must find a path to get away. Soils stay wet because there is no place for the water to go. Creating an escape route for this water will keep the turf from staying soggy and will improve the soil structure to support healthy turf and golf-related traffic.

Drainage will make the playing surface now acceptable for golf. Drainage systems give subsurface water a place to go and remove the water out of the root zone. These systems consist of well-designed interconnected series of perforated pipes (often called drain tile) that use gravity to move water to streams, ponds, wetlands, and other collection basins. Drainage structure resembles an irrigation system except that they remove water using gravity to a discharge point. In some rare situations, pumps have been added to aid the process.

One must be thoroughly familiar with the lay of the land before installing a drainage system. Identifying the areas that stay wet the longest or areas that are repeatedly wet is an important first step. Aerial maps with topographic contour lines can help to see the overall property and delineate natural water flow. Drainage plans for the golf course can now be created, and a plan of action can be implemented. The scope of the project will determine if the plan will be a large-scale undertaking, and if so, it may be appropriate to bring in an outside consultant who has golf course experience. This latter criterion is important, and it should be noted that being able to drain a farm field does not qualify one to drain turf-covered soils. However, projects of smaller proportions can be done in-house, even if it involves renting a trencher and a surveyor's level.

TIP: Use aerial maps of the golf course to designate underground systems and keep them updated as changes are made.

TIP: The grade of a tile line can be checked by placing a small amount of water in the bottom of the trench and watching how the water flows.

INSTALLING DRAINAGE ON NEWLY CONSTRUCTED GREENS

Unless a green is built on top of a gravel pit, a bed of tiles should always be included in the construction of putting greens. Depending on the contours of a green, the tile drainage bed in the base is usually in the form of a herringbone system, which looks and works like the veins on a leaf, one main drain with several laterals (Figure 12.1). The tiles are embedded in pea gravel, and the preferred method of promoting water movement is to connect the outlet either to existing drains in the fairway or rough. Another method of draining water from the tile lines is to move the water into a sump, which is an underground pit filled with coarse gravel and covered with topsoil and grass. A sump accepts water from connecting tile lines quickly and disperses it slowly into surrounding soil.

Figure 12.1 *Subsurface drainage on a typical green construction project includes installing a herringbone tiling system.*

The tile lines under a green should be 5–15 feet apart. Greens that are built according to USGA specifications have a "smile drain," or inceptor drain added across the front of the green and connected to the main drain. This type of drain directs the movement of water away from this potentially wet area at the front of the green. This is precisely the area subject to most golfer and equipment traffic and, therefore, prone to wear and tear. Having the approach well drained will ensure good turf. The main drain through the center of the green is often extended through the rear apron, brought to the surface and capped making it easy and quick to flush the tile line. A drainage system installed in this manner will function for many years.

TIP: Mark the end of the green main drain lines with a detectible metal so they can be easily found if they become obscured over time.

A multiflow system can also be used to drain new greens. The system is most effective when the placement of the multiflow is horizontal. The system does not need to be trenched but does need to be rolled out over the subgrade. The horizontal system has a flat profile; the risk of damage is reduced. Lateral lines are located close together, approximately 12 feet apart, reducing the distance that water needs to travel. The system has filters that prevent sand from entering the channels. Once the system is installed, it should be backfilled.

DRAINING EXISTING GREENS

Unfortunately, greens were not always constructed with perfect drainage. In fact, many older courses featured pushup greens, and many were built with tiling systems omitted. Often these challenging situations made the superintendents face the problem to either improve the drainage or live with slow draining greens. There are several different choices today that might be considered when the drainage on greens needs improvement.

| TIP: Installing tiles in an existing green is tricky but by no means impossible.

XGD Drainage

XGD drainage relies on controlling the subsurface groundwater table to manageable levels. The system is based on practices that have been used on farms, with very few inlets and catch basins on the surface. This process provides an option for removing surface water and lowering the water table without reconstructing the green. This drainage method requires a main line that is laid along the edge of the green with lateral lines feeding into the main line from the rest of the green. This drainage process can be accomplished in-house but is usually a contracted service.

PC Drainage

Passive capillary drainage, known as PC drainage, is a solution for removing excess moisture where drainage problems exist on greens. The system uses a fiberglass ropelike material that draws water into a stainless steel mesh core and can move large amounts of water quickly. It is only installed on targeted areas with excess moisture, using gravity flow that drains moisture away with capillary suction. This method of drainage is cost-effective, but should be professionally installed (Figure 12.2).

Follow-up Treatment

After the drainage system is installed, any sod that has been removed should be replaced in its exact location. The sod must be watered continually to keep it moist. The green should be rolled and topdressing should be applied to ensure that the surface is perfectly smooth.

Figure 12.2 *Installing PC drainage system into an existing putting green requires a cable plow to pull the fiberglass rope into the existing soil profile.*
(Photo by Mark Bobb, Barrington Hills Country Club).

RAISING A LOW-LYING AREA ON AN EXISTING GREEN

A low-lying area on a green can be caused by underlying soil settling or faulty initial grading. After irrigation or a natural rainfall, puddling may occur that can interfere with putting and inhibit the growth of grass. Remove the excessive water manually with a squeegee roller or, in extreme cases, by using a suction pump, which can provide a temporary solution. The long-term solution is to remove the turf temporarily, raise the low area by adding a compatible sand or soil mix below the turf, and place the removed turf back to the treated area. Repair work of this nature exemplifies the essence of practical greenkeeping.

TIP: Many important skills are included in the process, and unless experienced in these skills one should probably not attempt such a repair, certainly not on the 18th green in view of the clubhouse.

Step 1

Identify the area by outlining it with a paint gun or small stakes. Set a surveyor's level off to the side and take readings to determine elevations as they exist and to calculate the elevations that are needed to correct the drainage problem. Next, record the elevations and outline the working area, making sure that it is two to three times the size of the actual low-lying area. The large working area is needed to make sure that the finished grade blends in well with the rest of the green. The level should be placed at the back of the green, where it should remain until completion of the project. The goal is to complete the project within the day.

Step 2

Next, while removing the sod, number each roll very carefully so that it may be replaced back in the exact location, and store the rolls of sod off to the side of the green.

Step 3

Gradually build up the depressed area with a compatible sand or soil mix a few inches at a time, and firm it as you go until the desired level is obtained. Apply a starter fertilizer or root-enhancing product at the recommended rate. Rake the surface smoothly and compact the mix by rolling with a water-filled roller.

Step 4

Measure the progress by taking readings with the level, and if necessary, add more sand or soil mix. Continue rolling and raking, preferably with a wide aluminum rake, occasionally turning the rake and using the backside with the straight edge.

Step 5

When you are completely satisfied that the desired level is obtained and surface drainage is ensured, it is time to replace the sod. The upmost care should be taken when the sod is replaced that the rolls of sod that were numbered are placed back exactly into the location from which it was removed. If any of the removed sod has been damaged or is weak, replace it with a strip of sod taken from the back of the green to keep the type of grass consistent with the other turf on the green. After sodding, roll in two different directions and check the levels one more time with the surveyor's level to be absolutely sure that water will now run off.

Step 6

The final step involves applying topdressing and working it into the grooves between the rolls of sod with a Levelawn or the backside of the aluminum rake. Wash the topdressing into the sod and between the grooves of the sod with water. This will help to keep the sod moist but not soggy until it is well rooted. As a courtesy to the golfers, this work area should be fenced with stakes and rope, and a GUR (Ground under Repair) or explanatory sign should be placed in the middle of the roped area. Once the newly sodded area is well rooted it should be ready for play in three to four weeks. This process is best performed during the shoulder seasons when environmental stresses are less and play is reduced.

DRAINING TEES

Tees are usually elevated and drain exceptionally well, and rarely require tiling for drainage. Low-lying tees, however, are a different matter. When tees are built in a low-lying area, it may be beneficial to install a main drain with several laterals, also known as a gridiron arrangement that drains the subsurface water away from the playing surface. Large flat tees, as well as driving range tees, should be treated as greens and drained accordingly.

Tees that are built into hillsides often require interceptor drains, which are subsurface drains designed to intercept water runoff. A pitched trench should be dug that is 6–12 inches wide and at least 24 inches deep. The bottom of the trench should be covered with a few inches of the appropriate gravel. Next, a 4- to 6-inch tile should be laid on top of the gravel, and then completely covered with pea gravel. Coarse sand may be added, if desired, for the last few inches, and make certain the trench is filled to the top. The drain will intercept the water that seeps from the hillside. The steeper the surface slope, the faster the surface water will be removed and will also prevent wetness on the tee. Interceptor tiles should also be used behind greens that are built in similar locations, as well as along steep banks that border fairways.

DRAINING BUNKERS

Bunkers are frequently flat at the bottom, which makes them particularly easy to drain. A tiling system similar to that used under greens is installed, and as under the greens, the tiles are covered with pea gravel. One method of covering the tile is to add pea gravel to a level that is 2 inches below grade so that it will not mix with the sand and damage golfers' wedges. The outlet of the tile empties into a catch basin, for easy clean-out, and is then connected to the main drain. Most important, one needs to remember that bunkers require just as many tiles as greens to guarantee good drainage.

TIP: A coarse layer of sand can be added in the last 2 inches, on top of the pea gravel and before adding the bunker sand, to prevent the fine bunker sand from filtering into the pea gravel.

TIP: Access points, also called "clean outs," should be installed on the high and low side of bunker drain lines so they may be periodically flushed with high pressure hoses with jetting nozzles.

Repairing poor drainage in an existing bunker is best accomplished by removing all the existing sand, shaping the bottom into a desirable form and firmness, and then trenching the lines and installing the tiles. Stockings should not be used around the tiles because the stockings can quickly become clogged with sand and finer particles, which will prevent all water movement (see Chapter 5, "Bunker Drainage").

DRAINAGE ON FAIRWAYS AND ROUGHS

Fairways and roughs that constantly have wet areas need to be drained to make certain that the turf is healthy and play is more enjoyable. The area that requires improved drainage should be identified by staking the wet area where a new drain tile needs to be installed using a gridiron or herringbone pattern (Figure 12.3). Next, locate an existing drain tile that can be connected to the new drain tile. When there is not an existing tile available for the connection, the new drain tile can be routed to drain directly into a creek or lake. Dig a trench using a trencher equipped with a laser depth-measuring device to make sure that the trench has the necessary slope for water to drain into the desired location.

A small amount of pea gravel is then placed in the bottom of the trench. Dragging a narrow trenching shovel across the gravel ensures a smooth bed for the tile. After installing the tile, covering the tile with pea gravel helps to promote the movement of water. The trench can then be completely filled with the gravel. Another method is to add pea gravel within a few

Figure 12.3 *Adding drainage to existing fairways is often accomplished during the shoulder seasons when play begins to wane and the turf will still recover.*

inches of the top of the trench and then fill the remaining area with coarse sand to the sod level, helping to ensure that water can enter the drainage system unobstructed. Soon the grass on the sides will grow in and cover the trench. Do not yield to the temptation to cover the trench with topsoil; covering the trench with topsoil or sod will quickly seal the surface and prevent water from entering the system.

When the grass completely covers the tile lines and forms a dense mat, it may become impervious to the movement of water. When, after heavy rains, puddles appear over the tile lines, the thatch layer needs to be punctured. A soil probe or pitch fork may be used for this purpose.

There should be numerous catch basins included in tiling systems, and the catch basins should be placed frequently, especially in long runs of tile lines. The grate on a catch basin provides an opening for additional surface water to enter into the system and also allows more accessibility to clean out the lines. Catch basins can provide an opening to observe the performance of the tiling system. During or shortly after heavy rains, superintendents should check how the system performs by lifting the grate and observing the flow of the water.

THE VERTIDRAIN

The vertidrain (as mentioned in Chapter 9) penetrates holes in the soil to a depth of more than 12 inches and can extract cores of various sizes. The deep-tine aeration by the vertidrain machine promotes internal drainage and breaks up layering in the soil profile. A tremendous amount of earth is removed from a playing surface when using tines that are 6 inches apart. After greens are aerated by the vertidrain, the holes can be refilled with approved sand to the top of the putting surface. In the process, the layers that exist in the green's profile will have been punctured in many places and the drainage in the vertical plain will have improved; however, the water still may need to be removed from the subsurface with drain tile. This process can be applied to tees, fairways, and rough to improve drainage.

SLIT TRENCHES AND FRENCH DRAINS

A slit trench is a type of subsurface vertical drain that is 2–3 inches wide and 2–4 feet deep. The trench is dug and then filled with pea gravel or crushed stone (not limestone) to the surface. The area is left open and excess surface water is moved downward. The official terminology of a French drain is a narrow trench filled from top to bottom with gravel, but without a pipe and was used to drain small areas. Today, a French drain consists of pea gravel as well as perforated drainage pipe. The gravel-piped channel is connected to a tile that moves the water toward the main drainage system or the discharge point. When draining small areas with little or no fall, a slit trench system or French drain is effective in the removal of water but is no substitute for complete tiling systems.

FRIGID ZONE DRAINAGE

Superintendents in northern climates should be aware that snow and ice can hinder the normal runoff of water on golf course turf. Banks of snow can freeze, forming obstructions in the path of the water, causing the submerged turf to die. This can be prevented by the simple routine of regularly patrolling the golf course during the winter months. Remove any obstructions that exist, allowing the trapped water to flow back into the direction of its normal course. Dedicated and experienced superintendents have been known to remove snow and ice from all greens and tees to

Figure 12.4 *Northern superintendents will go to great lengths to ensure survival of the grass, including penetrating ice in midwinter.*
(Photo courtesy of Verti-Drain, Redexim B.V.)

aid the survival of the grass during extended ice and snow cover. Such attention is to be commended (Figure 12.4).

MATERIALS USED FOR DRAINAGE

All drainage systems require several various types of materials to make the systems work properly. Every soil has unique properties that can affect drainage. Each situation is different, and the scope of the drainage improvement depends on the soil profile, slopes and topography of the land, the geographic region, climate, and available monies allocated for the project. The following is a descriptive list of the most often used materials for drainage projects.

Tiles and Drainage Pipes

Years ago, clay tiles were used for drainage on farms as well as golf courses. There are still factories that manufacture clay tiles for drainage. The clay tile permits water to seep through its wall into the cavity of the tile. Since clay tile installation is very expensive, few people buy and install clay tiles. Today, plastic pipes that are either solid wall or corrugated are prevalent.

Drain pipes that are made from PVC are more rigid and less flexible but are less difficult to maintain, if the pipe becomes clogged. These pipes can also be solid or perforated and are available with connections, and if necessary the connections can be easily glued or solvent welded. Tiles in excess of 6 inches in diameter are available as plastic or galvanized pipes.

Pipes that are corrugated are more flexible and can be perforated. Also, corrugated pipes are available with a solid wall inside. The pipes can come in various diameters from 2 inches to greater than 12 inches and lengths up to 1,000 feet. The pipes can snap together, and in such instances, they may not be watertight. Plastic corrugated pipe can come in rolls or links, making the pipe easy to handle and to install.

Gravel

Pea gravel has been proven to be the best gravel for drainage purposes. The characteristic smooth, round surface of the individual stone makes pea gravel ideal for the passage of water. The small, round stones allow the water to slide off their surface and flow freely into the tiles. Granite chips or clear limestone (not crushed limestone) can be used as an alternative. The drawback of using the clear limestone or granite chips is that the angular surfaces tend to become clogged with foreign materials such as grass clippings and soil. Stones larger than pea gravel that are rounded and uniform in size can be an acceptable alternative to pea gravel. However, in the long run, the performance of pea gravel is well worth the extra cost.

Catch Basins

Plastic catch basins come in all shapes and sizes and are characteristically lightweight. They are easy to install and easy to clean. The grate lifts out, which allows the flow of the water to be viewed and checked. Cement catch basins are very heavy and can be installed only with the help of a heavy-duty lifting device. Cement catch basins are used in conjunction with larger pipes, generally greater than 12 inches in diameter. If need be, catch basins can be hand-made from a large galvanized pipe; although the end product is not visually as pleasing, it will still work satisfactorily.

Trenchers

There are two important criteria to consider when buying or renting a trencher. The first is how deep will the trencher dig? The second is how wide of a trench needs to be dug? In most cases, a trencher that digs to a depth of 2–3 feet is adequate, and the recommended width for a 4-inch drain pipe is a trench that is 6 inches wide. Digging the trench wider or deeper than is necessary will only create extra work and excess fill.

There are trenchers that are designed to make narrow slit grooves that permit the installation of flat tiles encased in pea gravel. These flat tiles are generally joined into larger main pipes. Also available are trenchers equipped with a laser depth-measuring device to make sure that the trench has the necessary slope for water to drain into the desired location.

Miscellaneous Tools

A saw to cut the tile is a must. So is a narrow trenching shovel to clean the trench. A pick to dig out rocks or stones is also essential. A line level or hand level will give accurate readings if the line of sight is not over 100 feet; otherwise, it may be necessary to use an engineer's or surveyor's level.

> TIP: Immediately following a heavy rain event, superintendents are well served by videorecording low problem areas as the water puddles. The footage can be used to help plan projects and garner support from green committees who do not normally see these issues firsthand.

SUMMARY

Drainage, drainage, drainage: those three words are the most important words of practical golf course maintenance. The superintendent should always recommend drainage improvement projects to the committee and/ or management for consideration and approval, as such projects usually require committee or management involvement. Drains and catch basins should be installed to correct problem areas. Draining a full-sized course may take a significant amount of time, but it should be started, and once begun, little by little, it will be completed.

After, or if possible during, torrential rainstorms, the superintendent should inspect and observe the performance of the drainage system. There is great satisfaction in watching a drain function perfectly. The result is dry land that can be cut without leaving ruts, and turf that can be played from, without casual water. Remember that proper drainage can extend the golfing season by reducing or eliminating the need for course closures, as well as increasing the number of days that golf carts can be used on courses without cart paths.

13

Trees

Whispering pines, waving palms, giant sequoias, flowering jacarandas, weeping willows, and other varieties of trees line the fairways on many diverse golf courses around the world. Nevertheless, some golfers maintain that golf is a game for wide-open spaces, and furthermore, they have St. Andrews to prove their point. Other courses have been built with unassuming, clear-cut landscapes and have eliminated the demand for trees. These courses are usually typified by a scarceness of trees. There are many clubs that are proud of the trees that adorn their properties and often name the golf club after a favorite or native tree. The list is lengthy and includes many golf clubs such as Maple Ridge, Old Elm, Burnt Tree, Pine Valley, Magnolia, Royal Poinciana, and, of course, Cypress Point.

Beautiful trees provide the setting for the game to be played to its fullest enjoyment. The shapes of trees, the gnarly roots and strong trunks, the crooked branches, the towering heights, the whispering leaves, the cool shade, all combine to give trees an aura of splendor and at times an atmosphere that can be both forbidding and inviting.

When trees are tightly spaced and encroach upon the playing ground, often the golfer has a fear that tenses the muscles causing even the most expert players to make erratic golf shots. Trees at a distance provide peace of mind, relax the body, and make one swing freely. Single trees on the fairway between player and green are often best ignored and, as so often pointed out are mostly air anyway. On a bad golf day, trees can be therapeutic for a troubled mind. Only the most dispassionate golfer can possibly ignore the beauty of flowering magnolias in the spring or the brilliant hues of maples in the fall. This is the world in which superintendents live and apply their skills to make the landscape ever so beautiful.

Often the superintendent begins a career on a course that is in disrepair and needs improvement, providing a unique opportunity to leave a landscape legacy. Trees have a special place in society and man easily connects with them, this association is even greater with golf course trees. Often when returning to a golf course that one had previously managed after time away, a superintendent will comment how large the trees have become. It is important when maintaining and especially planting new trees on a golf course, attention and care is given to this task.

TREE SELECTION

State colleges, universities, botanic gardens, state and local forestry departments, and arboretums centers are just a few of the places that can be researched before making a decision on what type of tree will be most appropriate for planting. A visit to a neighboring golf course may further help in the decision making of what trees are indigenous, desirable, and available in the local region. Different varieties of trees need to be planted during different seasons to ensure healthy growth after being transplanted. Tree nurseries usually have a slow time in midsummer after the spring rush and before the fall planting season, making it a good time to examine the stock and mark trees for future planting. Although often sought after, perfect trees that are statuesque are usually hard to find. A tree with free flowing curves, rough trunk, and other noticeable characteristics can be just as prominent on a golf course.

Fast-growing, weak wooded trees share many undesirable characteristics and are often unsuitable for use in large quantities on golf courses. These trees have extensive fibrous root systems that compete with turfgrasses for water and nutrients. They are often messy shedding many twigs, branches and sometimes limbs with stormy weather. They often produce many seeds that can litter the turf and make it difficult to find an errant golf ball. Willows, poplars, cottonwoods, and silver maples all fall into this category and should be avoided as golf course trees.

Are there any trees that can be safely planted without arousing the ire of the golfers or the greens committee? We feel that there is a place for all trees. Certainly, some trees are more desirable than others, but all have a place. Proper selection of the right tree for the right place is the first step in the planning process. Time and time again, poorly placed trees on golf courses are topics of dispute during many green committee meetings. Golfers become attached to trees and feel a tree can "make a hole", while this be true in rare cases, when most golf courses were built or designed, trees were not part of the plan or intent of the designer. Trees should be carefully selected and planted.

Evergreens, such as pines and spruces, make for wonderful backdrops and fairway separations when planted out of the play area. After a number of years, a bed of needles will collect at the base of the evergreens that forms a cover, making it unnecessary to trim the grass. Beech and maple trees can be majestic and have spectacular color, but the trees can produce leaves in abundance and need to be placed accordingly on the golf course. The strong oak trees have a very long lifespan. The leaves of the oak tree stay attached (even though the leaves have turned brown and are dead), into the winter months, long after the golfing season has ended. However, in southern Florida and some other areas of the far south, planting native trees is important. Native trees that are acclimated to these areas and are easier to grow include: slash pines, cabbage palms, and red swamp maples. In the northern part of Florida native oaks grow well, especially in the areas that are not conducive for growing native palm trees.

The ideal selection of trees to be planted on any golf course should include a variety of numerous species. Planting a single species may be consequential. The Dutch elm disease killed many trees that had become landmarks and left golf courses that had planted only elm trees looking naked. Austrian pines were likewise decimated by the *Diplodia* fungus, which left brown skeletons in its wake. The Emerald Ash Borer has decimated many native trees in most recent years. In the event that disease strikes a particular species, having planted an assortment of species will help to avoid a complete devastation caused by the epidemic.

YOU ARE BARKING UP THE WRONG TREE

All trees are not friendly in the golf course environment and, if possible, some should be avoided.

- Groupings of Norway maples, although attractive and fast growing, are usually known to have bare ground at the bases.
- Soft maples have objectionable roots that stick up aboveground. The brittle branches often break, dropping branches and twigs, and are just as messy as willow and poplar trees.
- Certain varieties of maples have canopies that block sunlight, which results in dense shade, making it difficult for grass to grow under the drip line.
- Green ash trees are slow to leaf out in the spring and, before the leaves break bud, often appear to look dead.
- While catalpas grow rapidly when young, they frequently do not show leaves until June, and in the fall drop long messy pods.
- Although the male tree of the exotic ginkgo species is hardy and has withstood centuries of worldly devastation, the female tree produces fruit with a very objectionable odor.
- Many species of palm trees require annual pruning to remove dead and ugly fronds.

- Willow trees have large invasive roots that compete with grass for nutrients and clog drains.
- Avoid planting trees that are prone to have roots that grow aboveground that can interfere with mowing operations and present unplayable lies to golfers.

A TREE PLANTING PROGRAM

Not all golf courses are blessed with an abundance of native forests or widely spaced specimen trees. On courses where there are few inherent features such as streams, ponds, or hills and dales, trees can be planted to separate the fairways, to screen the perimeter, or to provide character to the holes.

Location, Location, Location

The placement of trees will have a long-term effect on the landscape of the golf course and, therefore, having a plan prepared by a landscape architect will be useful when determining the strategic location of planting new trees. Consider the following when selecting a location for tree planting:

- Groupings of trees break the monotony of an otherwise bleak landscape.
- Trees can be planted to accentuate the strategy of individual golf holes (Figure 13.1).
- Trees that are small when first planted are no hindrance, but they can quickly grow up to become formidable obstacles.
- Trees planted in the wrong places can obscure vistas and views.
- Trees and tees almost never go together.
- A tree planted too close to a green with an encompassing bunker becomes an undesirable double hazard.
- A strategic location of a planted tree can take the place of a bunker, eliminating the need for raking every day.

For all these reasons and more, a tree planting program is a necessity, but it must be carefully prepared. Since in most cases the location of the trees affects the strategy of the golf holes, a qualified architect should be engaged. The plan prepared by the architect should show where to plant trees. The plan should be preserved, encased in glass or foil, and hung in a prominent place where it can stay for a while, because planting trees is a long-term project. Often trees are donated by members or are planted to remember deceased golfers. These donated trees should coincide with

Figure 13.1 *A tree in the middle of the fairway is an interesting design element on this long par five. It forces many players to lay up on their second shot. As the tree grows, how will it change the hole?*

the approved tree plan and be tagged with both the common and Latin names. In conjunction with the superintendent, committees and officials should make a firm commitment to adhere to the plan.

TIP: "The best time to plant a tree was 20 years ago. The second best time is now."– Anonymous

The Tree Nursery

When there is additional space on the golf course property that is large enough to sustain a tree nursery, planting young trees can be a very rewarding and satisfying experience. Preferably, the tree nursery should be located near the maintenance building. If the only available location for a nursery is in some out-of-the-way spot on the golf course, special care must be taken by scheduling the maintenance of the tree plantings so as not to be forgotten and neglected. The advantage of having a tree nursery on-site is that there are always trees available for planting.

Trees selected for the nursery may be as little as a few inches, and the diameter might be as tiny as the small finger on one's hand. Small trees should be planted in fertile soil and should be watered as needed.

The saplings should be planted in rows, a few feet apart, and protected with tree guards or stakes. Small trees grow quickly and usually need to be transplanted after just a few years to avoid crowding among the other trees. Planting small trees provides an opportunity to grow several different species for future planting and have an assortment of trees available at a substantial savings. Also, there is an opportunity to plant unfamiliar varieties of trees in the nursery and observe how the trees adapt to local conditions. A nursery should be weeded regularly or treated with a non-selective herbicide labeled for use. The nursery will need constant attention, and if left unattended, the nursery can become overgrown with grass and weeds. Using string trimmers in small tree nurseries is not advisable because trimmers can cause permanent damage to the bark of small trees.

After a few years, a selection of the trees should be moved from the nursery to their permanent locations according to the master plan, leaving a few trees in the nursery for future planting. Rainy days are ideal for transplanting trees from the nursery. The work may be messy, but its success rate is very high.

Planting Trees

There is a preferred planting time for most trees. Small trees have a greater chance of survival after being transplanted than larger trees. After choosing a tree that is suitable for the region, check to make sure that it is the right time of the year for planting the tree. An ideal time to transplant some varieties of trees is when the soil is moist and the buds on the shoots have not broken, which is in the early spring; others are best to move in the fall during different growing cycles. The chances for survival can be improved if the following precautions are taken:

1. Prepare the area by digging a hole that is two times the size of the root ball, allowing for space for the roots to grow into the soil. If the existing soil is undesirable, as is often the case on new golf courses, add some superior topsoil. Keep the balls intact, by keeping as much soil around the roots as possible.
2. Plant the tree to the same depth as it grew before, or slightly higher. This is to encourage drainage. Freestanding water should not accumulate around the base of the tree. It will result in the tree's having wet feet, a condition that will ultimately lead to its death.
3. Backfill carefully around the roots of the tree. Use good-quality topsoil, and stamp it down with the heel of your boot. The earth around the tree must feel firm so that the tree is securely anchored and there are no air pockets in the soil surrounding the roots.

4. Create a dish around the base of the tree. This will hold water that will remain in place and gradually soak down to the roots every time the tree is given a drink. Newly planted trees have a compromised root system and must be watered regularly. The dish, however, will have to be leveled at a later date.
5. Trees that are subject to adverse weather conditions should be staked, providing stability and protection from the elements. Larger trees may need more than one stake and even guy wires to secure them in position. For safety purposes, the wires should be marked or flagged.
6. After the tree has been planted and the hole backfilled, the area should be mulched with 1–3 inches of quality mulching material. This will help to keep the ball from drying out and also helps to prevent damage to the root ball in areas where there is thawing and freezing.

All of these steps can be performed quickly by the simple expedient of using a tree spade. This piece of equipment comes in all shapes and sizes and can be used for small trees with a caliper of 4–6 inches but is often used to transplant very large trees. Tree spades can move trees with a caliper of up to 10–12 inches and a ball of earth measuring up to 8–9 feet and weighing more than 5 tons. Once the hole is dug and the plug has been removed, the smooth sidewalls need to be roughened, allowing the transplanted tree roots to spread into the surrounding soil. Several large trees can be planted quickly in a group by using a tree spade, which can create an instant landscape, or an instant hazard, depending on one's viewpoint. Trees that are planted with a large tree spade need extra care after they have been planted. If there is a small space between the tree root ball and the spaded hole, the space should be filled with topsoil, tamped down "with a shovel handle" and watered. Create a well around the base of the tree for water retention purposes. Large trees that are planted should be mulched and periodically watered. Smaller trees are usually planted manually, because the trees can be easily handled without using expensive machinery. On rare occasions, smaller trees can be planted with bare roots. These trees should be planted as soon as possible after purchase. Check to be sure that the roots have been kept moist and look for many fine root hairs to ensure the tree is healthy. The tree should be planted in a hole on top of a cone-shaped mound with the roots spread, forming a crown. The flare from the trunk of the tree should be about 2–3 inches above the ground. After the tree has been properly planted, the area surrounding the base of the tree needs to be mulched and watered.

TIP: Digging a tree hole too deep will sever the supply of oxygen and too narrow will inhibit the roots from expanding.

Figure 13.2 *Care should be taken (left photo) when planting groups of trees on golf courses. Ample room should be given between trees for them to grow and mowers to move between them compared to (right photo) when the golf course is built between native stands.*

Distance Between Trees

Before planting a tree, try to visualize the newly planted tree's estimated height and width. The mature size of the tree must always be considered before planting a tree or groups of trees. Trees need plenty of sun to grow and should be spaced away from other trees so as not to crowd each other (Figure 13.2). There must be sufficient space for mowers to get around and in between the trees to trim the grass. As trees mature, they should be pruned, and if a tree should become crowded by other trees, it may be necessary for the tree to be transplanted to another location.

When landscaping with trees on a golf course avoid planting in straight rows. Trees should be planted in an irregular manner, to create interest and to avoid monotony, even along a perimeter or fence line. There are many ways to plant groups of trees; however, planting groups of the same species can be cared for easily and will have an impressive visual effect.

TREE MAINTENANCE

Small trees must be watered and pruned to keep growth under control. Superintendents often carry a small set of pruning shears to nip off branches that look out of place, or trim low branches that hit the roofs of golf carts. Pruning, however, is not a part-time assignment for the superintendent. A regular schedule for pruning trees and shrubs should be part of the overall maintenance operation. This will help to ensure that the golfers can observe the intended areas designed for strategic play (Figure 13.3).

As trees grow larger, pruning becomes cumbersome and requires the services of tree experts who climb and are trained to sever branches. Deadwood must also be removed and crossing branches eliminated. Wood chippers are used to chop up the branches, and the larger limbs can be cut up for firewood.

Figure 13.3 *Shrubs and trees from above obstruct a view of the target and hazards, and should be trimmed periodically. Half of this tee (left side) is never used because of the trees that block the tee shot.*

Many golfers are offended by the cutting of trees that are past their prime or dying. Trees that were originally planted with good intentions may have lost their usefulness and become a hindrance. These trees may have become sacred to many golfers, and the removal of the trees sparks a rallying cry in hopes to stop a project. People can become quite emotional when it comes to the removal of trees. A responsible person never likes to heartlessly take down the giants of a forest or specimen trees on a golf course. In most cases, the trees that we planted many years ago eventually grow to maturity but, for whatever reason, may be no longer strategically located and need to be removed. Confrontations can be avoided by always seeking the advice of a golf course architect, the grounds committee, and a tree consultant or management company to help make the final decision. As a last resort, trees can be cut down when there are no golfers around. Remember to remove the stump and cover the area with fresh sod. Golfers rarely miss a tree once it has been removed. There is the tale of a superintendent who carried two chainsaws on the utility vehicle, one called "thunder" and the other "lightning."

Both were used to remove unwanted trees. When asked by golfers what had happened to certain familiar trees, the response was always the same: 'Thunder took it down" or "It was struck by lightning." The answer was the truth, but with a twist.

TIP: Branches that are brittle are a danger to golfers and present a maintenance problem and should be removed immediately.

LEAVES

As pretty as the colors of the leaves may be in the fall, tremendous problems can be caused for the golfers whose golf balls are lost among the leaves as well as the maintenance crew being faced with what seems to be an unending task. Screens are placed inside the cutting units, converting these powerful grass cutters into very useful leaf mulchers. These special mulching attachments are available for tractor-drawn and up-front rotary mowers. The fast-rotating blades grind the leaves into tiny snippets that disappear in between the grass blades. Mulching leaves in this manner quickly converts a leaf-strewn fairway or rough into a clean and playable turf. The snippets of leaves break down into organic matter and mix into the soil. Other practical methods of leaf removal involve blowing the leaves into piles or windrows, sweeping the leaves into hoppers, and then hauling the leaves away to be composted, mulched, or disposed of by other methods (Figure 13.4).

On golf courses that are well known for their abundance of trees, leaf removal becomes a big-time operation, involving numerous machines and several workers for many weeks. The highest order of priority is to keep the greens and surroundings clear of fallen leaves. Since leaves fall continuously but gradually, the greens may need to be cleared several times a day. The next order of importance is the landing areas, and after that the bunkers, the tees, and then the rough. The process is ongoing and not finished until the last leaf has fallen and has been removed.

TIP: Some superintendents will leave a handheld battery-operated blower by greens that often become covered throughout the day during the fall so players or their caddies may clear the line of a put quickly and easily.

In years past, superintendents disposed of the leaves by burning, but now the smell of burning leaves is just a fond memory in the minds of gray-haired greenkeepers. The practice is now forbidden by regulation, and the autumn fires have faded away from golf course maintenance just as hickory-shafted clubs have faded away from the golfing scene.

Figure 13.4 *A leaf blower pulled by a utility vehicle is a common sight on golf courses with deciduous trees each fall. Leaves are moved to the rough where they are mulched by mowers outfitted mulching blades and decks.*

THE TREE REMOVAL PLAN

A tree removal plan may seem odd, but many golf courses have been overplanted with trees. Just as a tree-planting plan requires the skillfull eye of a qualified designer, so too does the removal plan. There was a trend in the middle part of the 1900s to use trees to define fairways by creating corridors between golf holes. Now these tree lines have filled in to make even a slightly errant shot too penalizing for even an adept player. These trees have unintentionally impacted the game and often impacted the turf underneath their canopies in a negative way. Once recognized as an integral part of the course, many clubs and courses have now started removing many of these trees, recreating vistas and views that have not been seen in decades because of the overplanting of trees.

TIP: When beginning the process at a club, one adept superintendent marked every tree that was staying with florescent tape rather than each tree that was to be removed. He remarked how it changed the attitude of the golfers when they toured the course after seeing how many trees were not to be touched.

SUMMARY

There is a place for trees, and although some trees are more desirable than others, all have a place. In the event that disease strikes a particular species, having planted an assortment of species will help to avoid a complete devastation caused by an epidemic. When planting an assortment of species, make an attempt to group trees of the same species together to create an impressive visual effect. Young and inexperienced superintendents will often search for fast-growing trees without success. Keen superintendents begin to realize that most trees are fast-growing trees, and that somehow trees grow bigger and stronger as we grow older and wiser. Superintendents will continue to plant trees, not for themselves but for future generations, and hopefully when they leave this Earth, they will have left behind a living legacy of their toil.

14

Landscaping

The first impression a golfer perceives occurs upon entering the golf course grounds (Figure 14.1). This impression is usually a landscaped area, often setting the tone for what lies ahead. A well-presented flower bed, a weed-free lawn, and a smooth, unblemished pavement can be indicative of what the golf course or even the clubhouse will be like. Adding a friendly reception in the pro shop, some appetizing food cooked in the grill, and a well-manicured golf course makes for a truly memorable golfing experience. That is precisely why golf club management is so much a team effort. All the components of the team must work together supportively and cooperatively, like the gears in a well-oiled machine, to produce a smooth-running organization. The entrance to the golf club may have an elaborate rock garden with cascading waterfalls and splashing fountains, statues, hanging baskets, or creatively trimmed bushes, but these focal points can be costly and require an abundance of maintenance. The golfer in a rush to the first tee will barely notice such extravagances, but the subconscious will recollect the imperfections—the lawn has not been trimmed, weeds are seen among the petunias, and trash is on the pavement. Blemishes are registered indelibly on the mind, further reinforcing why an organized team effort is important in the overall landscape of the golf club.

ENHANCING THE CLUBHOUSE AREA

Landscaping around the clubhouse is intended to beautify the buildings and to create eye-catching and vibrant displays. Everyone enjoys spectacular flowers, shrubs, and specimen trees. Impressive landscaping is the ability to organize plantings to their optimum advantage. Even the most modest clubhouse should have a variety of landscape plantings to enhance its visual appeal.

Figure 14.1 *First impressions count. When the club entrance and the landscape is well maintained the golfer can only become more excited to play the course.*

On the golf course, the emphasis is on the quality of the turf and the design of the holes; around the clubhouse, there is an opportunity to showcase unusual trees, flowering shrubs, and rose gardens. Flowering crab trees, tulip trees, and Japanese cherry trees when planted in groupings can leave an impressive image of an individual golf hole, and with their spectacular displays, are also ideal for planting around the clubhouse. Groupings of showy shrubs look magnificent around the clubhouse. Plant material that may struggle on the golf course manages to survive because the clubhouse buildings offer shelter and protection from the wind and cold. Plant material will grow faster and mature more quickly around the strategic clubhouse location, which provides growing conditions that are more favorable than anywhere else on the golf course grounds. These optimum growing conditions make it necessary to frequently trim and maintain the landscaping around the clubhouse.

Visiting golfers need a place to drop off their clubs, and a bag rack should be provided for this purpose. There are many functional and attractively designed bag racks available that should be considered when enhancing the clubhouse area.

Service areas should be screened with suitable plantings that can hide oversized storage units and trash containers. Groupings of dense evergreens or deciduous shrubs can immediately conceal the service areas.

TIP: Small, unobtrusive signs for guests are very well appreciated directing flow of traffic, parking, and bag drop areas.

THE LANDSCAPE PLAN

Designing the shape of a flower bed takes artistic ability. Unless the superintendent, the gardener, or horticulturalist has specific knowledge of landscape design, one should engage the services of a landscape architect. Professionals can prepare plans that show the shapes, locations, and the various plant materials of all the beds, as well as existing features such as rock gardens and waterfalls. Often the trees are already in place by the time the landscape architect is retained. Most of the trees will be preserved and others added in prominent places. The architect's primary function is to create a plan with flowing lines that coincides with the existing buildings. Once the plan is in place, the superintendent and the gardener combine their talents and make the plan a reality.

TIP: Courses that use a wide variety of landscape plants can install small signs indicating the plant name and variety.

PREPARING FLOWER BEDS

The use of high-quality topsoil is just as important for the flower beds as the topsoil is under the turf on the golf course. A new flower bed should be dug out to a depth of 8–12 inches. After excavating, fill the flower bed with a premixed bedding material or high-quality topsoil that is rich in organic matter.

Organic matter will encourage earthworm activity and also will increase the nutrient levels of the soil and water-holding capability, encouraging the plants' roots to penetrate into the earth. There are many types of different organic matter available to amend a planting bed's soil. It is best to know the source of material used to ensure it has not been contaminated with herbicides and is properly composted to kill any weed seeds.

Annuals, perennials, ornamental grasses, flowering bulbs, roses, and wildflowers all require different types and rates of fertilizers. The specific kind of fertilizer will be determined by the types of plantings in the various flower beds. Add the recommended amount of fertilizer to the top 4–6 inches of soil in the new flower beds. After the beds have been planted, a second or even third application of fertilizer may be necessary, often in liquid form. Adding more than the suggested amounts of compost or organic matter can create soil nutrient levels that are too high and actually result in unhealthy plant growth. A well-prepared and carefully maintained flower bed, rich in fertility, will grow large plants with huge blossoms for many years.

FLOWERING BULBS

Flowering bulbs that blossom in spring are essential in any garden. A display of vibrant tulips and daffodils will attract attention and a border created with colorful crocuses and hyacinths can be very appealing. Flowering bulbs randomly planted along a tree line with southern exposures can create a natural flowing array of color. Natural grassy areas can be eye-catching if bulbs are planted in a casual display, which can be accomplished by unsystematically planting a bag full of bulbs. Planting methods that are planned and prearranged usually result with gardens and beds that have monotonous straight lines and look unnatural. Once the bulbs have bloomed, the grass in between cannot be cut without spoiling the naturalized appearance of the area. Bulbs should be left in place until the leaves begin to brown. As soon as all the leaves have faded, the grass can be cut as well as the remains of the flower stems and leaves. This natural process helps to return nutrients and food back into the bulb, which is below ground, and ensures that there will be plenty of blossoms during the next season.

TIP: A battery-operated drill with an auger bit attached makes for quick work of planting bulbs in the fall. The proper depth to plant can be marked right on the auger bit and staff can be let loose to plant bulbs in intended areas.

Bulbs can be planted any time in the fall before the ground freezes and allow for enough time for the roots systems to grow. Check to be sure that the selections of bulbs are appropriate for the climate and planting zone. Make sure that the selection includes different sizes and heights of flower blooms and that the bulbs will bloom during various times of the season. Dig a hole to a depth that is at least two and half times the bulb's diameter when planting single bulbs. Bulbs planted in groups should always be planted using an odd number. Use a spade to dig the hole so that the bulbs can be placed side by side. After planting, water the soil lightly to encourage root growth. Overwatering can cause the bulbs to mold and eventually rot, and then the bulbs will be totally destroyed. Planting a mix of perennials around the bulbs will ensure a constant display of color.

When flower bulbs have faded that were planted in a bed that were mixed with annual flowers, the bulbs must be dug up and then stored for replanting before the ground freezes. Flower bulbs will go dormant during the winter months and will reappear in the spring. Their early blossoms will greet the golfers when they return to the course for their first game in the spring.

TIP: Try to plant flower bulbs, plants, and shrubs in groups with odd numbers. Appearance and balance will be improved because the group will be viewed as a single mass.

ANNUALS AND PERENNIALS

There are many annuals to choose from each spring, and it takes some experience to make the right selections. Annual flowers last only one season, so these flowers must be planted from year to year. In regions where the growing season is short, plant the annuals close together. If the budget is restrictive, allowing for more distance between plants will help to provide a colorful flower garden that will fill in as the season progresses. Newly planted annuals need lots of water to encourage their root systems. Once the plants have rooted, hoe regularly to break up the crusty earth and let in the air. Timely fertilizer applications are also essential. Annual flowers are generally more colorful than perennial flowers and are excellent in hanging baskets and garden pots.

Perennial flowers can offer a variety of color and character to a garden. The plant selection should be based on color, height, and tolerance to sun and shade. Since perennials return year after year, replanting is usually unnecessary. There are a multitude of perennial plants that blossom all season long and provide color and interest on a continual basis (Figure 14.2).

Figure 14.2 *A golf course planting of perennials always has something in bloom and is a great way to involve members who enjoy gardening for the benefit of the club.*

A planting method that is frequently applied to individual beds uses just one type of flower all one color or a variety of colors, and then the garden is highlighted with a colorful border. Planting various types of species (both annual and perennial) with an assortment of colors that blend together can also provide a spectacular show. The height of the plant material is important. When there is a backdrop, always plant the tallest specimens at the back and the smaller plants up front. When planting in a circular garden, plant the tallest specimens toward the middle, and gradually lower the height of the plantings until reaching the border.

Interested club members can be asked to help with the gardens. A Garden Committee may lend valuable support to the superintendent. Combining the talents of volunteers with those of the professional can lead to a profusion of color around the clubhouse.

PHOTO AREAS AND VIEWING OPPORTUNITIES

Golf courses are favorite settings for weddings, anniversaries, graduations, and other important events. Photos and videos are often recorded during these memorable occasions. The most suitable locations for photo and video opportunities are usually identified and enhanced with flowers, gardens, arbors, or garden furniture. Visitors to the golf club also like to observe golfers in action. Perhaps there is an opportunity to provide a vista of the property from a high vantage point. Such a viewing area should include a comfortable bench, possibly a table and some chairs, and potted flowers.

> TIP: Movable containers, whether hanging or placed on the ground, can be rotated quite easily from the maintenance area to places of high impact to change the colors and look with peaking blooms around the clubhouse and entrance.

At exclusive country clubs, the extent of the landscaping can become quite extravagant. One may find some of the most elaborate rock gardens with cascading waterfalls and fountains spraying colored water. Impressive as such landscaping may be, it should never be done at the expense of the golf course. The vast majority of the club's customers come to play golf and not to look at an artificially created landscape. The natural landscape consisting of grass, trees, water, and sand is a piece of beauty seldom equaled around the clubhouse.

A GARDENER/HORTICULTURALIST

Extensive clubhouse landscaping will require the attention of a gardener or horticulturalist. The daily routine includes watering, weeding, and trimming the shrubs and grass. The work is never-ending, with peak periods of activity in the spring, which will require additional assistance, followed by regular routines during the season. Sprinklers must be set properly to ensure that both the grass and the landscape plants are watered properly.

A gardener's reputation depends entirely on the quality of the work that is produced. When visitors want to know the names of plant materials, an astute gardener knows that the good work is being appreciated.

Almost any professional gardener will want the convenience of having a greenhouse. It can be used to start new flowers from seed, to pot plants, and to create hanging baskets. The greenhouse is a perfect place to overwinter plants that might otherwise not survive. Today, many superintendents contract with an outside grower to provide most of the annual plantings. These outside suppliers can provide an assortment of flowers that are hardy and grow profusely in the proposed planting area. These growers are a great source of information on new plant material and can help the designer create memorable landscapes. It is a good idea to invite a grower to the golf course and let them see how their plants are being used so their ideas and suggestions in the future are most beneficial.

NATIVE PLANT MATERIAL AND EDIBLE GARDENS

Many golf courses and clubs are using native plants for gardens and showcases. When properly placed, these plants are very hardy and require less inputs (water and fertilizers) than other plants. They may not be as showy as annuals that flower all summer long, but they can offer different textures, colors, and habitat and food for pollinators and other animals.

Some golf course superintendents have worked with their executive chefs to plant edible gardens that can be harvested and used in the clubhouse. This relationship often starts small with several common herb plants used in the clubhouse kitchen and slowly expands over the course of time to include commonly used fruits and vegetables. For a superintendent, it can give some of the members a whole new way to enjoy the fruits of their labor.

SUMMARY

That all-important first impression starts with the appearance of the clubhouse grounds. Some clubs go to great lengths to beautify their grounds, and a competent gardener is invariably the person who makes the clubhouse grounds stunning. Beautiful landscape beds require a great deal of care, and maintaining the beds can be very costly and time consuming. Consideration should be taken before adding this expense to already strained golf course budgets. Although landscaping can be very extravagant, it should be thoughtfully composed for each property so that it may be practically maintained and neatly tended.

15

Traffic and Paths

Traffic from golf carts, players, and maintenance can wear out areas of turf. These areas make for poor lies and bad bounces on golf courses, and such conditions are unacceptable to observant golfers. Superintendents are expected to repair the worn areas and also try to prevent further damage by dispersing the traffic. There are certain situations when there is damage caused by foot and/or cart traffic that is so severe that it needs to be improved by other means. When this occurs, plans need to be made to construct footpaths and/or cart paths. Although sometimes difficult, golfers should be encouraged to walk or drive around these damaged areas. Superintendents need to be inventive and creative, by devising ways and means to control traffic on the golf course as well as exploiting a system of functional paths.

FOOT TRAFFIC, PATHS, AND STAIRS

Architects should be urged to build gently sloped tee banks with slopes that are less difficult to maintain. Gentle slopes will reduce foot damage to the turf, and will lessen the necessity for paths and steps.

Championship or back tees tend to be constructed behind the other tees and elevated, often making the construction of a path, combined with steps, a necessity. Since these tees are used less frequently, foot traffic damage is limited near these tees.

When golfers are ascending or descending from a steep tee, firmer foot pressure is essential to avoid slipping. The extra foot pressure can quickly wear out the turf. The first inclination is to install a set of stairs, but rarely are stairs the best solution. Almost immediately after installation, the grass near where the steps begin, the top of the stairs, and the tee deck will start to show signs of wear. Stairs tend to concentrate the wear pattern instead of spreading the traffic out. In addition, they are usually very costly to install and maintain, and they create another hard-surfaced tripping hazard on the property. The location of the stairs can interfere with mowing patterns. A railing can be added to a set of steep stairs to give golfers a sense of security; however, it may also accentuate the unnatural appearance of the stairway (Figure 15.1).

In the fairway areas, most of the wear typically occurs near the bunkers and the hazards. Wherever there is a concentration of foot traffic, such as between closely placed bunkers, near streams, ponds, and especially near pedestrian bridges, foot traffic will damage and weaken the grass. The benefit of using very small bridges is that the entire structure can be moved at regular intervals, which helps to alleviate wear patterns that can occur at both ends of the bridge.

Wear patterns near the green inevitably develop between the edge of the green and adjacent bunkers. If the bunker is inappropriately located in a direct line of foot traffic, it will be necessary from time to time to occasionally stop all foot traffic by means of temporary obstruction devices such as stakes, ropes, or a thin metal bar, partially bent like a hoop.

Figure 15.1 *Stairs should be made of treads that provide traction and a handrail is always welcome. Stairs do concentrate foot traffic at the top and bottom and the turf needs special attention in these areas to thrive.*

On occasion, steep slopes near the green necessitate the installation of stairs. Stairs, just like those near tees, are a maintenance headache and should be avoided if at all possible.

While many golfers now ride, a core group of health-conscious players prefer to walk, and they should be encouraged to do so. Although there can be some wear and tear caused by the walking golfers, the damage from foot traffic is minimal.

PROVIDING FOOTPATHS

Providing sure, nonslip footing is the most important consideration when selecting materials or methods for footpath construction. A path of scattered flagstones may have eye appeal, but these stones are very slippery when wet. Rough-textured paving stones or rubberized tiles can provide a good grip for golfers' footwear. Slippery wooden bridges can be covered with nonskid rubberized mats to provide secure footing.

After golfers drive the ball off the tee, some of the shots will slice, some will hook, and a few drives will go down the middle of the fairway. Paths often develop quite naturally when walking off the tee, even more so if avoiding an obstruction such as a watercourse or a gorge. A natural curving path through a stand of tall fescue can be quite eye appealing. Its presence lends aesthetics to a golf hole and often tranquility to a golfer's turbulent mind.

Cutting a closely cropped swath that is 4 to 6 feet wide that extends from the front of the tee to the beginning of the fairway will help prevent walking golfers from getting their feet wet when there is dew on the grass. This type of grass strip is commonly known as a dew or pro walk.

GOLF CARTS

While golf carts are a great source of revenue and profit, they cause considerable damage to the turf. The traffic patterns of carts must be controlled and the damage constantly repaired. As soon as more than 10 golf carts are regularly used on an 18-hole golf course, wear will start to show – at first, only near the tees, but signs of wear will soon appear near the greens and the bunkers. In the beginning, the damage can be reduced by changing the traffic patterns and by keeping the grass healthy and strong. With the increased use of golf carts, the need for a system of paths, for at least part of the course, will become apparent.

When the threshold level of 50 golf carts is reached; tee-to-green paths on par 3 holes becomes essential. When there are between 60 and 75 golf carts on an 18-hole course, a continuous path from the first tee to the

18th green is advisable. The use of golf carts by many golfers has become the norm; some are not even aware that golf can be played on foot.

On 18-hole golf courses with extreme drainage problems, a continuous cart path should be considered, thus avoiding wear on the turf caused by power carts. This will encourage play, which in turn becomes a continuous stream of income – more play, more pay.

DIRECTING THE TRAFFIC

While cart-driving golfers would probably prefer to drive almost anywhere, some restrictions must apply to protect the turf. The best way to minimize the stress of golf cart traffic on turf is to spread the traffic over varied areas. If a golf course has a continuous cart path system (on every hole from tee to green), carts may be limited to the path after heavy rains until the course dries out. Courses that do not have continuous paths may limit cart traffic to the rough only, while others may prefer players to drive in the adequately drained fairways until they reach the green complexes. Different types of turf tolerate different amounts of traffic. Older golf courses that possess bentgrass fairways infested with Poa annua may not want cart traffic in persistently wet areas. Bermuda grass is stronger and tolerates wear, while rye grass and bluegrass fairways are in between with regard to wear tolerance.

Limiting the carts to the primary rough is usually unsatisfactory because the turf in concentrated areas will quickly deteriorate, and restricting carts to the rough also slows down play. As a compromise, some have instituted the "90-degree rule." Under this rule, carts may enter the fairway at a 90-degree angle, and after golfers have hit their shots, they must return directly to the rough, also in a 90-degree direction.

There are other well-known traffic-diverting methods that involve the use of unobtrusive barricades, ropes, stakes, and signs to divert cart traffic away from sensitive areas. It's important to realize golfers in carts will invariably drive right up to the obstacle before changing their course. Therefore, these obstacles should be movable to change traffic patterns and make it easier for the green staff members to mow or trim around. These methods include the following:

1. *Exit stakes, uniformly painted either brown or green, can be placed in the rough a short distance from the green on either or both sides of the fairway.* These stakes provide warnings to golfers that they are no longer permitted on the fairways beyond that point. In fact, if paths are nearby, golfers are expected to access a path at that point. These stakes range in height from 2 to 3 feet and are spiked at the bottom, so that they can be placed and removed with ease.

2. *On some golf courses, a line is painted in front of the green across the fairway as a reminder that carts cannot advance and must proceed to the roughs.* The line must be repainted to remain visible, and must be moved often to avoid wear caused by carts that are driven along the line.

3. *Ropes suspended on stakes can be used as physical barriers to stop carts from approaching the green.* Ropes are effective but visually unattractive, and can often deflect golf balls, and get in the way of golfer's swings. They can be a tripping hazard and are time consuming to move and/or set up. Because of this, some superintendents opt not to use stakes, instead stapling the ropes to the grass.

4. *Signs reminding golfers not to proceed can be effective.* Moving and changing the signs can aid the golfers by pinpointing the correct direction to travel with the cart. A series of small stakes, placed in a row just far enough apart for pull carts to pass through, can form an effective barrier to divert power carts.

5. *Near the green, when there are no paths for carts to drive on, the 30-foot rule should be observed.* This rule dictates that power carts should not be parked or driven closer than 30 feet or 10 paces from the green. The intention is to protect the turf and to provide acceptable lies for golfers.

6. *Golf courses that possess golf carts equipped with GPS can program "no access" areas into the system.* Then the only way out is for the driver to back out of the area slowly. This has reduced the need for on-course traffic control measures.

Whatever strategies are used to direct the traffic, all need timely attention. If the traffic diversions have been moved by the mower operators or golfers, it is important to remember that they must be replaced or put back. Controlling the flow of traffic is a difficult assignment that should be attended to on a daily basis.

TIP: The person assigned this responsibility should have a thorough understanding of the need to balance the demands of the golfers with what is best for the grass.

NO CARTS TODAY!

There comes a time when a very unpopular decision needs to be made about cart usage. It happens after a heavy rain, a sudden downpour, or a violent storm. The sodden ground on the course is soft and not suitable for cart traffic on courses without continuous cart paths. The weight of the cart, combined with that of the golfers and their clubs, can damage the turf. In extreme cases, rutting could occur, and carts traversing slippery slopes may even lose traction and spin out.

Who should have the ultimate authority to decide the fate of carts on these wet days?

It should be the person who is:

- Best trained to measure the agronomic impact of the potential damage that cart traffic can do to rain-soaked soil and turf
- On the job assessing the potential danger that may occur to golfers when carts slip and slide
- Deriving no direct financial benefits from cart revenue
- Committed to doing what is best for the grass and for the golfers

In all cases, that person is usually the superintendent and, in some cases, the green committee.

Conveying the Decision

Once the superintendent has made the decision about cart usage, the adverse news, "no carts – for part or all of the day," must be conveyed immediately to the golf shop:

1. The decision should be delivered in a professional manner.
2. Notices should be posted and should include the anticipated time that the ban will be lifted. This information should also be sent to member email, posted on the club web page, and placed on social media.
3. Annoyed golfers with important guests will try to persuade the superintendent to reverse the decision. Be visible and ready to explain; reasonable people understand thorough explanations.
4. Irate golfers will want to vent their anger, and a considerate, understanding superintendent should be available to act as a good listening board.
5. A superintendent's unwillingness to speak to the golfers on these occasions is unacceptable. Without being willing to provide a thorough explanation, the superintendent conveys the impression that an error in judgment has been made.

   The golf professional, the manager, the club's president, and most of all, the green chairman, should support the superintendent in these cases. Making unpopular decisions requires the total support of the management team.

Managing by the Decision

On courses without continuous cart paths, there are a number of things a superintendent should do to improve one's professional image on "no cart days":

1. All golf course equipment should be kept off the course entirely, with the exception of equipment being used to alleviate excessive water conditions.
2. Golf course workers should restrict their excursions in maintenance vehicles, and these vehicles should be used only for emergency maintenance.
3. A conscientious superintendent should walk and set an example during course inspections.
4. Golfers will respect a superintendent who adheres to the rules that are good for everyone.

TIP: Remember that it is often possible to make exceptions for situations that can financially benefit the club and its members while having minor negative impact on the turf conditions.

CART PATHS

Increased play intensifies the demand for cart paths near tees and greens. Par 3 holes, which are often characterized by spectacular changes in elevation, water hazards, and sand bunkers, should have safe paths provided for golfers to drive from tee to green. Once a few paths are strategically located and the number of cart rounds continues to increase, a continuous path system often becomes a necessity. A week-long period of wet conditions that restricts the use of golf carts and curtails cart revenue will hasten the process of installing continuous or tee-to-green paths on all golf holes.

Cart Path Location

Golfers rarely agree on where cart paths should be located on the course. Walkers, who usually prefer not to have paths, will reluctantly agree to locate the paths as far away as possible from the playing areas. Riders, on the contrary, want cart paths in the roughs but close to the fairway, so the walks to the balls are short, especially on the days when carts are restricted to paths only. A compromise between the two extremes is difficult. The solution is to hire a golf course architect. This trained professional with experience and knowledge is the most qualified to make the final decision. Since every golf hole is different, an architect who has seen numerous golf courses and golf holes is capable of clearly visualizing where the paths should be located. After careful study, the architect will lay out a routing plan for the paths that will become the groundwork for a construction program.

The routing plan prepared by the architect should provide details about the location of the paths and also specifics that relate to cutting and filling areas that have mounds. The architect will try to hide the paths from view (Figure 15.2), allowing for the natural beauty of the golf hole. This can often be accomplished by curving a path and placing mounds in strategic places. Nothing is more boring and visually unattractive than a straight line of asphalt or cement along either or both sides of a fairway. An artistic architect will create a design that is practical and visually appealing. Placing trees strategically can assist the hiding and directing of paths in an appealing and functional manner. The strategic placement of a tree canopy over a path will also help to filter golf shots and prevent, or at least reduce, the severity of bad bounces.

Figure 15.2 *The best cart paths are the ones that are part of the landscape and don't impact play. Signs directing traffic are always welcome when playing a course for the first time.*

Cart Path Construction

When first implemented, cart paths were designed narrow and barely wide enough for a single cart. Now, the suggested width for a single cart path is 8 to 10 feet, and paths that are used for two-way traffic should be 12 feet wide. Narrow paths tend to crumble at the edges and the turf deteriorates quickly along the sides. The wider paths can accommodate two-way traffic as well as most golf course maintenance equipment.

Paths should be excavated to a depth of 6 to 8 inches. The excavated material can be used to help create mounds that are used to screen paths or can be hauled away for future projects. Most granular materials that are not too coarse are satisfactory for use as a foundation. Ground-up asphalt forms a solid base and can be used as an intermediary path until funds are available for a permanent surface. As opposed to screenings or fine limestone, ground asphalt does not kick up dust during dry periods. In fact, the heat of summer will solidify the asphalt, and what may have started as a temporary plan may become part of a permanent solution.

Draining the area around the cart path is very important. Puddles on a path after a rain are unacceptable. Paths should be slanted slightly so that water will run off. Slanting the path slightly toward the fairway will also help golf balls that bounce or land on the path to stay in bounds. When constructing cart paths, distance markers at regular intervals can also be included in the design. Distance markers help golfers decide what club to use for the next shot. When a cart path blocks the natural flow of surface water, installing a catch basin and/or tile will help to alleviate water backup.

TIP: No matter what material is used, a solid foundation that extends beyond the finished width of the path will help to keep the surface of the path intact.

What's the Best Surface for a Cart Path?

A number of options are available when selecting surfaces for cart paths. Most cart path material consists of one of the following: concrete, asphalt, paving blocks, gravel, recycled asphalt, decomposed granite, crushed bluestone or recycled stone mixes, and natural or synthetic woodchips. Consider investigating cart path surfaces with a neighboring golf course superintendent to determine which product will work best in conjunction with local climate and soil conditions:

- *Concrete produces a high-quality cart path.* Depending on soil conditions and usage, concrete should be poured to a thickness of at least 4 inches; a steel mesh should be included for strength and have expansion joints with cuts provided at regular intervals. It should be brush- or broom-finished while still wet to provide better traction. Even though a base for a concrete path is properly prepared, heavy equipment traffic or freezing and thawing in cold climates may lead to surface cracks that are unsightly and difficult to repair.

- *Asphalt is more flexible than concrete, making it easier to repair cracks and holes.* A proper base should be constructed to make a solid foundation for an asphalt path. Since no forms are required, installation is easier. More than one layer of asphalt may be necessary to provide extra strength for golf course maintenance equipment.

- *Paving stones or blocks provide another alternative.* Paths paved with stones or blocks are very appealing, provide excellent traction for carts and walkers, and are easy to repair. The cost of the initial installation can be expensive, but in the long term the path should maintain its exceptional integrity, while requiring little repair, thus making it cost-effective.

- *Gravel cart paths are usually limited to flat terrain since gravel can wash out on hillsides.* The use of gravel has its limitations because graveled cart paths can develop potholes and ruts. If so desired, gravel cart paths can be paved at a later date as funds become available.

- *Recycled asphalt can be used to construct cart paths.* During the heat of summer, the ground-up material melds and forms a smooth-riding, solid surface that does not wash away on sloped areas.

- *Decomposed granite, crushed bluestone, or recycled stone mixes have become alternative materials used for the construction of cart paths.* The products all have limitations, but are natural looking, affordable, and can provide firm pathways for pedestrian and vehicular traffic on flat terrain.

- *Natural wood chips or synthetic mulch are options for cart paths with flat surfaces in areas where the chips will not wash away.* Paths made from natural wood chips can break down, and the chips will need to be replaced.

Curbing and Turnarounds

The installation of curbs on paths will help to keep carts out of restricted areas. Curbs help to keep carts away from tees, greens, and other sensitive areas. The curbs should be 4 to 6 inches in height and can be poured from concrete or shaped from asphalt. Curbing can also be done with the use

Figure 15.3 *Cart turnarounds should be large enough for the operator to easily turn the cart around like this newly constructed one of concrete.*

of prefabricated concrete, which can be installed whenever desired. Some superintendents use pressure-treated timbers or railroad ties; however, these require maintenance and when left unkempt can become unsightly. When installing a curb, topsoil should be added level to the top of the curb, graded, and covered with sod.

When installing a path that requires a turnaround, the recommended area that should be allotted for easily turning the golf cart should be approximately 30 feet in diameter. An area of this size will allow for safe turning while keeping the carts from driving over the edge of the turnaround unto the grass (Figure 15.3).

End of the Path Diversions

When a path comes to a sudden end, the inevitable result is for the grass to weaken and die because of concentrated cart traffic. This damage can be minimized by flaring the path to either the right or the left and adding barricades that can be moved systematically, giving direction to where carts may exit. Some paths include grooves, stoppers, or speed bumps on the surface to indicate that the path is about to end, alerting cart drivers to exit from either left or right before reaching the end of the path.

PATH MAINTENANCE

Both footpaths and cart paths need to be maintained on a regular basis. Asphalt needs to be patched when potholes develop. Cracks on the path need to be filled and sealed to prolong the life of the paths. Paths need to be kept clean and cleared of debris, and the grass along the edges needs to be trimmed on a regular basis. Poorly maintained paths can give a shoddy impression of the entire golf course.

> TIP: All green staff should be trained on the use of cart paths, making sure to keep their wheels on the path, especially when parking their equipment. There is a tendency to pull over into the adjacent grass when parking. Keeping all tires on the path, especially by staff, will help to maintain clean edges and protect the turf from avoidable damage.

SUMMARY

Golfer traffic will find its way across the golf course in the quickest and shortest way possible. A qualified architect is engaged to determine the best location for the paths, thus avoiding a compromised committee design with results that are inadequate. Whatever surface is used, the path must be thoroughly maintained. Remember to keep most of the golf course equipment off the course on days when there are "no carts allowed." Always set a time later in the day to reevaluate the "no cart" decision and notify golfers when cart usage will be permitted. Green staff must be trained to modify their routes, especially those who perform the same task daily. It is human nature to take the same path each day – potential problems can be avoided by encouraging staff to take a different route each day.

16

Changing Cups, Flagsticks, and Tee Markers

How the game is enjoyed on a daily basis is not only the result of the state of mind of individual golfers, but also reflects the skill and attitude of the superintendent and crew on their ability to properly set up the course.

Making sure that tee markers are pointed to the center of the fairway and the flagstick is in a reasonable position on the green will give golfers a favorable impression as they play the first hole. Nothing annoys an ardent player more than a course that has been set up thoughtlessly. Golfers can be finicky, and for the superintendent to be careless about their wants and needs is jeopardizing his or her professional status. Delegating the course setup to an inexperienced worker is poor management and irresponsible. It also shows lack of concern for the needs of the golfers and for the integrity of the game.

CUTTING HOLES AND CHANGING CUPS

The skills of a proficient golf course worker are prominently demonstrated during the process of cutting a fresh hole into the green and filling and repairing the old hole. The process is quite simple, yet so many things can and do go wrong. The hole may be mistakenly cut on a slant, which makes the hole slightly oblong instead of circular. The cup may be too far below the surface of the green, or worse, too close to the surface. When the lip of the cup is less than an inch below the grass surface, golf balls that were destined to drop to the bottom of the cup may instead hit the high lip, be deflected, and bounce out. If it happens to the tee shot on a par 3 hole, it may result in the thrill of an ace spoiled. The plug that is replaced in

Figure 16.1 *The hole is the aim of every shot a golfer takes and should be placed and cut with care by conscientious, knowledgeable staff members.*

the old hole is often put down either too deep or not deep enough. Both cases are unacceptable but unfortunately happen often on many courses (Figure 16.1).

The following seven steps should be strictly followed when changing a hole:

1. The hole cutter should be in a good working condition. The blade must be super sharp, and in order to keep it that way, it should be routinely sharpened or filed. If the hole cutter has been in use for more than five years, it could be time to purchase a new, improved model.
2. In addition to the all-important hole cutter, several other items are part of the necessary equipment and should be carried in the maintenance vehicle:

   - A cup puller and a cup setter
   - A sponge or towel to clean the cup
   - A water bottle to water the replaced plugs
   - A knife or a flat screwdriver
   - Greens mix, soil, or sand for low plugs

   All of these items can be carried in a "cup cutting" or tool caddy.
3. Select the place on the green where the new hole is to be cut. Usually, superintendents systematically set up the course hole placements and predetermine the hole location, which is shown on pin locator sheets. There should be a minimum of a 2- to 3-foot level area surrounding the hole. First, plunge the hole cutter vertically into the green. Next, twist it down a few inches farther, carefully extract

the plug, remove it from the hole cutter, place the plug in the pail, and then make the second cut to the desirable depth. Painting a white mark on the cutter blade to designate the depth of the hole is a helpful visual aid.

4. Remove the cup from the old hole, and use a moist sponge to clean the inside of the cup thoroughly. Replace the neatly cleaned cup into the new hole and use the cup setter to press it down firmly to the desired depth. Brush away any bits of soil that remain around the new hole. Extremely particular superintendents will use a pair of scissors to snip off any misplaced blades of grass hanging over the lip of the hole. Keeping the cutter blade sharp will make this step unnecessary. Try to keep an extra set of cups on hand to change the cups periodically during the season. Keep the cups clean and fresh looking all the time, and you'll be a hit with the golfers (Figure 16.2).

5. Replace the plugs into the old hole, while checking to make sure that the plug is level with the green. If necessary, use a knife or a screwdriver to scrape the green mix between the lower and the upper plug, which will help the roots find their way downward. Press down with your foot on the plug to level it with the surrounding grass. Water the plug around the edge to form a seal with the surrounding turf, thus making sure the plug will survive the heat of day. Clean up and make sure that any evidence of an old hole has been removed. If the plugs have too little green mix, the grass plug

Figure 16.2 *Painting the soil above the cup liner is a touch some superintendents will do for special events.*

will sink; if the plugs have too much green mix, the plug will be scalped by the greens mower.

6. If colored flags are used for hole location, select the appropriate color flag for the new pin position to complete the process. Visually and physically check how the pin fits into the hole of the cup. If the fitting is loose, it probably means that either the pin or the cup should be replaced. A loose-fitting flagstick can easily bend with a brisk wind and at times may lean inside the cup in such a way as to prevent golf balls from entering the hole.

7. Finally, when the hole has been changed, observe from a distance, making sure that the flagstick is standing straight in the cup.

In addition to changing the hole, the person charged with that duty should also be responsible for other minor repairs on the green. Small scars on a green can be removed with a hole cutter and replaced with healthy plugs that are removed from inconspicuous areas along the back edge of the green. Also, old plugs that have been scalped or have turned brown can be replaced in this manner. The hole changer's duties may include repairing ball marks as well as always scouting for the first signs of disease. The hole changer is usually the first to know if the green is lacking moisture content. The need for additional water on the greens should be communicated to the superintendent or the person in charge of irrigation. The responsibilities of the hole changer are complex and time consuming, and therefore some 18-hole golf courses employ two people to change holes: one for the front nine and one for the back nine.

The hole on the green should be changed after approximately 200–250 golfers have played, which in many cases is after a day's play. Changing holes should be a daily routine, except in the shoulder season, when some days can be skipped. In the event that the holes have not been changed, the cups should still be checked and if the edge of the hole has been damaged, it should be changed, regardless of how many people have played the course. However, once a competition is in progress, the location of a cup cannot be changed.

CUP PLACEMENT AND FLAGS ON THE GREEN

Routinely moving the hole or the cup on the green can contribute significantly to the overall quality of the green. Moving the cup on large greens can easily spread the wear, but on small greens, changing the location of the cup and maintaining quality turf usually requires a well-thought-out system. The problem is frequently exacerbated by undulations in the putting surface that limit the number of hole locations.

Most systems that have been devised and implemented to institute a regular process for locating hole placements from the front to the center and to the back usually work well on large, sprawling greens. The hole can be placed almost anywhere, provided that the adjacent surface is reasonably level and the location is away from the edges of the green. The next day, the hole can be moved as planned in accordance with the selected system, which allows the turf to receive plenty of rest between days of play. On smaller greens, the hole often needs to be closer to the edge of the green. Contrary to popular belief, there is no rule in golf that dictates pin placement. The recommended distance is 12 feet, or four paces from the edge of the green. Often, the flagpole is used as a yardstick for measuring the placement of the cup location, which should be slightly beyond the length of the flagpole and away from the edge on a level area of the green (Figure 16.3). Some superintendents systematically set up the course hole placements: six hole placements in the front third of the green, six in the center of the green, and six in the back of the green. There are a number of other options when using this simple, straightforward method, but most are more complex. Other superintendents divide each green into six equal parts, with each part being numbered 1 to 6. A pin locator sheet, which shows all the hole placements, is then posted near the first tee or visually displayed on the golf cart. During tournaments and other competitions, pin locator sheets are made available to the players, which

Figure 16.3 *Hole locations can be placed close to the edge of the putting green, provided the area is relatively flat and no closer than a few paces or the length of a normal flagstick.*

provide detailed information in feet about the exact location of the cup. The majority of golfers are content to see their shots land on any portion of the green, and for those golfers, the front, center, and back method is more than adequate.

Several systems have been devised to help golfers determine where the hole is located on the green:

- *Colored flags are often used for designating pin placement.* Different colors can represent different locations. For example: blue flags can be used when the hole is at the back, white flags when the hole is in the center, and red flags when the hole is in the front; this or any variation of color designating placements can be used. This method requires that the hole changer carry extra flags or flagsticks with colored flags attached.
- *Most golfers now employ the use of a handheld laser measuring device.* When aimed at a flagstick (sometimes equipped with a reflector) an instantaneous yardage is provided. This technology has reduced the need for other hole location methods.
- *Decreasing in popularity are pin placement indicator flags that are attached to the flagstick and slide freely.* The downward movement of the indicator flag is impeded by a tight rubber ring. The position of the pin placement indicator flag reveals the location of the hole and can also provide suggestions such as "please repair ball marks." A variation of the placement flags is the use of colored plastic balls that slide up and down the flagstick.
- *Pin placement software is available that picks hole locations for each green.* These systems offer diversity, keep track of hole location history, and convey daily placement to staff and golfers using personal phone applications.

THE TEEING GROUND

Golfers have a choice of several tees on the course from which to play, which can include the center tee, the forward tee, the championship tee, and possibly other alternative tees. Each golf hole usually has a center tee, which is used by a majority of golfers for daily play; a forward tee, often used by women, senior, and some junior players; and the championship tee, which is the furthest back and usually used for championship play or by golf professionals or occasionally by low-handicap golfers.

The center tee should be the largest, since it receives most of the play. There needs to be plenty of room to move the tee markers, both back and forth and often sideways. Total teeing area on par 4 and par 5 holes should be at least equal to that of the green. Usually, par 3 holes have a teeing area that is twice as large as the target green.

The forward tees are usually smaller. These tees are important and must be enjoyable, not only for women and seniors but also for beginners, because this is where they learn to play the game. Some golf courses have placed a marker in the fairway for families or young juniors to play the game.

The back tees or championship tees receive very little play; the tees may not be large in area but must be maintained with the same care as the other tees.

All tee surfaces should be closely mowed, and the surrounds need to be trimmed to an acceptable height. The length of the grass at the back of the tee must not interfere with the swing of the club, nor should long grass at the front obstruct or deflect a golf ball. The standard of maintenance should be the same for all tees. There are always players who take the game very seriously and will voice their displeasure when the tees are not set up correctly.

PLACING THE TEE MARKERS

The location of the markers (Figure 16.4) on the tee is very important. There is a school of thought that believes the length of a hole should not vary from day to day. When the markers are at the front of the tee, the flagstick should be toward the back of the green. This method ensures that the overall length of the course is always the same. Another variation on

Figure 16.4 *Tee markers come in all shapes and sizes. Horseshoes (right side up, of course) are used at Wild Horse Golf Club in Gothenburg, NE.*

this way of thinking is to make six holes long, six short, and six medium each day to keep the course playing at the overall same length. Those setting up just need to make sure variation exists so not all the par 3 holes are playing long or short on a given day. There are other procedures that create interesting variations in the length of individual holes, yet the overall length of the course remains the same.

A diligent hole changer will keep track of the total yardage while proceeding from one hole to the next. Some holes may be set up a little shorter than indicated on the card and others will be somewhat longer, but each of the 18 holes will play different and offer a different challenge; nevertheless, the total yardage played will always be as stated on the card.

The crew members that have the responsibility of setting the tee markers can use various methods to align the markers with the center of the landing area. One method is to stand between the markers with arms stretched wide and with one hand pointed to each marker. Bring the arms forward in a regular uninterrupted motion and, where the hands meet, the fingers should be pointed to the center of the fairway. Another method, not as widely used, involves the use of a T-square made from PVC pipe (this can be made with three ½-inch pipes that are 6 inches long and a ½-inch connector T). Place the T-square with the stem pointing between the markers toward the center of the fairway, then, if necessary, move one of the tee markers, making sure that it lines up properly. These devices work well to train new employees on proper tee marker setup. Problems often arise on dogleg holes. The center of the fairway for long hitters is different from that for short hitters. In the case of doglegs, first determine where the pivot point is – that is, the point where the hole changes direction – and line up the markers with the pivot point. Some players will need a driver to reach the pivot point; for others, it may be a long iron, but in each case the center of the fairway at the pivot point will be the same.

From a greenkeeping point of view, the wear on tees must be spread in the most efficient manner possible so that no areas develop that are void of grass. This could mean spacing the tee markers across the entire width of the tee, or it may be necessary to force golfers to use a corner or the edge of the tee in order to give other sections of the turf a chance to recover. Unless play is very light, tee markers should be changed daily.

TIP: On "Ladies' Day" or for special events that include female golfers, consider using potted plants or baskets of flowers for tee markers. This extra touch is always appreciated.

OTHER ACCESSORIES

In addition to the tee markers, several other accessories are standard on many golf courses. These accessories may include the following: benches, ball washers, permanent yardage markers, trash and recycle containers, and informational signs:

1. *Benches are placed in the tee area for the golfers' comfort and provide a place to rest on while waiting to make their tee shot.* Benches should be placed out of the way of errant shots from all tees. Benches should be lightweight so as to be moved easily, but heavy enough to withstand a stiff wind. The bench should be made of durable material because it will be out in the open and exposed to the elements (Figure 16.5). The benches must be cleaned, scrubbed, and, if necessary, repainted or stained from time to time. Moving the benches daily will ensure that the grass will not grow up around the legs of the bench and also help prevent worn areas on the grass. On golf courses where power carts are mandatory, benches are unnecessary.

2. *Ball washers (including clean towels) were always fundamental accessories of many tee complexes but are now slowly disappearing from use.* There are two reasons for this. Some golf carts have a ball washer on them and/or most players will clean their ball prior to putting on the previous green making a ball washer on every tee redundant. However, when they are used, a malfunctioning ball washer and soiled towels can be a major source of irritation to golfers. Occasionally, ball washers lack soap and water, the

Figure 16.5 *Course accessories should be carefully placed to not disrupt play and be kept in fine condition. When setting up this tee, the bench and ball washer/trash receptacle are moved to minimize turf wear and encourage use.*

mechanism is broken, or the brushes are worn. If courses still use them, ball washers and towels need to be checked on a daily basis. A schedule should be set to maintain the ball washers, which includes emptying, cleaning thoroughly with soap and water, and scrubbing the tops with a soft brush or cloth so that the paint looks fresh. Some superintendents use a portable power washer for cleaning. Most golfers expect soap to be added to the water in ball washers. Soap certainly helps to make the golf balls sparkle, but too much soap can cause a buildup of grime and often causes foul odor.

TIP: Try adding a small quantity of wetting agent or omitting soap altogether to help keep the ball washers odor free.

3. *To avoid damage by mowers, permanent yardage markers should be embedded into the tee just below the surface.* Permanent yardage markers are made from granite, concrete, brass, or other durable materials. A permanent marker is placed precisely at the point from which the hole is measured, usually off to the side of the tee deck but clearly visible. In addition to the yardage, the hole number can also be displayed on the permanent marker. The distance of the hole is measured from the center of the tee deck to the center of the green. If it becomes evident that there is more wear in the front portion of the tee, it could be a sign that the hole habitually plays shorter than indicated on the scorecard. In order to distribute play to all areas of the tee, the markers should be moved daily.

4. *Placing trash and recycle containers on or near the tee is a must.* Providing receptacles that are easily accessible to golfers will help to alleviate blowing trash on the golf course (Figure 16.5). Containers should be adequate in size, unobtrusive, and blend with the landscape around the tees. All on-course trash receptacles should be emptied daily by the person responsible for tee or green setup as they traverse the course.

5. Signs are found on most tees indicating the hole number, the par, the handicap, and the length of the golf hole. This information is valuable to first-time players and guests. On private courses, where members play the same course regularly, there is less need for this detailed information. In addition to tee signs, many courses display signs reminding golfers to fix divots, repair ball marks, and rake the bunkers. While all of this information is important, avoid the tendency to clutter tees with excess signs.

TIP: A private course that has no directional signage for regular member play can benefit from having a temporary set of directional signs for use during guest events and non-member play.

SUMMARY

Course setup is very a important part of the daily routine for a green staff and should not be overlooked. A poorly placed hole will create more negative conversation amongst players than any other imperfection on a golf course. Tee and green setup is the "icing on the cake" each day, and mishaps must be avoided by setting up the course in a fair and reasonable way. There are times when course setup can be altered to compensate for extenuating circumstances. During the beginning of the season, especially in the northern areas (when scores are not recorded for handicaps), consideration should be given to the placement of the tee markers so that the markers are located in the forward area of the tees. The weather may be cooler and the fairways softer, making the distance that the ball travels shorter. This can also be done during stretches of wet weather or heavy irrigation during the growing season when the course is playing longer. The goal should be to provide the golfers with the opportunity to have enjoyable rounds, encouraging them to continue to play the game.

Golf is a game that is difficult for most, and there is no reason to make it more so by placing holes in unfair locations and stretching the length of a course to its tips. It is during course setup that superintendents have the greatest opportunity to positively affect golfers' state of mind by their vigilant placement of tee markers and their thorough attention to detail when changing holes.

17

Rules of Golf That Affect Maintenance

The superintendent is often requested by the golf professional to assist with setting up the course so that it can be played precisely and effortlessly within the rules. A superintendent should be prepared to accurately define the course, the out of bounds, the penalty areas, ground under repair, obstructions, and other integral parts of the course. Staking and marking must be accomplished in such a manner that even the most critical interpreters of the rules will be satisfied. Therefore, it is advantageous for the superintendent to play golf and be familiar with the rules of the game.

PENALTY AREAS

Many courses have penalty areas, which are bodies of water or other areas defined by the rules where a golf ball is often lost or unable to be played. For a one-stroke penalty, players may use specific relief options to play a ball from outside the penalty area. Therefore, golf course superintendents must work with their golf committee to properly define and mark these areas so players know when and where to take relief. Red or yellow colored stakes and/or lines are used to define the margins of the penalty area (Figure 17.1). Water to the side of a hole offers lateral relief from the penalty area and should be marked with red stakes and/or red lines. When play crosses a body of water, the area is generally marked with yellow stakes and/or yellow lines. When painting lines, the superintendent should use the natural contour and limit of the penalty area and stakes can be used to identify the penalty area from a distance. In this instance,

Figure 17.1 *This lake bank is clearly marked for play. The stake can notify the golfer that there is a penalty area from afar and the painted line provides the actual boundary of the penalty area.*

it is recommended to place these stakes on the outside edge of the painted line, so if they are removed and fall, players may take free relief from the hole made by the stake. Stakes defining the margins of the area should be placed in the grass as nearly as possible along the natural limits of the area. The distance between stakes is important. At all times, an imaginary line between two adjacent stakes must be on dry land and the line of sight must be visibly apparent when one lines up behind one stake and looks toward the other. The stakes cannot be too far apart or else the margin of the hazard may be hard to define. The recommendation is for penalty stakes to be placed approximately 15 to 20 yards apart; however, good judgment may dictate that the stakes need to be closer together or further apart. Stakes should be placed closer together when play occurs around an irregularly shaped lake or riverbank. When possible, painted lines should be used to remove any conjecture or speculation for the players especially during tournament play.

Stakes used to identify a penalty area or margins are considered "movable" obstructions (Figure 17.1). These stakes are often moved by both golfers and maintenance personnel. It can be difficult to replace a stake in its original place when the hole cannot be found in long grass. When stakes are occasionally removed, dropped carelessly, or not replaced, it may cause confusion and irritation for the golfers. The alert superintendent will know where stakes should be and take notice when they are missing, lost, or moved.

| TIP: After allowing the painted line to dry, some superintendents will follow with an application of growth regulator applied through a handheld spray to the painted turf to prolong the painting application frequency.

OUT OF BOUNDS

When the out of bounds is identified by fence or stakes, it is determined by the inside point at ground level of the fence or stake. The recommendation is for the out-of-bound stakes to be placed approximately 30 paces apart so players can clearly see the base of one stake to the next to determine if the ball is out of bounds. When the out of bounds is identified with a line, the line itself is out of bounds, and the line extends vertically upward and downward. A ball is considered out of bounds when the entire ball lies out of bounds. However, if the ball is deemed to be in bounds, it may be hit by the player standing out of bounds. Stakes can also be used in conjunction with painted lines to make the boundary visible from a distance. Stakes identifying out of bounds are not obstructions and are deemed to be fixed. Boundary stakes and paint should be white and clearly marked.

At most courses, the perimeter of the property is clearly marked with fences that serve as boundaries, which makes it easier to determine whether a golf ball is in bounds or out of bounds. In other situations, the out of bounds may be determined by walls, or the edges of other permanent structures like roads or buildings. In the absence of property fences, out of bounds (OB) is designated with stakes. These stakes should be routinely checked and rechecked to be sure that they are clearly visible and in the proper position to identify the out of bounds.

The actual out-of-bounds line may need to be painted for important events. When the out-of-bounds line is used continually in lieu of stakes, the line should be painted on a continuous basis. In some instances, a local rule may establish boundaries between two adjacent holes to protect players or maintain the character of the hole as found on a dogleg-shaped hole. Other areas that might be out of bounds and need to be clearly marked are the clubhouse grounds, maintenance facility, and practice areas, even though they are part of the course's property.

GROUND UNDER REPAIR

There are often areas on a golf course in less than perfect condition that are scheduled to be repaired in the near future. These areas should be marked as "Ground Under Repair," also known as GUR, as approved by the golf committee or its authorized representative, which in most cases is the superintendent. The GUR can be designated by using a "Ground Under Repair" sign in a roped off area and/or an area that has been painted with white or blue lines, that distinctly outlines the limits of the work area (Figure 17.2). An irrigation leak that was recently repaired may be marked off and designated GUR, the same as a scar or a scrape caused by a maintenance vehicle. Dead turf caused by winter injury or summer heat stress can also be marked off and designated as GUR.

For tournaments and important events, GUR areas are outlined with paint by a club official, golf professional, or the superintendent. It should be noted that GUR areas should rarely be painted beyond the fairway and the adjacent primary rough. Careful consideration should be applied in determining GUR looking at the whole course and the conditioning. Landing areas on the fairway and areas near putting greens are usually the locations that need to be checked for turf that may have unplayable lies and if need be should be marked GUR.

Grass clippings that are left in piles to be picked up later are considered GUR, and golfers once again get to move their ball, if they are in or close to the pile. Grass clippings, poorly spread in the rough, can provide unplayable lies, but no relief is granted. Superintendents need to be

Figure 17.2 *The area above can be marked as ground under repair by encircling it with a white line. While players are not required to take a drop from the area, they should to protect the new seedlings.*

cognizant of this unacceptable situation and make certain that the crew members are trained to properly spread the grass clippings.

Even during nontournament play, superintendents and assistants should keep white spray paint on their utility vehicles for marking areas that are GUR. Areas that need repair can be quickly identified and marked on the spot. All GUR areas should be placed on the maintenance schedule and checked off when they have been repaired.

TEMPORARY WATER

As stated by the USGA *The Rules of Golf*, "temporary water" is not in a penalty area, and can be seen before or after the player takes a stance (without pressing down excessively with his or her feet). Snow and natural ice, other than frost, are either temporary water or loose impediments, at the option of the player. Manufactured ice is an obstruction. Dew and frost are not temporary water.

A ball is in temporary water when it lies in or any part of it touches the water. Golfers may take free relief from this temporary accumulation of water on the course, as long as the accumulation is not part of a penalty area. A player is entitled to relief from temporary water with no penalty (Figure 17.3).

Figure 17.3 *When bunkers hold water, players are forced to play from the water or take relief within the bunker from the nearest point. Pumps are used to remove standing water to avoid this ruling all together.*

When temporary water is a continuing problem on the golf course, the causes should be explored. Invariably, such conditions are drainage related and should be addressed. Temporary water during the heat of summer can lead to scald, the actual cooking of the grass in freestanding water that is heated by the sun. This is a condition that can happen occasionally and may be preventable by the simple expedient of removing water with a squeegee or pumping the excess water away when possible.

OBSTRUCTIONS

There are different types of obstructions found on the golf course that interfere with the game of golf. An obstruction includes anything artificial, like surfaced roads and paths, curbing, buildings, signs, and other man-made objects. There are three types of obstructions: immovable, movable, and temporary immovable. The Rules of Golf or the committee defines what type and relief procedure is inherent to each. Obstructions do not include fences, stakes, railings, and objects defining out of bounds.

Maintenance equipment is usually considered an obstruction and is typically movable (Figure 17.4). More permanent or immovable obstructions include bridge abutments, drainage grates, sprinkler heads,

Figure 17.4 *Under normal circumstances, golf course maintenance equipment is consid-ered a movable obstruction unless the superintendent is using it to create a different challenge on "Superintendent's Revenge Day" at the club.*

irrigation control boxes, rain shelters, signposts, and installed benches. Temporary immovable obstructions need to be defined and are regulated by Local Rules but are typically items like grandstands, scoreboards, signage, and portable toilets. During tournament play, it is best for the superintendent to limit the number of instances of a necessitated ruling by reducing or eliminating all nonessential equipment on the golf course. The USGA book *The Rules of Golf* offers recommendations and guidelines for these situations.

LOCAL RULES

Local Rules are supplementary regulations to *The Rules of Golf* that deal with abnormal conditions, special relief, or course boundaries. When local abnormal conditions interfere with the play of the game and the committee finds it necessary to modify a rule of golf, authorization must be obtained from the USGA. Local Rules may apply to newly planted trees that need to be protected from erratic golf swings. A Local Rule may state that relief may be taken from staked trees or at the start of the season when conditions are less than perfect; club officials may decree that "winter rules apply," allowing golfers to move the ball.

Local Rules can also provide for the establishment of special areas, known as dropping zones. These drop zones are identified areas on which balls may be dropped when it is not practical to proceed exactly in conformity with the rules of golf that pertain to immovable obstructions, abnormal ground conditions, penalty areas, ball unplayable, or other like conditions.

Local Rules can also be instituted when major construction projects are under way. Newly laid sod, a bunker renovation, and the installation of a water line all involve temporary inconveniences to golfers. Under the provision of Local Rules, areas on the golf course that are under construction can be declared GUR. When communicated properly there is no fuss or bother; golfers simply take their balls from these areas and drop them at the nearest point of relief, no closer to the hole.

KEY RULES EVERY SUPERINTENDENT MUST KNOW

Anyone who has ever read *The Rules of Golf* realizes that they are simple and meant to uphold the spirit of the game. However, those who have read the Official Guide on *The Rules of Golf,* once known as the Decisions on the *Rules of Golf,* quickly realize the interpretations of the *Rules of Golf* is not as straightforward. By knowing which *Rules of Golf* are impacted by golf course maintenance practices, the shrewd superintendent can avoid the ire of the golfers as well as negatively impacting the game.

The core principle of the game is that each player shall play the course as they find it and play the ball as it lies. If the latter is not a motivating force to provide a consistent playing surface throughout the property, a career change may need to be pondered. Superintendents should continually look to improve and repair damaged or weak areas on the golf course. This includes divots, bare spots, thin turf, areas prone to holding water, and the like. Bunkers should be properly raked with adequate and consistent sand depths and with easily defined boundaries. A superintendent should always be striving to eliminate abnormal course conditions.

While all *The Rules of Golf* are important, there are several a superintendent should especially know and keep:

The teeing area is the rectangular area between the tee markers and two club lengths deep. Therefore, tee markers should always be placed at least two club lengths in front of the rear boundary of a teeing surface.

Most golf courses use a hole liner or "cup" that holds the flagstick. This liner must be sunk at least 1 inch (25.4 mm) below the surface of the putting green.

Edges should be well maintained and easily identifiable for putting greens, bunkers, penalty areas and out of bounds. Applications of *The Rules of Golf* are different for these areas and if they are not clearly marked, *The Rules of Golf* become muddled.

The flagstick must be circular in cross section and cannot be greater than 2 inches in diameter from the top of the pole to a point no less then 3 inches above the putting green surface whereas it must have a constant diameter no greater than ¾ of an inch to 3 inches below the putting green surface. Use a proper flagstick, especially for tournament play.

TIP: Keep your cups, flags, and flagsticks in prime condition. It's a good practice to have extra sets of cups on hand and keep painted, and extra set of laundered flags and flagsticks with the new ferrules that fit the cup and keep the flagstick upright.

SUMMARY

Superintendents, as well as their assistants, need to be familiar with the Rules of Golf as they apply to their daily operations. Furthermore, superintendents should study *The Rules of Golf* and be proficient in their application. It is common for a golfer to waive down a superintendent to solve a dispute or answer a Rule question while on the course. Knowing the Rules serves superintendents well, and many local golf associations provide seminars for their officials that superintendents should attend in the off-season. Rules knowledge will help to keep the golf professional updated on the condition of the course so that golfers can be advised on what rules apply and what type of relief is permitted. Superintendents need to work with their golf professionals to make sure that the course is marked correctly and consistently, letting golfers know what conditions to expect on the course, which makes playing by the rules effortless.

18

Golf Course Budgeting

Many golf operations, such as resorts, privately owned courses, leased facilities, or those owned and operated by management companies are businesses and are expected to produce a profit. Today municipally owned golf courses are expected to operate in the black and turn a profit rather than a loss. Member-owned golf courses expect to break even, and an occasional loss is divided among all members and charged as an assessment.

For superintendents, knowing and understanding the business side of golf is as important as knowing how to grow fine turf. Their decisions directly affect the bottom line, so they should understand the business model of the facility in which they operate. This process begins with creating the golf course maintenance budget.

THE BUDGET

A budget is a financial plan that forecasts expenditures for the coming year. Some budgets start as a wish list by an optimistic superintendent but are pared down by the realities of expected revenues. In most instances, a budget is based on financial records of the previous year. At times, administrators may wish to start from scratch and require detailed justification for every expense that may be incurred on the golf course. In order to prepare a detailed budget, superintendents need to know many specific items to breakdown costs and expenditures. The largest part of any golf course budget is labor. Each daily task on the golf course can be measured in terms of labor-hours worked. For instance, it may take two people to rake all the bunkers on a course 6 hours apiece. Therefore, it takes 12 labor hours every time bunkers need to be raked. If this occurs three times per week, that's 36 hours spent on raking bunkers. Each task can be defined this way and used to justify not only the budget but the expectations and standards provided by the superintendent and his/her staff.

Using satellite imagery freely found on the internet, the superintendent can accurately measure each golf course feature like fairways, greens, and tees to figure out how much fertilizer and plant protectants are needed. Of course, astute recordkeeping and how monies were spent in previous years also provides valuable information for many other itemized expenses. Complete and detailed records will enable the superintendent to accurately estimate the yearly budget.

There are two types of expenses that turf managers need to be proficient in budgeting: capital budgets and operating budgets. Capital budgets define expenditures of items called assets that can be new purchases or add value to a current item already owned by the course. Operating budgets detail the expenses needed for the day-to-day functioning of the maintenance of the golf course.

Capital Budget Line Items

All capital expenses, including the following, show up on the Balance Sheet as increases in assets. These items will be depreciated annually based on their projected life span:

- Equipment purchases
- Major golf course repairs, for example, new green and tee construction
- Installation of a new irrigation system or upgrades to the current system
- A new pump house or a well
- New cart paths and bridges (Figure 18.1)

Operating Budget Line Items

All operating expenses, including the following, show up as line items on the Statement of Revenue and Expenses and have a direct impact on the profit or loss of the operation.

- Salaries, wages, and benefits
- Administrative costs, computers, and phone
- Uniform and/or laundry expense
- Heating and cooling
- Materials such as sand, soil, gravel, divot mix, and mulch

Figure 18.1 *Repaving cart paths is a capital expense and requires outside contractors when installing permanent surfaces.*

- Utilities
- Fertilizers
- Pesticides and plant protectants
- Seed, sod, sprigs, and other plant materials
- Repairs and parts
- Fuel and oil
- Equipment rentals
- Educational, travel, and training expenses for the superintendent, assistant, and equipment technicians
- Staff training

BUDGETING FOR EQUIPMENT AND TOOLS

A minimum number of mowers, tractors, and various other machines and implements – collectively known as the "tools of the trade" or equipment fleet – are required to maintain a golf course. The size of the fleet may vary from one golf course to another, and the number and kind of individual units depends on the size of the course, the maintenance expectations, labor pool, and the available budget. Most golf courses, especially those built around residential areas, are restricted by noise ordinances, and noise from workers operating loud machinery is not tolerated. Today's modern machinery (many of these machines are battery operated and quiet) permits crews to quietly start their maintenance programs before daybreak, thus allowing the maintenance work to be done early in the morning without disturbing residents and in advance of the golfers' play. Some courses have very little equipment and perform admirably; others have a plentiful arsenal and at times achieve only mediocre results. While the equipment budget is often the limiting factor that constrains the fleet, the level of maintenance depends on the expertise of the superintendent to expend the budget wisely (Figure 18.2).

Leasing versus Buying

At times, a golf operation lacks resources to purchase new equipment. Leasing then becomes an attractive alternative. Leasing makes it possible to acquire all new equipment at one time, and doing so makes it possible to dispose of outdated old machinery that requires constant repair. The monthly lease payments are a direct expense against revenue instead of the yearly depreciation. New leased equipment comes with extended warranties, which can substantially reduce the cost of repairs. Several machines are usually included in the leasing contract, and the initial

Figure 18.2 *Updating sprayers that utilize GPS and computer application controls is an investment that saves money by using less product and labor.*

output of monies tends to be less than when equipment is purchased outright. However, leasing does involve finance charges and equipment is never owned, unless purchased outright at the end of the lease. Those golf clubs with ample resources that buy their machinery outright escape these finance charges.

Budgeting for the Cut

Each golf course property is different; the following are guidelines for an average 18-hole golf course equipment fleet (Figure 18.3). It is best to figure equipment needs based on the busiest part of the golf season and when the turf is most actively growing. Special events and circumstances like shotgun starts, member/guest tournaments, or equipment breakdowns need to be factored into the number of units available for use on any given day. For instance, when there is a shotgun tournament scheduled early in the morning, there may be only one hour available to cut all the greens before the course is full of players. On a normal day, this task could be accomplished by three staff members each working for two hours.

Figure 18.3 *Trade shows like the GCSAA's Conference and Show is a place where superintendents can see the latest innovations and discuss them with vendors and other superintendents.*

In order to accomplish this task in an hour, it will require three more staff members, each with their own mower. There are ways to work around this by adding lights to the mowers and having staff start earlier. However, since cutting greens is such a critical part of golf course grooming, extra units should always be on hand in case of breakdown.

Cutting the tees usually requires one or two riding mowers, or if walking mowers are used, the number should be doubled. If the golfers start early or many shotgun tournaments and crossovers are scheduled by the pro shop, additional units may be necessary to complete cutting so as not to interfere with play.

There are various directional patterns to cut fairways, and for that reason the cutting may require the use of two or more mowers, and some clubs will maintain several more. One should always be prepared for emergencies and make certain that backup units are available, which can often save the day, especially when important functions are scheduled.

All golf courses need at least one specialty mower and preferably two. These mowers are used for cutting around bunkers, tees, and other hard-to-get-at areas. Frequently, these areas are composed of steep slopes and require a very experienced mower operator to deliver satisfactory results. These specialty mowers should be sturdy machines with good climbing ability.

The roughs encompass the largest areas on most golf courses and, therefore, also require the most machinery to cut the grass. It is necessary to have at least two large rotary mowers and perhaps one or two triplex-reel-type trim mowers dedicated to mowing the rough on an 18-hole golf course. Maintaining the rough is a never-ending job and requires lots of attention and dependable machines to stay ahead of the fast-growing grass. For the finishing touches, include four to six walk-behind rotary mowers and string trimmers.

Cultivating and Topdressing Machines

A variety of machines are used to cultivate the grass. Walking aerators are often used to cultivate tees and greens. Larger, tractor-drawn machines are used to aerate the fairways. Spikers and overseeders are important machines as well (when used to augment the aerators) and are also useful as a means of introducing seed into established turf. Verticut units are necessary to thin the turf on greens and tees and are often also used to pulverize the cores that remain after aerating. These units or core processors can be used for the same purpose on fairways. There are other means worth considering, such as drag mats or brushes. Much of the aerating equipment is used infrequently, and many golf courses have contracted out this type of work, thus eliminating the need to invest in and maintain expensive equipment.

Topdressers are regularly used on tees and greens, and every golf course should have at least one or two of these machines. Topdressing fairways is gaining widespread acceptance. Many courses now include fairway topdressing machines in their inventory.

Maintenance Vehicles

As a rule, almost half the greens staff needs to be mobile. Therefore, 5 to 10 maintenance vehicles are usually required for an 18-hole golf course. It is necessary for the greens staff to move about the course in order to change holes, move tee markers, make irrigation repairs, empty trash receptacles, and perform many other small tasks. There are many personnel carriers available, and the ones equipped with hydraulic lift boxes and extra seats are usually the most practical.

Sprayers and Spreaders

Self-propelled computer-operated sprayers are commonly used for spraying tees, greens, and fairways. If there is a condition that requires spraying on a regular basis, a backup spraying unit may be necessary. Consideration should also be given to obtain a sprayer that is solely used for the application of herbicides. Reliable fertilizer spreaders, both large and small, are needed to apply fertilizer to fairways, tees, greens, and roughs.

Tractors, Loaders, and Trailers

There is a basic need for two or three tractors, equipped with turf-type tires, which can be used to help accomplish miscellaneous work on an 18-hole course. At least one of these units could be equipped with a backhoe. Mini-excavators or small backhoes are becoming more commonplace on golf courses and are proving to be a valuable piece of equipment for various digging tasks and projects. A skid loader can be used to move heavy items from place to place. Several small utility trailers are needed for construction work and cleanup assignments.

Trucks

One pickup truck and, if possible, a small dump truck are a must on most golf courses. The pickup truck is used primarily as a runabout, both on and off the golf course. The dump truck is handy for construction work and, in northern climates, can be equipped with an appropriate attachment to be used as a snowplow and salt spreader.

Bunker Rakes

At least two powered bunker rakes are needed to rake the 50 or more bunkers on the average 18-hole course. When bunkers are small, they may be raked by hand. Also, in addition to rakes, power edgers are essential to trim the edge of the bunkers.

Rollers, Blowers, and More

Most golf courses have one or two power-operated greens rollers. These units have become essential in many operations to increase green speeds and help to make the ball roll true. Small and powerful pull-behind blowers allow operators to nimbly and quickly clear areas of leaves, clippings, and other debris. Two or three pull-behind blowers are a necessity, especially on tree-lined courses. A new category of equipment that is gaining popularity is the compact tractor that offers a variety of attachments to complete specific tasks on golf courses. They are versatile pieces of equipment and, with the proper attachment, can do the work of what used to take several different self-driven units or handwork. Different attachments allow mowing of steep slopes, flail mowing, cutting sod, aerating, trenching, blowing, deep-brush mowing, and even stump grinding. Golf courses that have steep slopes and undulating terrain can benefit by having one of these tractors in their inventory.

Practical Essentials

There are many practical maintenance items needed to keep a golf course in the proper playing condition. The following are necessary power-operated pieces:

- A sod cutter
- A trencher to install both irrigation and drainage pipes
- A woodchipper to grind up branches and twigs
- A generator
- Water pumps
- A power washer
- Bed knife and reel grinders
- Several-sized chainsaws

- Line and hedge trimmers
- Backpack blowers

When a superintendent is let loose in a hardware store, there will not be a shopping cart big enough for all that is needed on the golf course and in the grounds maintenance facility.

Specialty Greenkeeping Tools

Our profession requires certain tools to carry out practical golf course maintenance, and one must learn to be proficient in their use. The tools that are specifically greenkeeping tools include the following:

- Several cupcutters and the necessary cup-changing equipment.
- A sod knife is used to lift sod and to make small repairs on tees, greens, and even fairways.
- A turf doctor (also known as a square-hole turf repair tool) makes it possible for square pieces of thick sod to butt up against each other for an instantly playable surface. These turf repair tools come in many shapes and sizes.
- A Levelawn is used to spread topdressing and to work aerating cores into the turf by pushing the Levelawn back and forth.
- A large square-mouthed shovel can be used to apply topdressing to small areas.
- Whipping poles that are made from fiberglass can be used to whip the dew off the green. These poles also come in handy to clean spilled grass clippings from the apron.
- A push-type sod cutter with a narrow blade is useful when replacing the turf killed by a hydraulic spill or fuel leak.
- Portable soil moisture meters used to measure available water on putting greens and fairways.

Many other specialty greenkeeping tools designed for use on the golf course can help to make daily maintenance tasks easier.

KEEPING AN INVENTORY

There is a significant number of basic requisites and maintenance tools that are needed by each individual golf course. It all depends on golfer expectations and the size of the budget. There are many other items that a golf course needs to operate on a daily basis. Items like hoses and nozzles, irrigation fittings and movable sprinklers, landscape tools, shop tools, equipment lifts, and air compressors make up the equipment inventory of a golf course. The list can be quite extensive, and a recorded inventory should be kept updated throughout the year. Computerized recordkeeping is a task that can be completed in the offseason and updated yearly. There are many inventory programs available today that make this task easy to accomplish without much input. Records like equipment purchase dates, costs, models and serial numbers, maintenance records, and replacement schedules help to preserve the value of the asset and make future budgeting easier and more complete.

SUMMARY

In some instances, the total replacement cost of all the equipment and machinery for an 18-hole golf course can exceed millions of dollars. This amount may seem excessive; however, the vast majority of golf courses manage with much less. Large resorts, exclusive private country clubs, and courses that host televised tournaments are often endowed with the latest and the best equipment. There are many mom-and-pop-type operations scattered across the globe that manage with much less and are able to provide plenty of enjoyment to everyday golfers. It is up to the superintendent to manage the equipment fleet by matching the needs of the golf course with the available budget to get the task accomplished.

19

The Grounds Maintenance Facility

Golf course maintenance facilities are sometimes on the boundaries of the property; other times, they are located in the center of the course. No matter where it is physically located, the maintenance facility is the epicenter of action for all greenkeeping activities. It is a complex that stores equipment and tools and also houses offices and workspace for equipment technicians, meeting and break rooms, locker rooms, and showers. It has specific and specially designed storage locations for fuel, chemicals, and other dedicated areas to wash and clean equipment. There are designated areas to store bulk items like soil and sand, and specialized filling and mixing spaces for sprayers and other application equipment. There are parts rooms for irrigation and mowing equipment, and at some facilities there may even be a dog dish or two for a superintendent's four-legged friend.

Each day, often before dawn, many important decisions are being made and implemented that affect the daily condition of the playing surface. The day begins once the staff arrives. The superintendent or the assistant gives out assignments and last-minute instructions – sometimes by posting them online or writing them on a whiteboard – and updates the tasks throughout the day. Machines are started up, carts are loaded with the required tools and materials, and sprayers are readied and calibrated to make applications for the morning tasks at hand. The maintenance area is a beehive of activity all day long, but especially early in the morning with workers prepping and leaving for their assigned tasks.

In years past, the maintenance building may have been a decrepit barn or a small shed and was, not surprisingly, called the shop or barn. As the golf course maintenance profession became more sophisticated, so too the old buildings gave way to a modern facility. At many golf courses, this building has become known as the *grounds maintenance facility*. The new term was an attempt to upgrade the status of the place that houses the superintendents' office, the workshop and machinery, and the area where the crew assembles. It was much like a facelift with words, to gain acceptance as an important element in the framework of the golfing operation. The name "Grounds Maintenance Facility" is often displayed on the side of the building or on a prominent sign so that both golfers and passersby can easily see and become familiar with the name and the image. Other names for the grounds maintenance facility include turf care center, grounds department, or golf maintenance facility, for example.

Well-planned maintenance facilities offer indoor storage for the many pieces of valuable machinery and adequate space for the golf course equipment technician to work. There are specific areas for staff members to wash off their equipment after each use that captures and filters the rinse water. Many have self-contained tanks for fuel storage. The area or compound is laid out in an efficient manner for the flow of equipment coming in and going out on the course. Most are located somewhere in middle of the property, minimizing travel time to the farthest corners of the property. Some facilities even have nurseries and greenhouses to grow turf, trees, and plants for use on the course. Others have housing for staff members to live comfortably onsite. Most facilities are as different as the courses they service; however, a clean, well-organized facility typically leads to exceptional golf course conditioning.

THE MEETING ROOM

Every maintenance building should have a room that is large enough to accommodate the entire crew for daily meetings. The meeting room should be well lit, and there should be chairs available for the entire staff to sit. There should be a white, chalk, or digital board for writing each individuals assignment and making sketches or outlines of the day's projects. A sound system will only be necessary if there are a large number of crew members. A room that can be darkened is a bonus since it can be used to show presentations and training videos on rainy days.

The general purpose of this room is for the superintendent or assistant to address the staff at the beginning of the work day. Daily work assignments are announced, and as a result of this meeting, everyone on the crew will know exactly what to do as well as what is expected of everyone else on the team. During this briefing, there is an opportunity to single out individual staff members who have done exceptional work and should be praised for their efforts in front of their peers. This is the time to discuss special events that will take place on the golf course and the importance of the occasion. Golfers' positive comments that have been received by the superintendent can also be passed on to the workers to boost morale and raise their spirits.

At the same time, criticism of course conditions should also be shared with the crew.

> TIP: Always introduce visiting superintendents, traveling agronomists, and club officials to the assembled staff. This introduction can make everyone feel an important part of the team.

THE OFFICE

Superintendent's offices come in many different sizes. Sometimes they are shared with assistants and equipment technicians with several work areas; other times, they are separate. Like all industries, the personal computer and cell phone has changed the way the superintendent manages the business side of golf maintenance. Larger operations may employ an administrative assistant to help with many office-related tasks. Many superintendents take care of the day-to-day recordkeeping in their office and while on the course via their phones, tablets, and other electronic devices.

The superintendent's office is an important area and should be kept clean, well-organized, and inviting for employees, vendors, and club officials to meet as needed. Most offices contain the typical furniture – a desk, filing cabinets, bookshelves and at least one computer for the management of the operation and the irrigation system (Figure 19.1).

Figure 19.1 *Irrigation computers and course maps are a common sight within the offices of a golf course maintenance facility.*

ESSENTIAL RECORDS

No matter how small the operation, there is a need for some degree of recordkeeping. A detailed record of all operations still needs to be maintained, either in a handwritten journal or as a retrievable computer document:

- *An inventory of all equipment and machinery must be maintained and updated yearly.* The equipment should be permanently marked in an inconspicuous spot and all serial numbers be recorded for insurance and identification purposes. The year and cost of acquisition as well as an estimate of the replacement cost should also be recorded.
- *Maintenance and repairs must be recorded.* The equipment technician should record all maintenance and repairs to equipment, including their costs, and keep an accurate inventory of parts.
- *Fertilizer and pesticide applications should be recorded in detail, and should include the rate, method of application, and the prevailing weather conditions.* An inventory of all fertilizer and pesticide materials should also be maintained that includes date purchased, vendor and pertinent registration, and lot numbers.
- *A daily journal of weather conditions, unusual situations, and all maintenance-related activities that are performed by the green staff should be kept.* The assistant is often delegated this task of recording the daily events.
- *Daily time records for employees are maintained, including the number of hours that are devoted to the various tasks and projects.* All employee records and information should be securely maintained, and performance evaluations need to be recorded yearly.
- *Expenditures must be documented and tallied against the budget.* This makes it possible for the superintendent to provide current information on a timely basis instead of waiting for monthly reports from the club's office.

Computer programs specifically designed for golf course maintenance recordkeeping are commercially available. Most are cloud based, allowing access to the data from any location or device and making it easy to enter the information. Others design their own recordkeeping system, utilizing custom spreadsheets to log the data required to maintain a golf course.

No matter the system, it is important to back up all this information on a regular basis and keep a copy off site. Losing essential information because of computer breakdown or other incident can be devastating.

In addition to recordkeeping, the superintendent or the assistant typically produces a monthly or seasonal report that includes updates on the maintenance program. These reports and other communications are presented at the regular club and/or green committee meetings. Often, the superintendent is responsible for taking minutes at the meetings, and the recorded minutes should be filed for future reference. Newsletters, correspondence, and letters, as well as information that are generated for the golf club newsletter, should also be maintained.

WORKERS' STAFF ROOMS

The staff room needs to be comfortable, offering a respite from the outside weather. It should be warm in the winter and cool in the summer. The room should offer a relaxing place for staff to converse with coworkers, enjoy a cup of coffee or cold drink, and eat meals. Many of these rooms are equipped with a TV that can be used for training or entertainment during down times. There should be a separate location in the facility with space available for the workers to change clothing, wash, or shower, especially for those who have been applying hazardous materials.

The room should also be equipped with plenty of lockers, as well as spacious tables and sturdy chairs. There should be a refrigerator, a counter, and at least one microwave or other appliance to heat meals. Some facilities will provide a coffeepot and/or an electric tea kettle, and when the weather turns warm, water or cold drinks may also be made available. Always remember the need for hardworking people to have a place to eat and quench their thirst.

Who should clean the staff room, the shop, and the washrooms? In large operations, one person is frequently assigned this duty on a full- or part-time basis. Smaller operations are often cleaned by a junior staff member. The staff room should be cleaned and swept daily, preferably immediately after lunch. The washrooms and the floors need to be swept and washed daily. The entire staff area should look presentable at all times. Cleanliness benefits all the workers whose home away from home is the grounds maintenance facility. Visitors can drop in unexpectedly, and no one wants to be embarrassed and feel a need to apologize for an unsightly work area (Figure 19.2).

Figure 19.2 *A clean and well-lit break room is an inviting place for employees to fuel up and ready themselves for the next task at hand.*

THE EQUIPMENT TECHNICIANS' SHOP AND OTHER WORK AREAS

The equipment technicians' shop is where all the repairs and maintenance takes place on the grounds equipment. The shop is like a big garage, where equipment can be raised and lowered. It's a place full of drills, welders, grinding wheels, air compressors, and washup solutions. There are workbenches, tool chests, and bins full of parts. Vises, jacks, saws, hammers, and wrenches all can be found in an organized location within the shop. Most equipment technicians are very particular about the placement of their tools and prefer that their shop areas be kept neat, clean, and organized. A dedicated equipment technician with the encouragement of the superintendent will always maintain a shop in this manner. Many superintendents take great pride in the cleanliness of their work areas, and often there is a healthy competition amongst neighboring superintendents as to who can provide the cleanest, neatest, and most organized facility (Figure 19.3).

A computer, which is connected to the maintenance facility network, should be in place in the shop to keep an inventory of all the equipment and technical information. Long gone are the days when new equipment was shipped with a parts manual and maintenance schedule. Manufacturers now provide online manuals, parts breakdowns, and online tutorials for the golf course equipment technician to keep the equipment in top working order. Parts can be looked up and ordered online and often shipped the same day, alleviating the need to store many odd parts at the golf course.

Figure 19.3 *An equipment lift is an essential tool that aids equipment technician to adjust mowers with precision.*

It is still a good practice to keep commonly used or needed parts to minimize down time on key equipment. Keeping an inventory of equipment and parts will help the equipment technician when it comes time to locate parts for repairs and equipment replacements.

One of the important jobs for the golf course equipment technician is to sharpen the specialized mowers used on the golf course. Specialized grinders are used to sharpen the reel and bed knife of each mower, often several times a year. Some maintenance facilities have special rooms or areas that house these grinders to compartmentalize the dust and noise produced during the process. Newer sharpeners are fully enclosed, limiting the need for extra ventilation and noise abatement.

It is not uncommon for the maintenance facility to be used for different work throughout the year. Many courses will do carpentry work during the winter or off-season. Talented superintendents and staff members create tee blocks, signs, benches, shelters, railings, and other wood items, sometimes created from trees that once grew on the golf course. Others are talented metalsmiths and may create some of these items from steel and iron. Many pieces of equipment and course accessories are painted each year during the down time. It is important that the proper tools are used by trained employees and that above-adequate safety precautions are in place for these seasonal tasks and projects. The maintenance facility is used in many ways in addition to storing equipment.

CLEANUP AREA

When the workers return from their tasks on the golf course, there needs to be a place where the mowers and all other equipment can be cleaned and washed. Today's golf course superintendents are conscious of how various materials affect the environment. Clippings, bits of soil, or traces of fertilizer residues make for an undesirable mixture; this can be lessened by recycling and operating a cleanup area that is environmentally friendly.

Fully aware that an accumulation of such residues is not beneficial and more than likely detrimental, a prudent superintendent will install a prewash station, equipped with forced air. At the end of the day, air hoses are used to blow away all loose materials that accumulate on the mowers (Figure 19.4). Once the loose material has been blown off, the mowers can then be washed. Using forced air as an intermediary step drastically reduces the amount of solids in the washup water. At many facilities, wastewater is filtered and recycled (Figure 19.5).

After the machinery has been washed, the machines should be dried, refueled, and then returned to the storage area. There should always be time to clean and wash machinery, even if it means overtime. Everyone likes to start the next morning with a clean machine. Now and then, the machinery should be polished. There may not always be time for polishing and shining, but perhaps a rainy day will come along, and instead of sending workers home, consider keeping them around to shine the machines.

Figure 19.4 Prewash *station using forced air to blow away loose material at the Old Collier Golf Club, Naples, Florida.*
(Photo provided by Tim Hiers.)

Figure 19.5 *Washing off mowers after use is a standard maintenance practice. A container is used to collect the wastewater for recycling at the Old Collier Golf Club, Naples, Florida. (Photo provided by Tim Hiers.)*

TIP: The golf course equipment technician should train new employees how to properly clean and store equipment after each use. The equipment technician knows what areas should not be sprayed with water and other special areas that may need attention.

STORAGE AREAS

Equipment Storage

Seldom is a building for equipment storage large enough to hold all the golf course equipment and machinery (Figure 19.6). When space is insufficient, there is no choice but to store some items outside, exposed to the elements. Tractor-drawn implements such as tillers, graders, trailers, and large rotary mowers can be stored outside for extended periods. Ultimately, to preserve the equipment, arrangements should be made to have a roof over all implements. Many maintenance areas include an

Figure 19.6 *Most golf maintenance facilities have limited indoor storage for their equipment fleet.*

out-of-the-way place for castoffs and relics. Unless these items are well hidden, they detract from the overall appearance of the facility.

TIP: Castoffs and other usable metal items should be sold for scrap metal and other unusable items should be discarded or recycled.

Fuel Storage

Most municipalities have strict rules and regulations that control how fuel must be stored. In some places, double-walled storage tanks are sufficient for storing fuel. Many times tanks are stored on cement spill pads that have enclosed areas that will contain leakage. Tanks can be covered with a roof for protection from sun and rain, and should have a space that is open between the roof and walls to provide ventilation. The tanks are equipped with an electric pump to disperse the fuel. The system should include an emergency shutoff switch, which should be easily accessible and located away from the tank to provide safe access for shutting off the power. Steel posts filled with cement should be strategically placed to protect the tanks from accidentally being bumped, and each tank should be well marked with the type of fuel that it contains.

Pesticide Storage

Self-contained units that meet the conditions of government regulations are available for the storage of pesticides. Although these buildings are functional and serve a specific purpose, the unit is seldom a thing of beauty. Some superintendents may wish to construct their own buildings that are functional, blend in architecturally with the surrounding buildings, and are in compliance with regulations and codes.

Pesticide storage building units should be ventilated 24 hours a day to prevent the accumulation of noxious vapors. The unit should be heated in the winter to avoid the freezing of liquids. The floor should be raised and enclosed in cement, steel, or other leak-proof material so that in the event a spill occurs, the liquids will be safely contained. The building that is used for storing pesticides should be kept under lock and key at all times.

A record of the contents in the building must be kept on file and should be available to anyone who is in authority to see the list. In spite of all the precautions, the air inside a building where pesticides are stored can have an offensive odor, and breathing the fumes is not good for one's health.

TIP: Wear a protective face mask when inside a pesticide storage building.

Storing Materials at the Facility

Every golf course uses a variety of materials, including sand, topsoil, gravel, wood chips, and other provisions. For ease of handling, these materials must be kept separate, and inventive superintendents have designed a series of bins that are constructed with sturdy walls. Since many of the materials are delivered by dump trucks that deposit the load by backing into the bins, the minimum width of the bin should be approximately 12 feet (4 m). This size of an opening is necessary for the loaders to scoop up the materials that can then be dumped into maintenance vehicles. The walls should be constructed with heavy timbers or large solid cement blocks that are sturdy, and must also be built sufficiently high to ensure that materials do not spill over into adjacent bins. Some superintendents prefer to cover the storage area with a roof so that the materials will stay dry, ensuring that the materials are always ready for use.

Many superintendents prefer to purchase large quantities of fertilizer in hopes that there will be a substantial savings. In most cases, the price per bag or per ton of fertilizer declines as the quantity increases. Fertilizer that is stored, even if the fertilizer is in sealed bags, must be carefully tended, and should be stored in a completely dry space to further ensure that moisture does not seep into the product. Keeping the fertilizer dry and the bags intact will help to maximize the initial savings with the bulk purchase. The best policy is to practice moderation and limit supplies to quantities that can be stored properly.

Grass seed is available in plastic pails or bags. One of the advantages of purchasing seed in tamper-proof plastic pails is the prevention of intrusion by rodents such as mice and even rats. Smaller quantities of seed can be stored in sealed metal containers that are rodent proof. Timing the delivery of seed is important. Prolonged storage of seed in warm temperatures can affect germination. Large quantities of seed for overseeding or new seeding should be used soon after delivery. Low temperatures for prolonged periods during the winter do not significantly affect the rate of grass seed germination.

SUMMARY

The appearance of the grounds maintenance facility is a reflection of the superintendent. The meeting room, office, workers' staff room, and restrooms need to be kept clean, organized, and free of clutter. A tidy work area will encourage workers to grasp the importance of their responsibilities and employ these principles when completing their assigned tasks on the golf course.

Proper maintenance of the equipment technicians' shop, and of the equipment, material, fuel, and pesticide storage areas, will help increase savings by preventing waste and by extending the life of the stored items.

20

Managing People

Managing the crew is just as critical as selecting the right pesticides and fertilizers for the course. Internal management is the backbone of a successful golf course and is just as vital as the external management of the golf course. Selecting the right person that is qualified for the assigned task is one of the most important management skills that challenges a superintendent.

The green staff arrives early in the morning, sometimes before the crack of dawn. Each will be assigned specific tasks impacting the condition of the golf course that day. Their training and skill directly influence the golfers' enjoyment of their game. As a rule, many of the decisions of who does what and who goes where have already been made the day before, but there are often last-minute changes caused by weather conditions, an event, or employee attendance. The superintendent is in charge of managing the labor force and using this expense wisely (Figure 20.1).

DAILY STAFF MEETING

In most cases, the superintendent, the assistant, and often the equipment technician will have a last-minute meeting to discuss the objectives for the day. Often other key players, including the spray and irrigation technicians, are also involved. After the preliminary discussion, the superintendent or assistant should address the crew. Speaking to the assembled workers requires preparation and poise. If the superintendent addresses the crew, then the assistant should be close at hand to help look after the details.

The address to the crew should not be long, and it should be kept precise and to the point. A long-winded chat quickly loses its effectiveness. If golfers have made favorable comments, try starting the meeting by communicating these remarks. This way the day begins with a positive approach.

Figure 20.1 *Successful superintendents know that it takes a team of well-trained and dedicated staff members to manage any golf course. The superintendents who continue to work on their own leadership skills excel in their profession.*

Next, assign all individual routine tasks, such as mowing, changing holes, and raking bunkers, to specific crew members. Address them by their first names, and always make them feel that their tasks are important. Change the sequence of assignments frequently. If bunker raking is always the last job mentioned, the employee will feel that bunker raking is least important, and the quality of the work may suffer. Start with the rough cutters one day and finish with the hole changers, then rearrange the order of the assignments. If a certain worker has started earlier than usual, inform the rest of the staff what is taking place.

If a greens cutter is expected to be finished early, make sure that assignments are given for work that needs to be completed during the rest of the day. Therefore, be specific in assignments and be sure to include this information on the assignment board. Emphasize the need to repair ball marks to the greens cutters, and offer reminders to the hole changers about the importance of keeping hole cups clean.

When speaking to the crew, always include general information about what kind of events are taking place on the golf course that day. This is a good time to also mention future outings and functions that are scheduled. Perhaps there is a major tournament in the offing and special preparations need to be addressed. At the end of the opening remarks, try to single out one or two employees who have performed well the previous day or week and praise them in front of their peers. Such public praise is great for the morale of the crew. Praising a crew member will often increase work efforts, while nitpicking will usually decrease productivity.

| TIP: Criticism is easier to withstand when one is also praised.

CHECK, AND CHECK AGAIN

Shortly after the crew has left to work on their assignments, the superintendent should do a thorough check of all activities taking place on the golf course. Check the greens to make sure the mowers are cutting properly and the lines are straight. Observe hole locations to check that the placements are on level ground. Pull up on a ball washer handle to test for soap and water, and check the placement of the tee markers, making sure the markers line up with the center of the fairway. Stop and check on the bunker raker, and help rake the edge of a bunker. It shows you care, while at the same time setting a good example. By all means, pick up any litter as you travel across the golf course, either by foot or in a cart. Praise the jobs that are well done. Assist those who need extra help or additional training. A wave of the hand or a smile for the crew member on a passing fairway mower or rough cutter will do wonders for the morale and the attitude of the workers. The workers will be reassured that the boss appreciates their hard work.

The superintendent should occasionally stop and converse with the golfers, but without intruding on their game and concentration. Always try to remember the names of regular golfers, and be approachable with all the golfers, especially if they give the impression that they want to have a conversation. Listen to their concerns with undivided attention, even if you have heard their particular gripes on numerous occasions. Apologize for work that may interfere with their game and explain the reasons for inconveniences. At all times, present a congenial image, even when the grass is wilting and the machines are breaking down.

LOOK THE PART

A professional-looking superintendent will command respect from other managers, staff, and golfers. In years past, greenkeepers usually wore collared shirts and ties, and even sport coats, for their daily attire. The dress code is more casual today, but worn jeans and shorts are not acceptable around any golf course. Even when the golfers wear blue jeans around the clubhouse and sometimes on the course, it still behooves the superintendent who wants to be well thought of to look and dress respectably. Many times, the manner in which one dresses correlates with how one is treated. If the golfers cannot distinguish the superintendent from the workers, respect for the position most likely will diminish. A fashion statement is not necessary; wearing clean, suitable clothing for the position is usually sufficient. It is not difficult to find clothing made from durable materials composed of cotton blends that are somewhat stylish and very appropriate for the superintendent.

When golfing, a superintendent should look the part of a golfer, wearing a clean collared shirt, golf shoes, and pressed shorts or trousers. Attire for board or green committee meetings should include dress slacks, a jacket, and possibly a tie. Looking the part of the professional staff, much the same way as the manager or golf professional, is important at these meetings and can be advantageous. Remember that a hat is never appropriately worn indoors or during a meeting.

BREAKS AND LUNCHTIME

Regulations require that workers be given several breaks during the work day. This regulated break time may vary from place to place. We all like to sit down from time to time, to relax and have a coffee or a soft drink. The green staff is no exception. A break from manual labor and other activities can result in rejuvenating the mind and the physical demeanor of the workers. At lunchtime, all staff members are expected to return to the maintenance facility, or in some cases the clubhouse, to eat, to rest, or to take a break. While they eat their meal, there is time to socialize and establish friendships. After the conclusion of the lunch period, the superintendent or the assistant may discuss changes in the work assignments for the rest of the day. Usually, this is a reiteration of the information that was decided earlier in the morning, but sometimes there are changes and the staff needs to be advised of what is expected.

CHECKING, CHECKING, AND CHECKING AGAIN

Checking persistently and observing the workers will ensure the superintendent or assistant that all the work is being implemented properly. Occasionally observing and checking the work of well-trained personnel shows an interest that is contagious, leads to high-quality performance, and promotes workers' self-esteem. In addition, many of the little things that are sometimes overlooked by conscientious workers can be addressed and corrected during the timely visit.

TIP: Checking, checking, and checking again are basic functions of "Practical Golf Course Maintenance."

THE END OF THE DAY

At most golf courses, the end of the day for the hourly workers comes at midafternoon. This is the time of day when all the machine operators and their machines make their way back to the maintenance facility. Now is the time for:

- Using air pressure to clean off machinery
- Washing the machinery
- Topping off fuel tanks
- Cleaning and putting away equipment in an orderly manner
- Sweeping the floors
- Cleaning the washrooms
- Tidying the staff room

On a weekly basis, one of the crew members should be appointed for cleanup and lockup duty. Prepare a checklist and have the appointed person check to make sure that everything is being overseen. Tools and equipment should be properly stored and locked up safely. Once the checklist has been completed, the time has arrived for everyone to go home except those few who are working overtime – occasionally the irrigation crew, sometimes the assistant, and almost always the superintendent. When all is peaceful and quiet around the shop, there is an ideal opportunity to get caught up on the administrative work. File the day's report for any fertilizer or chemicals that may have been applied. Record all daily activities in a handwritten journal or stored in a computer file. Make telephone calls and check email. Plan the activities for the next day, and possibly write the assignments on the job board. Try to get ready for meetings with committee members or other department heads. Now is the time to take the cart for one last drive around the golf course, or perhaps relax for a while with a turf magazine before going home.

HIRING AND TRAINING THE RIGHT PERSON

Recruiting, interviewing, and providing training for the green staff is perhaps the most important aspect of the superintendents' responsibilities. The results from this process, as well as the already-trained green staff, will have an impact on the overall condition of the golf course. At most courses, there is a nucleus of workers who are hired for year-round work, as well as several seasonal employees.

Hiring a new employee requires time and careful consideration. Hiring a new person has the potential of being either a disaster or a great success.

There should always be a probationary period agreed upon during the initial hiring to ensure that the new recruit is suitable for the position. Workers are human beings with feelings, and at times need to be scolded or praised, encouraged or dissuaded, as well as trained to be hardworking and devoted greenkeepers. The object is to hire carefully.

Preparing for the Interview

The first phase of the interviewing process is preparing the help wanted advertisement. The announcement should include general information on the expected duties, requirements, hours worked, benefits, and possibly a salary range. Many local and regional golf course chapters can offer assistance by posting various positions through their communications. Advertising on job-related websites or other social media outlets may help to reach a wide audience of potential workers. Other options include posting help wanted ads on bulletin boards in local stores, as well as word of mouth through acquaintances and even a sign on the street may interest a passerby or local resident. Some of the senior workers with roots in the community can spread the word that the golf course is hiring.

Be wary of hiring the sons and daughters of golf club members – never hire workers who are difficult to fire. The greens chairman's son falls into this category, and so does the manager's daughter. Stay away from these potentially difficult situations. Hiring people who live locally may also be advantageous for everyone.

The interview is conducted in a quiet place where there will be no intrusions or interruptions by the phone. It can be helpful to have another person present to make sure that all the questions are acceptable, which will avoid any misunderstandings at a later time. If another qualified person is not available at this time, consider recording the interview with the consent of the applicant. Usually, there are many applications received for available jobs. Most of these applicants will be eliminated on the basis of their resumes or phone interviews. Check out the references of the selected applicants, particularly the ones from other golf courses. It makes no sense to hire someone else's problem. Interviews should then be scheduled for the remaining qualified applicants.

Picking the right person for the right job is an acquired ability that is learned after considerable practice and some mistakes. The first impression of any new recruit can be crucial. If there are still concerns or unanswered questions after the first interview, consider giving the applicant a second chance at making a more favorable impression. Never hire impulsively or reject quickly. Remember the need for all employees to fit into the golfing environment – inform the potential employee that start time is early in the morning, and working some weekends and holidays will be required.

Suitable employees are those who enjoy working hard in the outdoors, are friendly, and have a positive attitude.

Once a decision has been made, act promptly and bring the new recruit aboard as quickly as possible. Discuss the rules and regulations. The payroll or human resources department will have forms and documents that need to be signed for taxes and terms of employment.

Each new employee may need to be trained for several weeks or months. If, at the end of this training period, the new recruit proves to be unsuitable, then a large amount of time and money has been wasted. Hire carefully and avoid making impetuous decisions. Consider waiting until the following morning before making hiring decisions.

The Training Process

Once a new worker has been hired, the assistant or an experienced crew member can teach him or her the fundamentals. A training video that is provided by a manufacturer or turf-related educational company can provide visual assistance with this process. The training process can begin with the trainee observing a senior crew member, gaining experience visually and obtaining hands-on knowledge. After a few days of observation and supervised instruction, the time has come for the trainee to make a first solo attempt at his or her new position. Make sure that there is always a qualified employee present to help and supervise in the event the trainee requires assistance. Everyone needs to learn to be patient with the newcomers, and remember that all things are difficult before they are easy. Unlikely as it may seem at first, trainees will eventually turn into valuable workers. In the future, some may even become superintendents.

TIP: Create laminated maps of the golf course with all the holes numbered and other key locations like the maintenance facility, clubhouse, and parking lots delineated for new employees to carry. This will help them learn the locations of all the holes and assimilate more quickly with the rest of the staff.

Hiring an Assistant

Hiring an assistant can be a time-consuming process but one that should be looked at as an opportunity to make a positive impact on the golf course and operation. There are many avenues to advertise the position: local superintendent chapters, social media, universities, and word of mouth. As the resumes begin to arrive, carefully select the best candidates to begin the interview process. Interviews should then be scheduled for at least an hour, and also allot ample time in between interviews. Try to arrange the interviews in a concentrated time period so that a decision can be made in a methodical manner. Use the following criteria as a basis of comparison, and rank each applicant according to merit:

- *Appearance.* A favorable appearance increases the chances of success in life as well as on the job. The all-important first impression opens doors or closes opportunities.
- *Education.* Educational requirements for turf managers have increased substantially as their duties have become more technical and complex. The requirement for assistants is a two-year diploma or at the very minimum a certificate from a recognized turf school. A bachelor of science (B.S.) degree in agronomy or related field is much more desirable but not always the case today.
- *Experience.* Several years on a golf course crew and familiarity with all operations are essential. Experience obtained from nine-hole golf courses can be valuable, since workers on these courses have to be more resourceful because of limited staff, equipment, and concentrated play.
- *Maturity.* Since an assistant will be a leader, you will need a person who will command respect. The degree of maturity that is desirable for the position is a subjective decision on the part of the interviewer.
- *Golfing ability.* While some outstanding superintendents are known to be non-golfers, in the golfing environment knowledge of and the ability to participate in golf is advantageous. The applicant does not need to be a single-digit handicap player, but having a working knowledge of the game and enjoy playing are helpful indicators of their viewpoint.
- *Attitude.* Without a positive attitude, all other criteria are meaningless.

After interviewing candidates for the position of assistant, always check the references of the applicants that ranked the highest, then arrange for two or three candidates to be interviewed for a second time. During the second interview, working conditions and salary may be discussed in greater detail.

Before making the final decision, ask yourself the following questions:

1. Can I work and get along with this person?
2. Will this person take direction and follow instructions?
3. Does this person have leadership qualities and the ability to get along with the staff and the golfers?
4. Will this person represent our club respectably?

On the basis of such a thorough process, mistakes are rarely made and the new assistant will almost invariably work out well and become a valuable asset. The same process, with minor alterations, may also be used for other key personnel.

PERFORMANCE REVIEWS

Each worker and all key personnel should have a file detailing the history of employment. Part of the recordkeeping process involves making timely notes in these files. Absenteeism, personal days, sick days, vacation periods, and lateness are all recorded in the employee's docket. Any unusual occurrences in which the employee was involved should also be noted for possible future reference. In addition, once a year there should be a thorough performance review. Reviews should be in writing and should include all the positive accomplishments that the employee has made during the past season, and shortcomings should also be noted. Perhaps a worker has been taking longer breaks than permitted. Possibly a worker has developed an unpleasant attitude. The performance review provides an opportunity to discuss behavioral problems. These inadequacies should be documented and be made part of the permanent record, and when talked over may serve as motivation for improving the worker's performance. The document is discussed and agreed upon, then signed by both the superintendent and the employee.

DISMISSAL

Selecting the wrong person for a job is a common mistake; failure to remove that person is a fatal weakness. New employees can easily be let go during the probationary period, but it becomes more difficult as time progresses. Workers who have been excellent performers for many years, but now have developed differing behavior, should be given every opportunity to rectify their situation. When all attempted discussions with the employee have failed, and there is no discernible improvement, further action needs to be taken. If both parties do not come to an agreement, a severance payment based on the period of time the worker has been employed will sweeten the sting. The reason for dismissal never makes sense to the person who is being let go, but if the transgressions are well documented, there can be very little argument about the decision. Never keep on an employee who has been dismissed. A crew will function to its optimum performance when all participants, workers, and managers alike, work as a team to the best of their ability.

INTERACTING WITH SALES REPRESENTATIVES

Sales representatives can be a great help to golf superintendents, especially those rookie superintendents who need assistance and often have few colleagues to call upon when they take a new position. Company representatives can provide a wealth of information about various products, but one should remember that their primary goal is to sell product. Modern technology makes searching for information much easier, and comparing products and prices can now be done on the web with ease. We should not become totally absorbed by the cost of products, because sales agents who offer superior service in addition to fair and reasonable pricing for their products should always be considered.

TIP: On occasion, allow your assistants to select a fertilizer or pesticide for an application. Encourage them to meet with vendors, discussing products, pricing, and effectiveness while mentoring them through the process.

SUMMARY

Building good working relationships with the employees who are part of the golf course family provides the basis for the foundation of effective management. This management style includes motivating the workers, making sure that work is completed, and often delegating certain tasks to assistants. One should always remember that workers are sometimes not recognized or rewarded for the work they do on the golf course. When a crew member performs extremely well, it may be a result of the treatment conveyed by the superintendent. When the superintendent recognizes a job well done, this will affirm respect and approval of the employee. Good management requires that the superintendent listen to issues presented by any of the workers and, if necessary, after a period of reflection, explore the problem and take appropriate action. Rarely should one act impulsively, because decisions made in haste are often regretted at a later date.

TIP: When managing people, always do so with RESPECT.

21

Greenkeeping Common Sense

There is no substitute for greenkeeping knowledge and know-how gained from a formal education, from training from a seasoned mentor, or from the experience of being a superintendent for many seasons. All of this prescribed training, education, and experience can place you at the pinnacle of the greenkeeping profession, but if you lack common sense, then the most important ingredient of your professional persona is missing. Much of greenkeeping is problem solving and being able to adapt to the ever-changing environment each day. If you are able to add a handful of common sense when seeking solutions you will avoid pitfalls and make it easier to confront the hurdles that are encountered daily.

Greenkeeping common sense is the knowledge that has been acquired and then passed on for over a hundred years from superintendent to assistant or, in some cases, from parent to child. This knowledge that was passed on in previous years is still applicable today, and much of what we practice today is based on experience and information that was attained from days past. Technology is always advancing the way we do things, but the fundamentals of greenkeeping have remained the same.

PRACTICAL SUGGESTIONS FOR GOLF COURSE MAINTENANCE

The following is a list of greenkeeping common sense suggestions advocating practical golf course maintenance:

- *Keep a clean house.* Many of the aspects of housekeeping are realized in greenkeeping! In addition to your college degree, general housekeeping on the golf course is the essence of our occupation. From the maintenance facility to the parking lot, there is never an excuse for trash or things out of place on a golf course. Many successful superintendents are also excellent housekeepers and are paid handsomely, especially when they succeed a messy predecessor. There may be a valid reason for some strange disease that's attacking the grass, but there is never an excuse for a messy golf course.

- *Plan your work and work the plan.* We have all heard these words before, but they remain true. Keep a list of projects to do, and post it in the staff room for everyone to see. Engage your staff by including them in the progress of tasks and enthusiastically cross off each one that has been completed. As they work the list, they will remind themselves not to postpone until tomorrow what can be done today.
- *Don't forget the little things.* These are the things people normally see, like a limb that needs trimming, a pothole on the path, or a bunker without a rake. If not addressed, they will come back to haunt you. These words can be attributed to Colonel Morley, the founder of our great golf course superintendents' association, who wrote them almost a century ago – and they are still true today. These are the low-hanging fruit that you need to pick each day; otherwise, someone else will, and they will use them against you when you least expect it. Many superintendents lose their jobs by forgetting the little things.
- *Never experiment on the 1st or the 18th green.* These greens are the ones that leave the first and last impression with the golfers. Always try to use the nursery green when experimenting with new machines or products.
- *First impressions count.* Drive your own vehicle into the club parking lot and see what others see when they come onto the property. Is the entrance welcoming, well-marked, and tidy?
- *The putting green is often the first green that golfers see on the golf course.* A favorable impression of your operation will be based on that first glimpse of the well-manicured and maintained putting green.
- *You can't get a clean shave with a dull razor!* Words from the writer-superintendent Leo Feser, who wrote articles during the Great Depression that kept the association's official publication alive. Leo knew the importance of cutting a green perfectly and communicated his philosophy in writing.
- *Smell your grass!* Just as you stop and smell the roses, you should stop and smell your grass. Get down on your hands and knees,

pick a little tuft, hold it up to the sun, and then bring it to your nose. Your nostrils may be far sharper than a lens in a microscope. Familiarize yourself with the smell of healthy grass – if the smell is offensive, get ready to spray.

- *Don't be afraid to make mistakes.* Your critics will be disarmed if you readily admit to having made a mistake. Just the same, try not to make the same mistake again.
- *Finish projects in a timely manner.* Procrastination can often be the reason that superintendents lose their jobs.
- *Ball marks happen.* Golfers will either fix them or they won't. It is up to you to create a program and instill care in your staff to take the time to fix them each day. Look at the whole problem – maybe things are a little too wet and the irrigation schedule needs adjustment.
- *Address problems before they keep you awake at night.* If a key staff member has started to underperform, find out why and rectify the situation before it compounds into greater problems. If attempts fail and the situation worsens, don't delay the inevitable. Take action.
- *When it comes to golf, you will remember the company you keep far longer than your score and the condition of the course.* Therefore, choose your friends carefully and be less critical of the course you play – unless it is your own. The most memorable golf games will often be played on unusual and scantily manicured courses. Playing the game will provide you with plenty of insight and passion when it comes to greenkeeping.
- *Look for the positives, too.* Superintendents are trained to seek out what needs to be fixed, and this serves them well. It can be a difficult hurdle to overcome, but see the good conditioning created by you and your staff too.
- *Play your golf course regularly with a notepad or voice recorder.* While it can be difficult to play your own course, you should see it from a golfer's perspective as often as needed. The notepad or voice recorder will help you remember the things that need to be addressed while you can still focus on your game.

During the initial euphoria of a new position, perhaps your first job, applying these truisms will help you succeed. You most likely will even develop some of your own guidelines. As the years progress, steer clear of falling into a rut so that you avoid having your professional life become a lackluster routine instead of an enthusiastic journey. Revitalize your focus with positive initiatives by taking time to read current turf articles and consider reviewing this chapter.

SEVEN DEADLY SINS

There are seven deadly sins that golf course superintendents and the greenkeeping staff must not commit at any cost. They are sins against the integrity of the profession. They are sins of neglect, omission, and lack of common sense. Any one of the following sins reflects poorly on the professional image of the person in charge:

1. *Fertilizer burns, anywhere on the course.* Accidents can and do happen, but there is rarely an excuse for burning turf with fertilizer. State-of-the-art fertilizers contain mostly slow-release-type nitrogen, but even these high-tech fertilizers should be tested first in the nursery or in the rough. Be completely confident that the material you are applying will not burn the grass on the greens, tees, or fairways. Always water in all fertilizers thoroughly to be on the safe side.

2. *Greens mower out of adjustment.* Possibly the cutting cylinder is not touching the bed knife, and the quality of cut is very poor. Improper adjustment can also be the cause for one side of the greens mower to cut lower than the other. Frequently, triplex mowers have a unit that is cutting at a different height than the other two units. In all instances, the result is a poorly cut green that has an unsightly appearance. If you're going to go through the process of mowing all the greens, make sure the mower is adjusted before it leaves the storage area.

3. *Scalped or sunken hole plug on the putting green.* Dead plugs caused by scalping can spoil the appearance of an otherwise-perfect putting green. If the plug is placed too high, it will be scalped by the greens mower and turn brown. Just the same, plugs that have been set too low below the surrounding surface can deflect putts and ruin the putting experience. Both instances are a result when the hole changer improperly fills the old hole when changing cups and should be avoided at all costs.

4. *A greens mower cutting into the apron.* Cutting into the apron is an ugly mistake that should not be tolerated. This can happen when a careless or new operator fails to lift the mower in time and cuts into the apron. Adequate training and supervision can help to avoid this issue.

5. *Letting new sod die.* Fresh sod properly laid is the culmination of a landscape project. The shapes and the alterations have been carried out to perfection. The new sod has been installed and staked, and the area has been marked as "Ground under Repair (GUR)." Three days later, the sod turns brown and dies from lack of water because someone just failed to properly care for the new sod. This careless

oversight advertises a greenkeeper's incompetence and is definitely a deadly sin.

6. *Losing turf on a putting green by manmade stress.* Today's weather forecasting technologies are more accurate than ever. When temperatures are on the rise, maintenance activities that add stress to putting greens should be curtailed until the weather changes. Topdressing, applying phytotoxic sprays and fertilizers, aeration, and/or multiple mowings are the types of activities that can wait. Sometimes we are better off just doing nothing during times of high turf stress.

7. *A messy golf course.* There may be an excuse for brown grass; there is never an excuse for an untidy golf course strewn with trash, leaves, and other debris. Greenkeeping and housekeeping are closely related. The superintendent should always set the example when it comes to both: Stop and pick up the litter. Remember: The golf course begins at the maintenance facility for the staff; a messy maintenance area will translate to conditions on the golf course. A messy golf course is the worst of the deadly sins because it is totally preventable. General housekeeping on the golf course is the essence of our occupation.

Mistakes happen on the golf course. Many of them can be avoided with proper training, supervision, and planning. When mistakes do happen, successful superintendents will use them as a learning opportunity for the whole staff, including themselves. These seven deadly sins are serious omissions that can be avoided and should never recur on any golf course. While some superintendents have posted pictures of some of the deadly sins in the break room, others post pictures of the good things, too. It is up to the superintendent which method works, as long as corrective actions are put into place to avoid these seven deadly sins.

SEVEN VENIAL SINS

Besides the seven deadly sins, there are seven venial sins. These are sins of a less serious nature, but sins just the same, and they should be avoided:

1. *Dirty, smelly water in a ball washer.* A schedule should be established to check all the ball washers and towels often, preferably daily. A program should also be in place to thoroughly clean the ball washers as well as replacing soiled towels. Don't forget to periodically check the brushes inside each ball washer to make sure they are in working order.

2. *Dirty putting cups.* Retrieving the ball from a grimy cup is a most unpleasant experience. The cup changer, in his or her daily routine, should carry along cleaning materials and use them to wipe off the inside of the cup. In addition, all cups should be replaced with new cups or cups that have been freshened with paint several times during a golfing season. New or refreshed cups should always be used for special events.

3. *Empty divot boxes on the tees.* On the occasion that a golfer will make the effort to fill in their divot on a tee, there is no excuse for them to lift the lid and find the box empty of mix. Those golfers who take pride in their golf course and want to help by filling divots should always have the adequate mix available.

4. *Misaligned tee markers.* Golfers will blame anything for their poor scores. High on their list is a set of imperfectly adjusted tee markers. The superintendent often gets blamed for errant shots when tee blocks are not properly aimed toward the middle of the fairway. Superintendents should make sure that the greens staff is well trained, ensuring proper placement of the tee markers on all tees.

5. *Piles of sand and tracks left in the bunker or on adjacent turf from the power rake.* All too often, when the operator of a rake exits the bunker, the machine leaves tracks and an ugly pile of sand that has been hastily left in the bunker or on the turf. After dispersing the tracks and piled sand, operators should also make sure that there are a sufficient number of rakes in each bunker. In addition, it is inexcusable to leave bunkers with broken or missing rakes. Rakes should have solid handles and no missing teeth.

6. *Torn flags and beat-up flagsticks.* The putting hole is what everyone aims for; keep the flag and flagstick in good shape by cleaning or replacing when needed. Additional flags should be stored in the event that some of the flags become damaged by weather or vandalized. A complete set of flags, flagsticks, and tee markers should always be available for emergencies. Always be prepared.

7. *Untrimmed areas and trees on the course.* Long grass growing around the bases of trees, signs, and fenceposts is a visible sign of negligence. This long grass looks very unsightly and can ruin the look of an otherwise well-manicured course. Likewise, tree limbs that are too low for a golf cart to pass underneath, or limbs that block a teeing area, should be trimmed regularly.

Venial sins, unlike deadly sins, can be quickly corrected. This list of sins should also be prominently displayed in the maintenance building for everyone to see. Members of the greens staff and the assistant should take notice of the conditions on the course to be sure that all the sins, the seven deadly and the seven venial, are not committed against the fine art of greenkeeping.

THE SUPER SUPERS

Wherever our travels in this world have taken us, we have always found that there are some superintendents who stand head and shoulders above all the rest. These individuals possess many special qualities that are evident. We have studied these individuals and prepared a list of the characteristics that all consistently have in common. These are the "Super Supers," and the following are their trademarks:

- *The best superintendents in the world are invariably great greenkeepers.* They can grow grass in places where others could not grow grass. Their greens are smooth and are in excellent condition, their tees are level and the grass is growing vigorously, and their fairways are always firm and the turf is healthy.
- *They are knowledgeable, well educated, and constantly increasing their refined wealth of information through further education, common sense, and hands-on experience.* They learn from and listen to other golf course superintendents, golf course architects, university researchers, and vendors, to enhance the golf course.
- *They maintain the best possible golf courses within the limits of their budgets.* They don't gripe about the lack of funds, but instead find innovative ways to accomplish their objectives.
- *They are environmentalists.* They realize their work takes place within the environment, not outside of it. They will do everything in their power to enhance and encourage animal and plant life on their courses. They share the concerns of their fellow citizens and use pesticides only when everything else has failed.
- *They are dedicated, hard workers.* They are up early in the morning and on the job until the last employee leaves. When necessary, they do evening checks on the computer or return personally to resolve unforeseen situations.
- *They have an excellent staff – knowledgeable and well trained.* Staff work with the superintendent, not for the superintendent. They are always concerned about the safety and well-being of their staff. They help the staff to reach their own professional goals, teaching and training them along way. They treat their coworkers and employees with respect and expect the same in return.
- *They demonstrate a positive attitude.* They are enthusiastic about their work, and they inspire their assistants to follow in their footsteps. They encourage each and every one to excel at whatever they are undertaking.
- *They are effective communicators.* They instruct their staff by both the written and the spoken word. They make information available to their golfers regularly by communicating through

newsletters, by emails, social media, and at meetings.
They respond to communications using thoughtful and
timely manners.

- They patiently listen to golfer complaints, and they avoid
giving lengthy technical explanations that all too often sound
like excuses.
- *They look the part by presenting a professional image.* They wear the
proper attire for the event or current setting – from a coat and tie
to their daily dress on the course.
- *They have their life priorities in order.* They devote time to their
families as well as their job. They keep current on local and world
events so as to have well-informed conversations with golfers and
staff. They are spiritual, hardworking, and play when there is time.
They enjoy golf and play respectably.
- *They are active professionally.* They serve in their professional
associations. They attend meetings, conferences, and seminars.
They stand up and speak when called upon.
- They are the SUPER SUPERS!

SUMMARY

The new generation of superintendents has different responsibilities
than those of past greenkeepers. Superintendents today are not only
greenkeepers but also administrators, something our predecessors would
never have thought possible. A balancing act must be accomplished so
as to avoid the danger of becoming bogged down in the office and losing
sight of our primary function on the golf course – which is maintaining
the golf course in a manner so that it is readily available, playable, and
enjoyable for the golfers.

Superintendents lose their jobs for many reasons, but more often
than not, the reason for dismissal is a clash of personalities, a failure to
communicate, or promises to perform that are not fully carried out. In all
instances, the person involved may possess excellent greenkeeping skills
but lack basic abilities that are necessary to accomplish daily undertakings.
Remember, to be successful, practice greenkeeping common sense, avoid
the pitfalls of greenkeeping sins, and master the skills that are demonstrated
by the "Super Supers."

22

Job Descriptions

The maintenance of a golf course takes a team of individuals with knowledge and expertise that spans many different areas and subjects. Above all, those who reach the top of the profession love to work outdoors and adapt to the ever-changing environment that each day brings. Those who excel possess an internal drive and work ethic to continually improve their surrounds to make things better for all. These common characteristics have guided many individuals through successful careers. The job of the golf course superintendent is never done.

GOLF COURSE SUPERINTENDENT

A golf course superintendent's primary responsibility is to maintain the golf course and provide service to golfers at a professional level, while always working in a manner that will provide golfers a great sense of pride in the course. A superintendent also needs to be proficient at budgeting, managing people, and communicating with golfers and staff. The superintendent should possess undisputed personal integrity and approach the job with the utmost standard of professional ethics.

The superintendent presents a congenial image, neatly groomed, smartly dressed, and always willing to answer questions and to share knowledge in a professional manner. A superintendent enjoys golfing, tries to play frequently, and networks with other local superintendents.

Above all, a superintendent must accomplish these objectives while still being mindful that the land that constitutes the golf course is a living habitat for all creatures, and that it must be conserved for future generations.

Education

Most superintendents possess a degree from a postsecondary institution in turfgrass management or a related field. Superintendents should belong to and participate in local, regional, national, and international professional associations. Attendance at seminars, conferences, and field days at universities where turfgrass research is conducted is essential. A superintendent should visit with colleagues to compare maintenance practices and play golf with neighboring superintendents.

A superintendent's education and training never ends. As technology and science advance the profession of greenkeeping, a superintendent must stay abreast of the innovations and evolutions. In their formative years, superintendents should consider attending a Dale Carnegie course or belong to the Toastmasters organization to improve communication skills. Participation in community groups is also highly recommended.

Qualifications

The qualifications of a superintendent are a combination of academic knowledge, technical training, and practical experience.

- A postsecondary diploma from an accredited turfgrass school is a minimum requirement. There are many superintendents who have bachelor's and/or master's degrees in turfgrass science or a related field.
- Specific technical training can be learned in seminars, webinars, and specialized short courses.
- Experience that has been acquired under the guidance of at least one established master in the art of greenkeeping; this practical experience may include trade secrets that can be learned only on the job.

Responsibilities

The maintenance of the golf course is the top priority on the list of the superintendent's daily duties. The heat of summer brings out the many pests that attack the grass, which requires extra attention from the superintendent to ensure the survival of the turf. Greenkeeping is an occupation that rarely knows time off, especially during the busy golfing season. The superintendent's duties usually include the following:

- Visually check the greens, tees, and fairways.
- Keep diseases, insect pests, and weeds under control.
- Oversee that the grass is cut regularly, the bunkers are raked, the tee markers are moved, and the cups are changed to provide a pleasurable golfing experience.
- Hire green staff very carefully, training them thoroughly and checking their performance repeatedly. The superintendent shall keep the staff well motivated throughout the season and train them to be considerate to the golfers while working on the course.
- Attend meetings with the manager and the golf professional, and often run green committee meetings.
- Schedule and conduct business with commercial suppliers of materials and equipment.
- At the end of a busy day, there are administrative duties such as recordkeeping, writing reports, answering emails, and returning phone calls that need to be addressed.

In addition to the golf course, many superintendents oversee the grounds around the clubhouse, swimming pools, and tennis courts.

Specific Required Skills and Knowledge

A superintendent should possess the following skills and knowledge:

- Know how to operate all machinery and equipment in the maintenance building and be capable of training others.
- Have a thorough knowledge of pesticides and fertilizers.
- Understanding the operation and use of the irrigation system is paramount, including the pumps, piping, sprinklers, and control system.
- Understand the needs of the golfers and the demands of the game.
- Know *The Rules of Golf* as they pertain to the maintenance of the course.
- In addition to being a competent greenkeeper, a superintendent needs to possess administrative skills to deal with the business aspects of golf course management.
- On occasion, a golf course superintendent is expected to address meetings and to present reports and budgets.
- Understand and know how to use computers, tablets, and technology.

The superintendent is often the spokesperson for everything outside at a golf course. An important responsibility of the superintendent is to be a steward of the environment. Successful superintendents communicate this often within their communities by proactively getting involved with groups and individuals who share similar environmental beliefs. Many superintendents host field trips for schoolchildren, lead bird-watching tours, keep bees, and maintain many native areas on their courses to show a community what an asset a golf course truly is. Superintendents demonstrate through their actions that they care about the land with which they have been entrusted. They are, in essence, and at all times, the ultimate conservationists.

ASSISTANT GOLF COURSE SUPERINTENDENT

The assistant golf course superintendent's primary responsibility is to assist the superintendent in all areas with regard to the maintenance of the golf course. The assistant, at all times, should function as an extra set of eyes, ears, and legs for the superintendent. The ultimate objective of both the superintendent and the assistant is to provide the best possible playing conditions within the limits of the operating budget.

Education

The qualifications of the assistant superintendent are a combination of education, experience, and technical training:

- A postsecondary degree; a bachelor's degree or master's degree in turfgrass science or a related field from an accredited institution is beneficial.
- A valid pesticide license is often required.
- Membership in professional associations is highly beneficial.
- Continuing education by attendance at turfgrass conferences, webinars, and/or seminars shows dedication to the profession.
- A valid operator's license for chain saws, string trimmers, and other such tools is sometimes necessary.

Qualifications

Assistant golf course superintendents should have the knowledge and understanding of the following:

- Familiarity with the operation of the pump house and the irrigation system; ability to troubleshoot and repair all components and parts of the system

- Familiarity with the chemicals and fertilizers used in turfgrass maintenance, as well as knowledge of application rates and calibration of sprayers
- Recognition of the correct mower settings, quality of cut, and mowing patterns
- Ability to operate most pieces of equipment that are required for golf course maintenance
- Ability to select suitable people for particular jobs and to motivate the crew
- Knowledge of the game and rules of golf, and ability to play golf reasonably well
- Ability to write reports and attend meetings
- Projects a professional demeanor

Responsibilities

The hiring and firing of the greens staff is the primary responsibility of the superintendent; however, the assistant may be involved in the preliminary screening of new staff. The assistant arrives at work before the majority of the greens staff to review the day's assignments, and if needed, to assist with unexpected emergencies:

- Daily work assignments are given to each individual member of the greens staff by the superintendent and/or the assistant.
- The assistant should guide the crew by helping to make sure that the machinery is operating properly and that the workers have started to leave to perform their assigned tasks.
- When not involved in a particular project, the assistant will go out on the golf course to check on the performance of the crew as well as the condition of the course.
- When necessary, the assistant should never hesitate to work with the crew on the course.
- The assistant will help the crew members by demonstrating how the assigned work needs to be satisfactorily completed.
- The assistant trains new crew members in the operation of machinery and various other tasks on the golf course.
- The assistant, with the superintendent, helps organize the crew to ensure that the work is accomplished efficiently.
- While working with the crew, the assistant visually observes the grass, checks for disease, weeds, insects, and any other imperfections, and reports all findings to the superintendent.
- The assistant should routinely check on inventories to ensure that materials and supplies are available when needed.

- The assistant meets with the superintendent to plan the work for the next day.
- A successful assistant shall possess some business knowledge and computer skills in order to assist the superintendent with office tasks.
- The assistant should be comfortable meeting with salespeople and suppliers as well as attending meetings with other facility managers.

GOLF COURSE EQUIPMENT MANAGER/TECHNICIAN

The golf course equipment manager's responsibility is to repair and maintain all the grounds equipment. The equipment manager should have the ability to make reel mower adjustments and sharpen reels to provide accurate cutting heights and cutting quality. The golf course equipment manager works under the supervision of the superintendent.

Education

In addition to several years of work experience, the golf course equipment manager should:

- Be licensed or certified via training programs.
- Possess a diploma or certificate in mechanics from a recognized institution.
- Participate in continuing education by attendance at seminars, workshops, or training programs.

Qualifications

The golf course equipment manager should be competent in the following fields:

- Small engine repairs
- Tractor engine repairs (gas and diesel)
- Hydraulics
- Welding
- Electronics
- Grinding and sharpening of reels and bed knives
- Operation of most equipment required for golf course maintenance

- Recordkeeping and computer skills
- Holding a valid driver's license

Responsibilities

The equipment manager is responsible for doing the following:

- Handle preventative maintenance, repairs, and setup of all equipment and licensed vehicles used by the crew at the grounds maintenance facility.
- Maintain an adequate inventory of parts and supplies.
- Organize maintenance records, parts manuals, and tools.
- Keep the shop clean and orderly.
- Oversee the assistant equipment manager and training operators on the proper use, cleaning and storage of equipment.

Often, the golf club shall provide the equipment manager with a set of tools or, at the very minimum, provide the specialized tools needed to maintain some golf course equipment.

GOLF COURSE SPRAY TECHNICIAN

The golf course spray technician works under the supervision of the superintendent and/or the assistant. The main areas of responsibility are the application of pesticides, fertilizers, plant protectants, and scouting for pest problems. The spray technician also participates in regular maintenance duties when time permits.

Education

The spray technician should have a strong background in disease identification, insect technology, weed identification, and nutrient deficiencies as they apply to turfgrass maintenance:

- The spray technician must either be working toward or already have a postsecondary education (degree or diploma) from a reputable institution.
- A valid pesticide applicator's license is a necessity.
- Participating in continuing education by attending seminars and conferences related to spraying and/or pest control for golf courses is highly recommended.

Qualifications

The following qualifications are recommended:

- Broad knowledge in the identification and life cycle of the diseases, weeds, and insects that invade fine turf
- Familiarity with pesticides and their phytotoxic characteristics
- Operation and calibration of all equipment used for spraying and fertilizing
- Knowledge of fertilizers and their mode of action, and residual effects

Responsibilities

The spray technician performs all spray operations exhibiting a total commitment to use safety precautions, for him- or herself and for others. The spray technician is responsible for reporting to the superintendent or the assistant all findings related to the following:

- Regularly check the golf course for pest- and nutrition-related problems.
- Report all spraying and fertilizer operations on the golf course under the direction of the superintendent or assistant superintendent.
- File accurate reports and records of all operations, which include application rates, spreader settings, weather conditions, pest symptoms, and quantities of materials that have been applied.
- Keep an up-to-date and accurate inventory of all pesticides and fertilizers.

IRRIGATION SPECIALIST

The irrigation specialist works under the supervision of the superintendent and/or the assistant. The prime responsibility is the operation and repair of, and at times, making additions to, the irrigation system. The responsibility of the irrigation specialist is to ensure that the system is totally functional any time irrigation is needed.

Education

The irrigation specialist should have experience and knowledge in the field of sprinkler operations and water distribution systems by means of the following:

- Must be either working toward or already have a postsecondary education (degree or diploma) from a reputable school related to turfgrass maintenance
- Sufficient on-the-job training to troubleshoot, repair, and operate all parts of the irrigation system
- Continuing education by attendance at seminars and conferences related to golf course irrigation

Qualifications

The following qualifications are recommended:

- Have basic knowledge of hydraulics relating to volume, pressure, and flow of water.
- Be familiar with the pumping stations as related to golf course irrigation.
- Be able to start up the irrigation system, locate isolation valves, and shut down the system when there is an irrigation problem.
- Know how to repair and operate all types of sprinkler heads, piping networks, and control systems.
- Understand soil/water relationships and turfgrass water requirements.
- Have basic knowledge of design and installation of irrigation systems.
- Be able to use electronics and computers required to operate and repair modern irrigation system components.
- Know how to winterize the water system if in a northern climate.

Responsibilities

The irrigation specialist is responsible for the following:

- Ensure that the irrigation system is totally functional when it is needed.
- Troubleshoot and repair all parts of the system as needed.
- Check the turf for drought stress symptoms and take immediate corrective actions.
- Make recommendations to the superintendent on the programming and scheduling of nightly irrigation.
- Add or change the design of the current system when required to do so by the superintendent.
- Ensure that all sprinkler heads are turned on, functioning properly, and distributing water evenly.

- Ensure that after a repair, the sprinkler heads and the surrounding areas are level with the adjacent turf.

GARDENER / HORTICULTURALIST

The gardener works under the supervision of the superintendent and/or the assistant. The gardener is responsible for the maintenance of the flower beds, clubhouse lawns, parking lots, and halfway house.

Education

The gardener should have a background and work experience in a horticultural-related field, including the following:

- A postsecondary education (certificate, degree, or diploma) from a reputable school related to horticulture
- A valid pesticide license and other applicable permits
- Continuing education by attendance at horticulture-related seminars and conferences

Qualifications

The following qualifications are recommended:

- Have broad knowledge of annuals, perennials, shrubs, trees, and other woody plants, including size, shape, time of flowering, seasonal colors, hardiness, and planting locations.
- Be familiar with common weeds, diseases, and insects.
- Know how to operate equipment necessary to prepare/maintain flower beds and clubhouse lawns.
- Be able to operate and program irrigation controllers in the landscaped areas.
- Understand pesticides and fertilizers pertaining to landscape plants.

Responsibilities

The gardener is responsible for doing the following:

- Talk to the superintendent, determining the annuals and perennials required for the flower beds.

- Keep the landscaped areas around the clubhouse clean and tidy, especially when plants are dormant.
- Prepare the beds for perennials and for planting annuals.
- Hand-water flower beds without irrigation.
- Remove annuals killed by frosts.
- Prepare the beds for planting spring-flowering bulbs.
- Winterize flower beds.

MAINTENANCE CREW MEMBERS

A maintenance crew member works under the supervision of the superintendent and/or the assistant superintendent, or crew leader. The crew member is part of the team that is responsible for the maintenance of the golf course grounds, which includes cutting, topdressing, aerifying, divoting, and any other general maintenance work that may be required.

Education

The maintenance crew member should have some basic landscape experience and the following:

- Some high school education
- Ability to write brief messages and to follow verbal and written instructions

Qualifications

The qualified crew member must possess a valid driver's license and have the ability to do the following:

- Drive a maintenance vehicle.
- Drive a tractor.
- Operate several different types of mowers.
- Operate string trimmers.
- Perform manual labor.

Responsibilities

The crew member's duties include:

- Work proficiently under the direction of supervisors, and completing assigned tasks within given time limits.
- Work safely while operating machinery.
- Occasionally apply fertilizer.
- Hand-water areas without irrigation.
- At the conclusion of the work period, clean up tools and equipment and store.

SUMMARY

No matter the size of the golf course maintenance operation, the budget, or number of employees on staff, the same jobs are completed on every golf course each day, week, month and throughout the season. Grass is fed, watered and mowed. Holes are cut, tee markers moved, and bunkers raked. Equipment is operated, maintained, and repaired. No matter the task, every one of them is under the direction of the golf course superintendent. This chapter provides an array of job descriptions for those who may be responsible for specific tasks on a golf course maintenance team with unlimited access to qualified and trained individuals. In reality, there are many jobs described in this chapter that are the responsibility of one or two individuals. We've done this purposefully to show the amount of knowledge and varied training it takes to successfully manage a golf course every day.

23

Communicating with Management

There are many different structures and forms of management that superintendents may work for and with throughout their careers. Many private country clubs employ a general manager that oversees the whole club, and the superintendent reports directly to the general manager. Other clubs may have a green committee in place that oversees the golf course maintenance operation, and the superintendent reports to the chairperson of this group. In the case of privately owned courses, superintendents may report to the sole owner or an owner's representative. Some golf courses are owned and operated by municipalities that have unique governing structures that oversee maintenance operations. Other golf courses are overseen by management companies.

Whatever the case, successful superintendents have learned to communicate effectively with those who govern and oversee their operations. For many facilities, the golf course is that entity's greatest asset. Volunteers (in the case of green committees) may help to oversee the maintenance operations because of their love of the game, their passion for the outdoors, their interest in golf course maintenance, or the history of the course and maybe even its architecture. For others, it may be part of their responsibility of their management position. It is important for superintendents to understand how their role impacts the maintenance operation and ultimately the golfing experience.

The superintendent profession is unique, and those who are new to the industry may not completely understand the knowledge and skillset it takes to be successful. Superintendents know they have accumulated a wealth of knowledge and education in turfgrass and environmental science that covers plant physiology, soil science, water, fertility, pesticides and plant protectants. Superintendents have significant experience in utilizing cultural practices like aerification, irrigation, mowing, and cultivation to keep the turf healthy. They manage a fleet of equipment from golf carts to GPS guided sprayers. (Just take a look at the topics contained in this book and understand we're covering most matters with a wide lens.) They oversee and manage diverse crews and mentor the next generation of leaders in the industry. They are often the "go-to" person on the property when something needs to be accomplished on the grounds, maintenance to the clubhouse, or when projects are being considered. They are a tremendous resource for the facility because of the breadth of knowledge and experience they possess, and most of all, they are experts at solving problems. While it can be difficult to discuss one's skillset, experience, and education with an employer, there are times when it is appropriate to do so, such as during a formal evaluation. There is always a need for more education, and a way to approach the subject is to share your current level of expertise and your desire to learn more in a given area.

MAINTENANCE STANDARDS

One of the most beneficial exercises a superintendent can undertake with the powers that be is to develop maintenance standards for their golf course. Standards clearly define the conditioning of the course and make it so there are no hidden or assumed expectations. Each segment of the golf course can be looked at in detail by management with guidance from the superintendent. For example, standards for the putting greens would define putting green speeds for everyday play, weekend play, and tournament play, with the understanding that a true roll is imperative.

Practicing the standards set forth, a superintendent will be able to develop mowing schedules, utilizing different mower types (walkers vs. riders), and employ rolling practices. While there isn't a number to define firmness of putting greens (yet), helping to define this characteristic in a putting green standard will provide guidance for the superintendent to manage irrigation, topdressing, and fertility programs utilized on the putting surfaces. Knowing the specific turf cultivar and soils underneath the greens can help the superintendent develop a complete program that meets the standards set forth.

Why are standards good? They provide an opportunity to educate and give anyone who is new to this side of the industry a starting place to discuss course conditions. They're also a great tool to use for a year-end review of the maintenance program to see what has been done well, what could use some attention, and what needs might be met for future improvement when making requests for capital expenses, course renovations, and even smaller projects to improve specific issues.

Setting standards helps to provide the cost basis for the maintenance budget. Superintendents are able to easily define the amount of time and man-hours specific tasks take. For example, it may take four staff members four hours to rake bunkers on any given day at your course. The labor cost to rake the bunkers, then, can be computed like this:

$$4 \text{ staff members} \times 4 \text{ hours each} = 16 \text{ labor hours}$$

$$\text{Labor hours} \times \text{Average labor cost} / \text{hour} = \text{Total labor cost to}$$
rake bunkers on any given day

This does not take into account fuel, equipment depreciation, or employee-related costs. However, a superintendent can accurately estimate the amount of monies maintaining bunkers will take based on a maintenance standard.

Not only does this help a superintendent to budget for labor costs, it shows where maintenance funds are spent and allocated. No program is perfect, but a standard will help the superintendent use discretion if there is a need to fully rake bunkers based on weather, irrigation, and labor scheduling. There may be days when bunkers just need a light touch up that can be accomplished by one staff member's morning task. Setting the standard for bunker raking helps to define the conditions and the expectations of the golfers during play, and as a superintendent it provides a solid understanding of the expectation of the level of bunker maintenance.

Another key component of defining maintenance standards is creating a basis for capital purchases, especially equipment and system upgrades. In the bunker raking example, each team of two staff members will use a motorized bunker rake and a utility vehicle first thing in the morning before play begins. Therefore, to meet the standard, two motorized bunker rakes and two utility vehicles will be needed to complete the task of raking bunkers. If the course only has one motorized bunker rake, it will be the limiting factor to completing the task in a timely manner, and this shortcoming will need to be addressed by the finance group when they are approving capital expenditure requests. Everything has its price.

THE LONG-RANGE OR MASTER PLAN

Every golf course, no matter who oversees or owns it, can benefit from a long-range or master plan. Golf courses and clubs that are volunteer based can benefit the most from a long-range plan. Having a long-range plan will counterbalance the transitory nature of this leadership and use resources wisely. Superintendents often span different boards and bring some continuity to the organization. When new leaders take over, the superintendent's accumulated knowledge will help to provide preplanned guidance for their future decisions.

The long-range or master plan seeks to improve the golf course and protect the asset – especially the components that deteriorate with time. Some courses are like a fine wine that will get better as they mature, but unlike the wine that will eventually be opened and enjoyed, a course will continue to have a life after it has matured, and if left with no preplanning, will often need help to be enjoyable again. Certainly, the golf course is much more complicated than a bottle on a temperature and light-controlled shelf. Not everything ages or degrades on a golf course at the same rate, further requiring a strategy to keep the golf course in the optimal condition required by the player of tomorrow.

As courses age and integral systems begin to fail (think irrigation, drainage, cart paths, trees, and bunkers), resources that were once used to maintain tip-top playing surfaces are now being allocated to failing infrastructure. This can lead to poor conditions, diminished player satisfaction, and an increase in maintenance costs. All systems have a life expectancy, and anticipating the eventual replacement or repair of each system can create the core of a long-range plan. When other remedies are desired – such as restoring a classic layout or characteristic feature set – these can and should be coupled with the infrastructure replacements to minimize course closure and maximize resources. The intertwining of these systems makes it necessary to include all the potential and desired changes or goals incorporated into the plan for the health of the golf course.

Many golf course architects, consulting firms, and designers will work closely with the superintendent to create a plan. This process takes input from many parts and is beyond the scope of this text but having such a plan will provide consistency, continuity, and protection of the asset with minimal inputs and disruption.

ENGAGING WITH PLAYERS AND KEEPING GOLF FUN

As a golf course superintendent, it is important that you engage with representatives of each group of players who use the golf course. Most clubs have a vocal minority of players who can be intimidating to the rest of the golfers. These individuals are often the better players who compete regularly and can be influential in their recommendations, comments, and advice when it comes to the care of the golf course. While most have good intentions to improve or change the playability of the course to their liking, their requests can negatively impact the playability of the course for the majority of those who play at the facility. One example that superintendents will often hear about is the putting green speeds – often to make them faster.

It is no secret that better players like to putt on faster greens, but even the pros have their limits. Remember the US Open at Shinnecock Hills in 2018 when the weather changed on the third day of play? The greens were already fast and the USGA chose difficult hole locations. By the afternoon, the best players in the world could not hold the greens with well-struck iron shots, nor get their putts to stop anywhere near the hole. The scoring average was 75.3, with only three players under par (and those three teed off early in the morning). While this example might be an extreme scenario, it shows that a golf course can get too difficult to enjoy for any level of player.

Superintendents need to match the playability of the course to those who use it. This is not always an easy task, but some practices will help. According to the USGA (usga.org – handicap statistics) the average handicap for men in the United States is 14.2; for women it is 27.5. Those are average numbers, so less than 5 percent of all male players hold a handicap under 10 and 0.75 percent of women hold the same rating. Knowing the demographics of the golfers playing and when different groups are more apt to play can alleviate unenjoyable rounds.

There are many different maintenance practices and combinations of maintenance practices that can be used to tweak the course for desired playability. A couple of the obvious practices include hole locations and tee marker positions. It is just as easy to tuck a hole behind a bunker on the corner of a green as it is to place it right in the middle. Holes can be shortened by moving the tee markers to the front or lengthened by "tipping it out" – moving them to the back.

Planned scheduling of certain maintenance practices can create desired conditions at different times when specific groups play the golf course. For example:

- Greens can be sped up for an afternoon men's league by delaying mowing and rolling the greens until just before that group tees off.
- Mowing the rough on Mondays can make the course play easier for a Tuesday ladies league while keeping the rough longer for weekend play.
- Hand-watering the dry areas rather than using the irrigation system will keep the majority of putting greens dry and fast.

It is just as easy to make a course more challenging to play as it is to make it easier. The key is to make the course enjoyable for the membership and keep it fun. It is easy to alienate sets of golfers by listening to one group only.

IMPACT OF WEATHER ON TURF

Superintendents know the weather has the greatest impact on turf, and they are continually monitoring the forecast to adapt maintenance programs to keep the turf as uniform and consistent for play as possible. Sometimes the changes are insignificant and don't impact the playability of the surfaces all that much; other times, they are greater and the adaptation of the turf is more apparent. Successful superintendents will communicate the course conditions using the weather as part of the descriptive terminology in daily updates via email or social media posts.

THE GREATEST ASSET

The maintenance of the golf course is too often only looked at as a cost center on the club's budget or balance sheet. Superintendents will serve themselves well to link the play of the golf course directly to the income side of the club's finances. At most facilities, the golf course is the main reason people come – to play golf. The upkeep of the golf course, including capital expenditures, should be thought of in terms of the cost of a product that is being created by the golf course superintendent and his/her maintenance team and is valued by the golfer. Without the golf course as the main feature or attraction, many of the other amenities offered at facilities would cease to exist or could not stand on their own. When looked at from this perspective, superintendents will find it easier to gain support for the short- and long-term maintenance of the course.

SEEING THE COURSE IN A DIFFERENT LIGHT

Listen to the players when they speak to each other and to you about the golf course. When you walk or play it, try and see the course from their point of view. It's too easy to only see it from the perspective that our own golf game experience allows. Play it from a different tee or use a different club to see how a player who doesn't hit it like you interacts with the course. You'll be able to address their needs from their perspective and provide a starting point for a meaningful conversation about a shared place of significance. Superintendents that communicate well are more successful and have the support of their golfing constituents.

SUMMARY

Every golf course is different. From the grasses that are grown on the surface to the soils that lie below, no two golf courses are alike. This is especially true from the perspective of how they are owned, operated, and managed. Superintendents who take the time to educate their employers about the intricacies of their golf course benefit in the long run. By doing so, superintendents and their owners are able to create effective strategies and develop tactics to preserve the value of the facility. Successful superintendents understand how the golf maintenance operation fits into the business model and are adept at managing all of their resources to create a desirable and value-driven product for the golfer, member, owner, or shareholder.

Index

About the Authors

Michael Bavier

Michael Bavier grew up in the small Minnesota town of Willmar. He developed his love for golf as a caddie at the Willmar Golf Club and later worked on the grounds crew while attending high school. While attending Pennsylvania State College, he did his internship and became the assistant under Warren Bidwell at the Olympia Fields Golf Club in Illinois. After graduation from Penn State in 1963, he continued to be the assistant at Olympia Fields.

In 1964, he began serving his country as a proud member of the US Marine Corps Reserve and was honorably discharged in 1970. During that time he became assistant superintendent at the Oak Ridge Country Club in Hopkins, Minnesota, and soon after served as superintendent for four years at the Calumet Country Club in Homewood, Illinois. After more than 40 years, Michael retired as the superintendent at the Inverness Golf Club in a suburb of Chicago.

Michael has always been active professionally, serving as director, secretary, and president of the Midwest Association of Golf Course Superintendents (MAGCS). After serving several years as director and vice-president, Michael was elected in 1981 as president of the Golf Course Superintendents Association of America (GCSAA). One of his proudest moments came when the GCSAA honored him with the Distinguished Service Award in 2000.

To this day, he is active in the Musser Foundation, an organization that raises money for students in their final year of a doctorate program in a turf-related field. For many years, Michael has had the honor of being a volunteer for the Masters Tournament in Augusta, Georgia. Michael is known in the Chicago area as a successful mentor of many turf students and actively assists with promoting their careers. Today, Michael remains active in turf-related fields by providing consulting services for golf courses and individuals.

Luke Cella

Like many others in the turf industry, Luke began his career working at a golf course during the summer months of his high school and college years. The golf course was Pottawatomie Golf Club, a nine-hole Robert

301

Trent Jones Sr. designed course in St. Charles, Illinois. It was here that Luke became the golf course superintendent at the age of 24 after completing his undergraduate and associate degree in English and Turf Management, respectively. Soon his passion for industry blossomed, seeking to improve the golf course while growing his knowledge of the profession.

Thereafter, Luke was offered an opportunity to return to school and complete a master's degree in Environmental Science at the University of Illinois while working for the turfgrass program under the direction of Dr. Tom Voigt. During this time, Luke learned to share his knowledge with others through teaching and developing his writing style. Always looking for ways to solve problems, Luke developed an instrument to effectively measure how a golf ball sits on a fairway, allowing researchers to compare turf types by this characteristic. It was developed in an effort to find suitable replacements for perennial ryegrass fairways after they were wiped out by a fungal disease in the Midwestern United States.

Luke then returned to the profession as the superintendent at the semi-private Tamarack Golf Club in Naperville, Illinois. In addition to his superintendent responsibilities, he began to teach turfgrass management at local community colleges and became active in the Midwest Association of Golf Course Superintendents, serving as a director. When the Midwest began their search for a full-time executive director, Luke was encouraged by his fellow members to apply for the position and was chosen to lead their organization, a role he currently holds. Through his work, Luke stays on the cutting edge of golf course management, screening topics for education, journals, articles, and many online resources to keep the membership informed with up-to-date practices and information pertaining to their profession.

In addition to managing the MAGCS, Luke also manages several similar organizations in the golf industry, including the Wee One Foundation. The Wee One Foundation helps those in the golf management profession who have been adversely impacted by medical hardship. Luke continues to be instrumental in growing the Wee One throughout the United States and the world.

Luke has been active in promoting the benefits of golf and golf courses since these early days, certifying Pottawatomie Golf Club as the first nine-hole course in the Audubon Cooperative Sanctuary System's program while being recognized as an environmental steward both locally and nationally. Through his travels, Luke continues to teach, write, and be a voice for the profession representing all that is good in the world and game of golf.